OUT PROUD

OUT PROUD

Stories of Pride, Courage, and Social Justice

EDITED BY DOUGLAS GOSSE

BREAKWATER BOOKS | EGALE CANADA HUMAN RIGHTS TRUST

P.O. BOX 2188, ST. JOHN'S, NL, CANADA, A1C 6E6
WWW.BREAKWATERBOOKS.COM

WWW.EGALE.CA

COPYRIGHT © 2014 Breakwater Books Ltd.
LIBRARY AND ARCHIVES CANADA CATALOGUING IN PUBLICATION
Out proud : stories of pride, courage, and social justice /
Douglas Gosse, editor.
Short stories.
ISBN 978-1-55081-487-3 (pbk.)
1. Sexual minorities--Canada--Biography. 2. Gays--Canada--
Biography. I. Gosse, Douglas, 1966-, editor of compilation
HQ73.3.C3O98 2014   306.76092'271   C2014-900562-8

We acknowledge the support of the Canada Council for the Arts which last year invested $24.3 million in writing and publishing throughout Canada. We acknowledge the Government of Canada through the Canada Book Fund and the Government of Newfoundland and Labrador through the Department of Tourism, Culture and Recreation for our publishing activities.

PRINTED AND BOUND IN CANADA.

 Canada Council
for the Arts
Conseil des Arts
du Canada

 Canada

Newfoundland
Labrador

Breakwater Books and Egale Canada Human Rights Trust are committed to choosing papers and materials for our books that help to protect our environment.

CONTENTS

PUBLISHER'S NOTE

The essays in this volume contain mature subject matter, and discretion is advised. *Out Proud* is an anthology of personal narratives collected in the spirit of diversity and freedom of expression. The opinions communicated here do not reflect the opinions of Breakwater Books or of Egale Canada Human Rights Trust.

INTRODUCTION

I am pleased to welcome you to *Out Proud: Stories of Pride, Courage and Social Justice*. This anthology is devoted to essays from a variety of Canadians who are lesbian, gay, bisexual, transsexual, transgender, trans*, intersex, interested, queer, questioning, two-spirited, asexual, or allies (LGBTTIQQ2SA). The acronym is long, and continually growing, as social activists attempt to be inclusive. While these essays have a central theme of "pride, courage, and social justice," they are additionally organized into sub-sections: Seeking Social Justice, Forging Families, Intersecting Identities, Constructing Communities, and Un-learning Learning.

In pop culture and academic circles, we sometimes hear that we are living in a post-gay era. However, these essays clearly express the ongoing and pivotal role sexual orientation plays in the daily lives of Canadians. Nevertheless, this anthology purposely highlights the fluidity of identity beyond sexual orientation. We all drift in and out of privilege depending on multiple factors, including race, class, gender, age, disability, geographical location, language and culture, and sexual orientation. In other words, several of these identity markers may overlap in a given situation. For instance, one may be working class, high-school educated, and living in a rural setting with few community resources, while another may be upper-class, university educated, and living in an urban setting, rich in community resources. While both may self-identify as gay or lesbian and persons of colour, their lived realities may be quite different. Even the thematically grouped sub-sections of this anthology have much overlap.

In "Seeking Social Justice," Kim Chee Lee, our eldest author, brings light to the underreported homophobic abuse of the elderly in "The KC Story." In "I Used to Be Alone," Kaylie Sorrenti tells how the medical system can pathologize trans* youth, and the importance of finding one's personal and collective voice. In her essay entitled, "Why?" Iona Sky talks to her child about the pivotal role of relentless questioning in seeking social justice for all people.

"Forging Families" is a collection of essays with the theme of family connections; some are about blood relations, foster families, or chosen families. In her essay, "The Cost of Living," Valérie Bah reflects on being raised in a Haitian-Beninese household in Ottawa, the realization of poverty, and the evolution in her familial relations. In "Come Out Come Out Whoever You Are," Joanne Brigden, with a tongue-in-cheek tone, manages to amuse and educate regarding stereotypes. In "Chosen Family," Jane Byers tells a moving story of foster care, adoption, religion, and love.

"Intersecting Identities" shows the fluidity of identities with several essays that connect with the medical field, desire, and social constructs of gay/straight. Margaret Robinson relates the complexities of bisexuality as an Aboriginal woman with white skin in "Two-Spirited Sexuality and Resisting Assimilation." In "Morning Has Broken: Leaving HIV!" Francisco Ibáñez-Carrasco relates twenty-five-plus years of history with HIV infection and AIDS; the health of men who have sex with men (MSM), drug users, Aboriginals, and heterosexuals seems to have slipped from public attention. In "Distant Touch," Bogdan Cheta traces his pathway from Europe to Western Canada, with a haunting tale of desire and unrest, which fuels his creativity as an artist. In "Living Out Every Day: An Effort to Fight Hegemony in its Many Incarnations," Amy Soule cleverly affirms her various identities as a gay educational assistant, vegan, and observant Jew.

"Constructing Communities" contains narratives that reflect the desire to belong, and to be understood. As LGBTTIQQ2SA Canadians, most of us must work hard at building social networks, due to the historical and ongoing exclusion we regularly face. In "Making History, Making Community: One Canadian Lesbian Story," Melissa Sky poignantly recalls:

> I listened as people who protested against the Bathhouse raids
> in 1981, Canada's Stonewall, recalled that turning point in
> Canadian queer history, and the growing sense of solidarity
> amongst the LGBTQ community.
>
> I bore witness as old men broke down, speaking of the
> legion of friends and lovers lost in the 1980s to the tragedy
> of AIDS.
>
> I cringed as assaults were remembered in halting,
> haunted voices.
>
> I was taken aback as a charming senior citizen marvelled,
> "I haven't been called a faggot for over a year now!"

Then, Kerri Mesner and Carl Leggo share "Six Moments" in their lives that navigate the theme of violence—bullying, tacit ignoring, and silencing—towards more affirmative and loving ways of knowing and interacting. In "After the Dancing," Valerie Windsor articulates years of social activism and community building, with the startling surprise of internalized homophobia when a family member comes out. She also relates the pros and cons of living in rural and urban sites.

"Un-learning Learning" provokes readers to question what is knowable, acceptable, and bearable as knowledge; it is a *queering* of educational stories. Jamie B. Laurie, the youngest author, confronted strict gender expectations as a Canadian boy and the indifference of teachers in addressing bullying. He emerges as an optimistic, self-affirming teenager. In "The Peaceful Child," Adam Carroll bravely converts a history of childhood bullying into an adult mantra of selflessness, understanding, and forgiveness—with a touch of fabulous *joie de vivre*! In "Queerly Hopeful: Moments of Educational Activism Beyond the GSA," educators Vanessa Russell and Louise Azzarello highlight extraordinary moments from their work at Oasis Alternative Secondary School in Toronto—of which the Triangle Program is part—still Canada's only secondary school classroom for queer youth. These and other essays show how LGBTTIQQ2SA Canadians find innovative ways to confront hostility, to challenge social norms, and to arise as transformational fighters and leaders.

I encourage you to find your own favourite essays in the anthology. These Canadian stories of pride, courage, and social justice show how far we have come but also the distance yet to be crossed.

Douglas Gosse
General Editor

SEEKING SOCIAL JUSTICE

"It all came down to the
fruits, in the end."

1

APPLES AND ORANGES

Gemma Hickey

"Count backwards from one hundred," the doctor said.

"I can't even do that when I'm sober."

She laughed. Humour was my defence. Shortly after, I was moved out of Emergency to the psychiatric ward.

I was sixteen years old; my last year of high school was just beginning. I was a good student and popular among my friends, so when word got around that I had attempted suicide, people were shocked.

I wanted to be dead because I hated myself. I didn't think twice about it. I drank a flask of rum and swallowed a bottle of pills as if they were medicine—as if they could cure my "disease." Death must be better than living as a gay person, I told myself.

Before my suicide attempt, I tried not to be gay. When I found myself feeling something for another girl, I took a cold bath. I started having sex with my boyfriend even though it felt wrong. I went to church each day and prayed to God at night. I read every book I could find on reparative therapy and even went to see a conversion therapist. When nothing worked, I wrote a goodbye note to my parents and put a plan in place.

Spending a few weeks on the psychiatric ward gave me a chance to clear my head. I became friends with another patient who was a gay man. He took me under his wing. I also met a nurse who was gay, and she was very kind. All of a sudden, gay people didn't seem so bad and I didn't feel alone.

The other patients were friendly, too. Because I was much younger, they showed me the ropes. They pointed out the nurses who let patients sleep in and told me the doctors to avoid. Fortunately, the one assigned to me wasn't on their list.

After a few sessions, I finally told the psychiatrist that I had tried to take my own life because I was gay. His response surprised me: he told me that homosexuality hadn't been considered a mental illness since the early 1970s.

"Where do you think all this hate comes from?" he asked.

"I was raised Roman Catholic, Doc, and spoon-fed Irish ballads as a baby. I thought being gay was a sin, and every song I ever heard my uncle sing was about the love between a man and a woman," I answered.

"It's no wonder you're in here," he said. "Irish ballads can do that to a person. There's nothing wrong with you. I'm sending you home."

He must be a Protestant, I thought.

After I left hospital, I gradually "came out" and realized that I had internalized my homophobia. No one kicked me out of my house or disowned me. No one beat me up or called me names or refused to be my friend like some gay people experience. I was one of the lucky ones.

My mother cried when I told her, but not because she was sad. She told me she had seen stories on the news about gay people being beaten, even killed, and she didn't want that to happen to her child. She wanted me to live a full life.

"You won't be able to get married now," she said, tears streaming down her face. "I kept my wedding dress for you."

"It's okay, Mom," I said. "I don't like wearing dresses anyway."

Almost a decade later, much had changed. In 2003, I was on a plane to Halifax to present a brief on same-sex marriage on behalf of the Lesbian, Bi-sexual, Gay, Transgendered (LBGT-MUN) resource centre I ran while attending Memorial University. At that time, the issue was a hot topic of debate, so the federal government formed a Standing Committee on Justice and Human Rights that travelled to every province (with the exception of Newfoundland and Labrador) and invited organizations to present position papers, both for and against.

The lobby of the Casino Nova Scotia Hotel was filled with protesters. I waded through them cautiously, as if walking in thick brush. I couldn't see their faces because they held their signs up high. But one man didn't have a sign. I'll always remember his face because he spit in mine. I eyed him while I wiped my face with my sleeve and made my way to the salon, trying not to appear shaken by what just happened.

The room was large with no windows and packed with people. Some were parents, who brought their children; some were pastors, who brought their flocks. One translator lined the back wall with her equipment, six politicians sat at a table in front of her. We activists sat in the middle of it all, not knowing what to expect.

After I delivered my brief, I felt empowered. I left the room and searched the lobby for the man who spit on me, but he was gone. I wanted to thank him for what he had done because being degraded in such a public way had influenced how I presented my brief that day. It had also inspired me to focus the next decade of my life to the gay rights movement, and to same-sex marriage specifically.

As a feminist, I had struggled with the historical implications of the concepts behind "marriage." Ultimately, for me, feminism means having the freedom to choose, and if some same-sex couples wished to marry, they should have that option.

After returning to St. John's, I became involved with Newfoundland Gays And Lesbians for Equality (NGALE) and soon was elected co-chair. I joined the St. John's Pride Committee and formed a chapter of Parents and Friends of Lesbians And Gays (PFLAG) in St. John's. I also developed an outreach project for Planned Parenthood Newfoundland and Labrador that coached doctors, nurses, social workers, teachers, youth care workers, and clergy on how to offer support to LBGT youth. It was the first project of its kind in the province.

My work locally was getting attention nationally, and I was encouraged by other gay activists to run for the position of Atlantic Rep with Egale Canada. Not long after I was elected, I became President of that national organization and was appointed to the executive of a newly formed group called Canadians for Equal Marriage. Working side-by-side with activists from all across Canada made me feel less alienated. Geographically, Newfoundland and Labrador is separated from the rest of Canada. Growing up on an island can be isolating, especially when you're gay and closeted.

By 2004, same-sex marriage was legal in seven provinces. Newfoundland and Labrador wasn't one of them. But I knew that many same-sex couples in my home province wanted to get married. I proposed orchestrating a court case in Newfoundland and Labrador to my colleagues at Canadians for Equal Marriage and Egale Canada.

My next step was to recruit same-sex couples to be involved in a court case. A month later, I found two lesbian couples who were willing to go public. Both couples had been together for many years and wanted to get married. I brought them to Vital Statistics to apply for marriage licences, and they were denied.

I called a lawyer from Nova Scotia who had represented same-sex couples in a similar court case there, to take on this case. Once he agreed, he filed suit against both the provincial and federal governments on behalf of the couples.

When our court date arrived, I met with the two couples in the courtroom to debrief before the proceedings began. The walls were covered in stained oak from top to bottom. Large windows hung from the wall like paintings in an art gallery.

There were long oak benches lined up like church pews in the back. I sat in the first row with the two couples. The lawyers were ahead of us, in a separate section, closer to the judge: the lawyer for the two couples, the lawyer for the Attorney General of Newfoundland and Labrador, and the lawyer for the Attorney General of Canada.

The judge granted limited intervener status to a pastor; he was up front, as well. The public were also allowed in the courtroom. Behind us, on one side, were activists and family members of the two couples. On the opposing side were members of the pastor's congregation.

The judge that presided over the case seemed so thorough that I doubted there would be grounds for appeal from either side.

"This isn't going to be a rubber-stamp courtroom," he warned.

After the lawyers spoke and informed the judge they would not oppose, the pastor was invited to present his case.

"You can't gut an orange and put an apple inside and still call it an orange, Mr. Justice," he argued.

The case began on the December 13, 2004. Eight days later, the judge ruled in favour of issuing marriage licences to same-sex couples in Newfoundland and Labrador.

"I like the pastor's analogy of the apple and orange," said the judge. "But instead of putting one inside the other, I'm going to put them side-by-side under the umbrella of equality."

The courtroom erupted in cheers.

"Order, order in this court room!" the judge shouted.

We barely heard the sound of the gavel hitting the wood.

The couples embraced one another in tears, and their family members and friends shouted joyfully. Some people even danced. I was elated. Not only had we come a long way as a community, I had come a long way personally. I was always proud to be a Newfoundlander, but for the first time, I was proud to be gay.

Outside on the steps of the courthouse, a scrum of reporters asked me for a comment.

"It all came down to the fruits, in the end," I said.

The next day, the lawyer emailed me a scanned copy of the order from the judge. I printed it and went straight to my mother's house.

"Look, Mom—now I can marry the person I love," I said.

She threw her arms around me, and we cried together. Not because we were sad.

"It takes a tremendous amount
of guts to live outside of the box and be honest
and open. By being ourselves we change
ourselves, the people around us, and sometimes
we change the world."

SMALL *A* ACTIVISM

Jenna Mackay

There is no single way to make a difference. Creating change takes many forms and takes place at multiple levels. Change can happen within our selves, families, friends, and communities. Institutions, society, and government can also change in positive ways to increase equity and inclusion, and these are the transformations we often see on a large scale. The individuals who exemplify social justice and change are big A activists with a public face and a strong voice.

There are visible signifiers of social justice for sexual and gender minority peoples in Canada. Many communities across Canada have Pride celebrations, many high schools have Gay-Straight Alliances (GSAs), and gay marriage has been legal since 2005. But for these big, visible differences to happen, a lot of less visible changes take place in the day-to-day lives of individuals.

Sometimes, because of the privileging of grand gestures, I feel like I am not doing enough, that my contributions could be more significant. I question whether my voice should be louder, and I wonder how I can harness my limited energy to organize around all of the issues I am passionate about.

There are so many invisible activists behind the scenes who are a tremendous force in transforming their communities. Invisible forms of activism take place all around us and have the capacity to change us in profound ways. The exciting thing about social change is that, by engaging in social justice thinking and organizing, we empower and change ourselves. We broaden our compassion and the lens with which we see the world. Our understanding of privilege, oppression, inclusion, exclusion, and our own position have the capacity to deepen (sometimes in frustrating and contradictory ways). The transformation on the individual level alters how we interact with and understand ourselves, as well as the people around us.

I am twenty-nine. Currently I identify as a queer/bisexual woman. In the past I have identified as a queer-dyke. When I was in high school, GSAs did not exist. And if they did exist I probably would have protested them for not disrupting binary thinking around sexuality. When I was a teenager there was no queer visibility, aside from middle-class stereotypes of gay males on *Will and Grace* and, later, *Queer as Folk*. Our sexual education was centralized around cis bodies in heterosexual relationships, and it was very uncommon to be out. In the four high schools I went to, I only remember one girl in grade eleven being vocal to the entire school about being a lesbian. Her tough, brazen, butchy attitude impressed me.

Despite the lack of LGBTQ visibility, I knew I was a queer. I don't know how I learned the concept (maybe from the homophobic slurs made by the adults around me), but from the age of five, I knew that I liked girls *and* I liked boys. I also knew there was nothing wrong with that. By twelve I knew that if people had a problem with it, it wasn't my problem. Where this resilient, *go fuck yourself* attitude came from, I do not know. Riot grrrl, punk rock, and feminism were all significant factors. In many ways, this attitude protected me during my teenage years as it gave me a voice to challenge and deconstruct any discriminatory remarks made by my peers about my unapologetic positioning of myself as a queer sexual being.

Although we lacked GSAs or other formal LGBTQ resources in our partly-rural-partly-suburban community, we found each other. Somehow, at each high school I attended, there was a magnetism that brought me closer to other queer students. We built strong-knit friendships and became very important in many aspects of each other's lives. We would support each other through oppressive home environments. We attempted to intervene when one friend developed a substance abuse issue. I supported two friends through mandatory homophobic church services. I would tell them that everything the pastor told them was wrong:

"There is nothing wrong with you."

"You are not a sinner."

"You were not molested as a child, and if you were sexually abused, the abuse isn't the origin of your sexuality."

Together we counted down the years to eighteen and fantasized about life in imaginary queer paradise—the city.

We didn't come together because we were queer. What brought us together was that we were different. We were artsy and political. We were the hippies, punks, goths, and nerds. Through the safety of our friendship, we explored our gender and/or sexuality and defined ourselves outside of the norm. Many of us came from challenging home lives, and together we struggled to be ourselves and to be healthy. We would envision a future outside of the norms ascribed to us and because of each other we believed it was possible.

In hindsight, our very friendship was a form of activism. Our friendships were based on the values, desires, and lives that we wanted to cultivate and not by what the rest of society had dictated to us. Together we explored who we wanted to be and what kind of life we wanted. I cannot speak for everyone (because I am not in contact with most of them today), but I think we made a difference in each other's lives. I know they made a difference in mine. Some of us were fiercely honest about who we were. We had named our desires and our differences. We were open and visible within our friendship circle as queer, gay, or a dyke. This claiming of a marginalized identity, despite homophobic parents, is itself a form of social justice. By refusing to fit into the script that society had expected us to conform to, we planted the courage for those around us to explore who they were. By being out and by having out friends, we created a space to express ourselves without judgment. We could play with gender and sexuality and be supported and understood.

The courage it takes to be who we are is immense, especially in high school. When you challenge the norm and are visible, you can easily become a target of hatred and violence, but you can also become a source of inspiration.

I will never forget the day I was sitting in grade nine social studies with a group of my athletic, popular, male peers asking to see my armpit hair and asking me about sex with women. Although that sentence reads as bullying, the moment did not feel malicious. There seemed to be a genuine curiosity, and they thought it was "cool" that I didn't feel the pressure to shave. I used the opportunity as a Sex Ed 101 and attempted to challenge their male gaze of sex between two women. One of them said to me, "You are so lucky. I wish I could be myself and not care what people think." That was not the last time that a "normal" or a popular student expressed such a sentiment to me. That moment taught me that even people I thought had it so easy in the high-school hierarchy may have been struggling internally. So many of us carry the burden of hiding who we truly are.

Being who we are and living our life and following our own dreams and values (and not those that are handed to us) is a change maker. It takes a tremendous amount of guts to live outside of the box and be honest and open. By being ourselves we change ourselves, the people around us, and sometimes we change the world.

To be a champion of social justice and create change for gender and sexual minority peoples in Canada, we don't have to be a big A activist that takes on the task of re-structuring our society and institutions. We don't have to be the founder of a GSA or take our high school to court (but it is pretty awesome if you do!). I think I can let go of judging whether I do enough in terms of activism. Instead of judging myself, I should use that energy to celebrate the small and not-so-small ways I do work every day to create change. Sometimes this is as simple as using inclusive language, being accepting and not-judging people, or having critical conversations with the people around me. Other times it looks like organizing groups or events and participating in research that aims to increase the health equity of sexual and gender minority peoples in Ontario.

The big changes are important and necessary, but they would not take root without those of us on the ground that have the courage to be open and honest about who we are. Being ourselves and having strong supportive friends is important because it deepens our compassion, politics, and belief in a better world. Without the small changes that I have experienced and participated in as a teenager, I am not sure I would have become a confident adult that believed I could make a difference in my community. Without my queer friends in high school, I am not sure I would have been able to cope with the discrimination and believe in myself. If we don't have spaces where we can be ourselves and learn to love and challenge and transform ourselves, how are we going to transform Canada?

> "Life is too short to live with
> shame instead of pride,
> pain instead of happiness,
> fear instead of love,
> and lies instead of truth."

KIND OF GAY

Paul Edward Fitzgerald

They make it look so easy; the movies and storybooks make it look so easy and uncomplicated. I mean, sure, there's an ogre or two and a wicked witch here or there, but in the end love wins out and the princess asleep in the tower is awakened by the kiss of her Prince Charming. Real love is much more complicated than that though. Real love is even more complicated if you just happen to be an actual "fairy."

I always found myself dreaming of that fairy-tale ending when he would come and just sweep me up in his arms and our lips would ever so gently touch. The look in his eyes would tell me that I was loved, that everything was going to be alright. Thinking back now I did have that moment, but as I learned from both experience and word of mouth, happy endings are merely for stories that have not finished yet.

Every person on this planet can remember that first time in their youth when there was a sexual awakening of sorts. At the time, no one really understands what it is. They just know that being touched a certain way or the feel of someone else's flesh against theirs brings them a physical tingle and inner warmth they cannot really describe, and it just feels good. It's a very confusing and scary time for some. It is especially confusing and scary when your male friend is talking to you about how cute this girl on the television show you are watching is and you find yourself as captivated with him as he is with the woman on screen.

I remember my first crush well. At the time, I never knew I was crushing on him. He was my friend, after all, and he spent so much time at my house that he was kind of like another brother. At least that is what I chalked my feelings up to. We would wrestle a lot and roll around in the backyard, and being intertwined with him felt pretty neat, for lack of a better word. Looking around, all the boys in our neighborhood wrestled, and I thought I had just figured out why. It was not just rough housing. It felt awesome! Although the rough housing was a big part of the dynamic I had with my childhood friend, there were also plenty of innocently sensual moments between us. I learned how to give massages on him after we saw it in a movie, and it was something we would do in secret, jumping apart if one of our brothers or a parent knocked on the bedroom door. Even though we were so young, it felt so good. I know it felt right and assumed he felt the same. I mean, why else would he want me touching him like that all the time?

We drifted as kids often do, but did later get together to reminisce and laugh about old times. Soon those little massage sessions came up. I smiled and asked him if he wanted one presently for old times' sake. At first he laughed uproariously, clearly assuming I was making some sort of wisecrack. Then, upon seeing the confusion in my eyes, responded, "I don't know, man. One guy rubbing another guy, it's…kind of gay."

"Kind of gay." That was really an early moment when it struck me. Was this how I actually was and how it was I was to describe myself? "Kind of gay." All my life I had only ever heard "that's gay" when it was meant in an unflattering light. So as many of us kids did during the infancy of the Internet, I decided to search up "gay" and…I liked what I saw! It was from that moment onward I did what many of us in this world tend to do; I repressed it.

The first real relationship I found myself in was one that was quite on the unhealthy side. Truthfully I found the secrecy of it quite fun. For me it was the thrill of almost getting caught that was part of the fun. The real problem came in with the fact my secret boyfriend was slightly unstable. That instability began to spill out onto me over the course of our relationship, and I felt him begin to resent me when he would unleash certain forms of abuse on me. That abuse left scars that I carried with me when I finally found him.

I had known him for years. He was somebody who, for whatever reason, I wanted to be friends with from the first day I met him. I did form a friendship with him, and it was the best friendship I had ever had. But I didn't look at him in the romantic sense. Then it just happened one summer.

It started with just a little rough housing and then that tingly feeling came from deep inside. Suddenly we were just close and intimate, connecting on what felt to be some other level that went beyond the physicality of the moment. I was one with him in that moment. There is no way anyone could ever tell me feeling that much warmth and love could ever be sinful or wrong.

I remember pondering to myself exactly what it meant because we didn't discuss it. It was most certainly "kind of gay" by most standards. This wasn't what male friends who hung out together did. I did not dare bring it up to him though. I was too afraid to bring it up to him and get a definite response. But soon he brought it up.

"You know we do kind of gay stuff, right?" he said with an expression I found utterly unreadable.

I did not know what to say to him. Should I agree with him? Should I deny the truth I knew lay within that statement? I knew I had to have some reaction or he would know something was up.

"Yeah."

After what seemed like hours of contemplating what to say next, the best I managed to come up with was a very flat "Yeah" followed by a forced and awkward chuckle.

Well, this is it, I can remember thinking to myself. He's going to leave now just like all the rest.

That's when I suddenly saw a smile sneaking across his face. It was this cheeky little grin on his face that made him look about ten years old, and it melted my heart every time I saw it. He leaned forward to me and said, barely able to contain his smile, "But I love it."

My heart could have leapt out of my chest because I loved it too. More importantly, I loved him and I could feel that he loved me. Looking back on that moment, it's hard to believe that we ended up in the place that we eventually did.

We were together in secret for many years and spent practically every weekend together having sleepovers at my house. We just fit together like two puzzle pieces. We were such different people but different in such a way that we just seemed to complement one another. But every relationship has problems, and that's exactly as it was for him and I.

I was still struggling with my own inner demons about being "kind of gay" and the abuse I had endured at the hands of my unstable, secret ex. Being entangled with someone like that for so long leaves its mark on you and those intense emotions were beginning to cause problems.

It started with us having fights over him blowing me off for a new stereotypically straight bunch of guys. I felt thrown over for these guys and this persona he was now forming. He had never really been very open with his emotions because he was, deep down, a sensitive boy. But soon he really began shutting off in a way where I found myself playing a game of "He loves me, he loves me not" in my head when we would be lying side-by-side together in bed. Suddenly this game of secrecy was not that fun anymore, and I felt like his dirty little secret. I began to feel like he was regretting what we had become to one another but did not know how to get rid of me. Was some of this my own mind and insecurities wandering? Perhaps. He certainly never told me either way.

Soon I started catching him in lies and would only see him once a month. Despite the fact it was over, we still carried on till Christmas that year. I gave him his present on Christmas Eve, and we embraced each other for such a brief moment. Sometimes when I think back hard enough, I can still feel his chest against my cheek and smell his body spray. We embraced and said goodbye, and this time it really was. After that he sent me a text message saying, "I can't keep doing this anymore. We keep hurting each other and I'm no help in this situation. I'm so sorry. But I'm done." I have not seen him again to this day.

I went to a very dark place when he left me. I found myself reviewing everything. I went back in my mind and tried to figure out exactly what happened in all my past relationships and ended up blaming myself until I finally discovered something.

When a relationship comes to an end, it is never a one-sided deal. As they say, it takes two to tango. But there was something else that had eaten at these relationships I had with those boys. That was the secrecy and shame that came with it. It was not something instinctual. It was not a shame that swells within you when you steal or wilfully hurt someone out of malice. It was a shame taught to us. It was a shame taught to us by the society around us. Why is that? It's because from the time we were children we learned that "kind of gay" had a negative connotation. Someone who was "kind of gay" was somebody who was, for some reason, less of a human being and to be treated as such. It was an insult of the highest regard. So those of us who were "kind of gay" or partook in "kind of gay" acts hid it for fear of being discovered as the sub-humans we had been raised to think our feelings made us.

Upon finally realizing this, I decided there would be no more secrets. I came out of the closet and can happily say that it's the most liberating thing I've ever done. I know some would expect me to say, "Oh, I wish I had done it sooner!" But I really don't. I learned more about the pain of having to hide who you truly are and who you truly love by living my life the way I had all through my youth than I probably ever would have cared to, but it makes me even more proud of who I am today. I learned that hiding something so natural and wonderful about yourself hurts far more than being "kind of gay" or being judged by those who are too ignorant to understand. That lack of honesty and truth to oneself eats away at you far worse than anything any hateful person could say or do to you. Most importantly I learned that living in a relationship and living a life that is not true is only a half-life and not one worth living. Life is too short to live with shame instead of pride, pain instead of happiness, fear instead of love, and lies instead of truth. And in the end it is okay to be "kind of gay."

"When my turn comes, I want
to make sure I will not be
put on the bottom of the list
or be neglected because
I am a gay old man."

THE KC STORY

Kim Chee Lee

I am an eighty-two-year-old gay Eurasian man born in St. Boniface, Manitoba. I am an active volunteer with The 519, in the older LGBT drop-in program, and at ACT. I retired early at the age of fifty-five to pursue personal interests: dancing, singing, Chinese brush painting, drawing, writing, and telling short stories.

I am very fortunate. When I was growing up, it did not make a difference who or what I was. It seemed normal for me to be gay. Perhaps my family was thankful that I was healthy, as children died from all kinds of disease back in the 1930s.

My auntie Annice was an important person in my life. She and I were very close. One of the things we did together was making clothes for dolls. I enjoyed and will treasure those moments with her. I have to remind myself that this world is not as liberal, as safe, or as gay friendly as we believe. We have come a long way, but we still have to educate people to be more gay friendly. I hear many negative stories about the lives of older LGBT. That disturbs me. This is one such story when my auntie was in a long-term health care home. I visited her almost every day.

There was a man, KC, who lived down the hall from her. He was somewhat confused. Sometimes, when told to get ready for his bath, he would remove his clothes and wait; however, his caregiver left him waiting for some time, unaware of the inappropriateness of his behavior, and KC would wander the halls in the nude. I discovered later from another resident that KC was put on the bottom of the list for his bath, as it was reported to me, "He's a gay."

It makes me feel very sad to think how some of us older LGBT are treated so badly because we are different. I am writing this story, because when my turn comes, I want to make sure I will not be put on the bottom of the list or be neglected because I am a gay old man.

"Addressing homophobia and sexual
orientation is not something straight people
should be able to walk away from."

ENGAGING TEACHER CANDIDATES IN ANTI-HOMOPHOBIA DISCUSSIONS: REFLECTIONS ON CAUTION, CARE, AND COMMITMENT

Leanne Taylor

I teach a diversity course for second-year concurrent education students. The course is designed to teach students about a range of issues of diversity and their impact in the classroom, including racism, classism, multiculturalism, ableism, sexism, and homophobia. As a social justice educator working with both teacher candidates and graduate students in a faculty of education in Ontario, I help students develop a critical reflective language that will hopefully support the transformation of inequities in schools and society. Part of my approach includes advancing students' awareness of the diverse needs and experiences of those in their classrooms. However, as a prerequisite to challenging difficult issues in school and society, I also insist that students unpack their identities, biases, and privileges, and consider who they are in relation to whom and what they are teaching.

Like most educators working toward social justice and equity goals, I often struggle with how to most effectively address and work through the tension and resistance that frequently accompanies challenging and difficult knowledge. In this short essay, I reflect on a recent experience facilitating an anti-homophobia activity in a class of 100 undergraduate students. The activity, often referred to as the Coming out Stars activity, is well known and readily available online. It is frequently used in positive space workshops, professional development courses, and in various classrooms. The purpose of the activity is to foster empathy for those who may be struggling with coming out, and to encourage participants to engage with difference through directed reflection. The thirty to sixty minute activity moves participants through several stages of coming out. Participants are each given a different coloured paper star. On each point of the star they are asked to record (1) a family member, (2) the name of a close friend, (3) a religious or community group, (4) their current work or ideal job, and (5) some of their hopes and dreams. The facilitator reads a script to guide participants through a range of scenarios that delineate various LGBT experiences with coming out. The experience varies according to the colour of the star they hold. Depending on the star one holds, participants are instructed either to keep intact, fold back, or tear off different points on their star. The action they take represents the effect that coming out can have on their relationships, aspirations, and goals.

I have used this activity in smaller contexts. At a different university, a representative from a local AIDS resource network presented the activity to my class of twenty-five teacher candidates. I also used the activity to co-facilitate a positive space workshop for a small group of staff and faculty. In both cases, participants noted how it helped them develop a clearer understanding of not only the potential challenges of coming out, but also their role and responsibility in creating a supportive and positive space for students and colleagues. I wanted to use the activity in my large diversity class to get students thinking even more deeply about issues of homophobia, heteronormativity, and related theoretical concepts. I also wanted students to think beyond lesson plans, curricula, and school policies as the only places where they can make a transformative impact. Unlike my previous experiences, I was growing concerned that the large lecture style format of this class was reinforcing apathy and keeping students dispassionate and distant from the issues. While I see it as imperative that students understand theoretical concepts and their sociocultural relevance, I also wanted to know that students were connecting to the issues—something I believe is necessary if we can have any hope for real change. I wanted students to not only engage but to feel transformed. But I was never sure how much was actually *getting in.*

Unlike before, I planned this stars activity more strategically, introducing it more than halfway through the course, and after students had spent time coming to grips with the reality that schools are not naturally equitable places, and that we need to start tuning in to our own identities and biases as teachers if we are ever going to make a difference in the lives of those we seek to teach. Before the activity, students were assigned Canadian readings on heterosexism and schooling, including Karleen Pendleton-Jimenez's 2009 article entitled, "Queering classrooms, curricula, and care: stories from those who dare" and another by Tara Goldstein, Vanessa Russell, and Andrea Daley entitled, "Safe, positive and queering moments in teaching education and schooling: A conceptual framework." Leading up to the activity, we watched various YouTube clips exploring heteronormativity and unpacked key terminology. We had discussed heterosexual privilege. Students were instructed to explore the Safe @ School website and consider in their tutorials how educational practices might be heteronormative. I also decided to follow the activity by screening the groundbreaking documentary *It's Elementary* (1996) and had prepared questions and a viewing guide. I hoped that by structuring the class in this way, students might connect more deeply with the course material, with student experiences, and with those who have successfully been addressing issues of homophobia, sexual orientation, and sexual diversity.

However, the day before class, as I was cutting out all the multi-coloured stars and was priming the script, I found myself getting nervous. I started to question whether this approach would actually be effective in this context. I realized I had not had much opportunity to connect with these students. In such a large class, I did not know who was in the room. I did not have the luxury of working with students in their small tutorials of fifteen to twenty students. These were monitored by my teaching assistants. I had no idea what kinds of experiences some students may have had, how they understood their sexual identities, or what traumas or triumphs they, or those close to them, may have faced. Although these challenges exist in all contexts, in such a large class I was concerned that I would not be able to effectively control, regulate, or address any side comments, jokes, or other homophobic acts that might arise—and which I might not even hear in a large lecture hall. How could I ensure this was a safe space for LGBTQQ students in the class? I feared I might inadvertently create an unsafe space for some students who would relive trauma through the exercise, who might have to recall (in silence) the ways that family, friends, co-workers, teachers, and others may have shut them out of their lives. I also feared that, without appropriate time to engage students in discussion, the exercise might position the coming out process from a deficit perspective and portray the experience of coming out (and living as LGBTQQ) as always inherently difficult and trying. The *last* thing I wanted to suggest was that LGBTQQ individuals are forever victims lacking in agency and, therefore, always in need of the help of good liberal-minded teachers to *pull* them out of the closet. Also, as a straight woman of colour, I wondered how my attempts to explore sexual diversity would be received or misinterpreted. I felt exposed and underprepared. I questioned whether large classes could ever allow for the kind of discussion necessary to nurture change.

Despite these reservations, I carried out the activity as planned but made sure I arrived armed with extra facilitation questions and allocated more time (in small groups) to unpack some of the challenges of the exercise. I was left wondering, again, what had gotten in until the end of class, when I found myself surrounded by students who wanted to share their thoughts on the activity and the class. One by one, I listened to their stories, and gave each of them space to articulate their thoughts and concerns. One student tearfully let me know that she was deeply affected and shocked that she didn't know this before. Some, who were instructed to tear off one or more points on their star, explained that they had never imagined losing connection with certain people in their lives. They thought about what it might be like to come out and lose the support of those on whom they currently depended. Another said she appreciated the small and large group follow-up discussions and learning that not all coming out stories are the same and that, while many are challenging and even traumatic, it can also be a positive experience. One student said they never thought of themselves as potentially being a point on someone else's star and asked me to send her resources so she could learn more about how to create a positive space in her future classrooms. Another student emailed me to tell me that her brother is gay and that she had struggled speaking about it with friends. She said she appreciated the exercise because it helped her friends understand some of the challenges she and her brother faced. Not all comments were positive, however. Two students admitted that while they appreciated the activity and "what I was trying to do," they remained doubtful that addressing "gay issues" in schools was appropriate. One student emailed me after class explaining that he doesn't believe in homosexuality but that it is his personal and religious right not to address the issue.

As a woman with heterosexual privilege, I operate from a

position of relative safety. Because of this location, I feel an added responsibility to address these issues and make sure they are always on the table. As a racialized minority, I know all to well the challenges of teaching about racism and have frequently been accused of "pushing my agenda." I often explain to students my belief that addressing homophobia and sexual orientation is not something straight people should be able to walk away from, just as white people must not and cannot turn a blind eye to racism. Oppression hurts us all.

As I reflect on this experience, I realize that even though such a large class is not the most ideal forum, and that there will always be tension, frustration, resistance and apathy (among students as well as colleagues), I believe the activity did make an impact. I see it as *one* way some educators might enter into conversations about LGBTQQ experiences. Certainly, the exercise is not perfect, nor can it stand alone. But I know it helped some students work through aspects of the course material, consider their relationships and friendships, and deepen their understanding of a teacher's role and responsibility.

A couple of weeks after the activity, a student suggested we should be focusing less on understanding structural causes of oppression or our teacher identities. He said we should instead devote our attention to creating anti-bullying policies. He felt that only the rigorous application and enforcement of such policies would make our schools safe and our students happy and successful. Before I could respond, another student chimed in and referred to the stars activity to make her point. I sat back and listened as she explained how she had once thought like the other student, but that after participating in the exercise, she realized our focus needs to be on more than anti-bullying strategies (although these are undoubted-ly important). She made the point that despite our good intentions and policies, teachers can still create unsafe classrooms and other spaces, particularly when they refuse to consider their biases and privilege or when they inadvertently send messages telling students what parts of themselves it is best to leave at the door. She said she now realizes it is not good enough to sit back and trust that the system is addressing the problem because the system is informed by larger structures and ideologies. She admitted that she doesn't know how she was going to make change yet, and although the idea scared her, she realized she must always try.

I approach my social justice and equity work with caution, care, and commitment. No activity is completely effective, nor can activities truly work in a vacuum or without contextualization. All require sensitivity in delivery, opportunities to follow up and reflect, and background information to guide students toward a critical appreciation of the broader and complex issues. From time to time, as instructors or facilitators, we will have to negotiate our own feelings of discomfort and hesitancy. But we also need to trust that we are making an impact and that this impact sometimes takes time to emerge. Sometimes, we may not even see it unfold in our classrooms but can only hope it surfaces later. In the end, I only ask that students make a commitment to move forward. We must all start from where we are, but as Richard Milner (2010) put it in his book *Start Where You Are, But Don't Stay There*, we must work to ensure that we "don't stay there."

"The fact that so many queers are social justice activists is an expression of our victory."

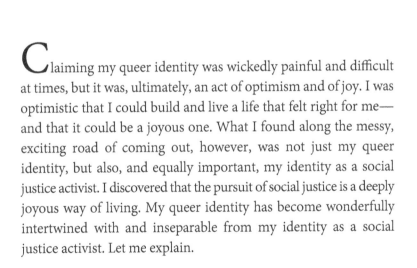

JOY—A QUEER GUIDE TO THE PURSUIT OF SOCIAL JUSTICE

Sarah Blackstock

Claiming my queer identity was wickedly painful and difficult at times, but it was, ultimately, an act of optimism and of joy. I was optimistic that I could build and live a life that felt right for me—and that it could be a joyous one. What I found along the messy, exciting road of coming out, however, was not just my queer identity, but also, and equally important, my identity as a social justice activist. I discovered that the pursuit of social justice is a deeply joyous way of living. My queer identity has become wonderfully intertwined with and inseparable from my identity as a social justice activist. Let me explain.

IN PURSUIT OF JOY

As a teenager in the 1980s, I sensed that life might be more than the sadness and defeat that had characterized my wretched childhood.

But I had no idea how to confirm if life could indeed be more—let alone how to pursue such a life. I inherited the sorrow and long-lasting ramifications of abuse. The few that hold me tight, sense it on their fingertips. The inherited despair and devastation bred ferocious mistrust—in people and in life. The balls of my feet have always been calloused—a result of the sudden pivots required to separate and distance myself from people, events, and moments that appeared threatening. Optimism, happiness, and the delight of simply being loved were largely absent. Life was to be endured, not pursued. Survival was the means and the end.

Still, I caught glimpses that there might be something worth pursuing. These glimpses were provided by bold, flashy queer activists who insisted that the opportunity to love and be loved was a battle for which they would forgo jobs, family, safety—just about everything. Their fifteen seconds on the nightly news and the heated debate they inspired in homes, communities, and hallowed halls were carving out possibilities for the massive societal change they sought, and for infinitesimal, albeit still significant change, in people like me. They fuelled the political and personal imaginations of millions, including myself. Witnessing the activists' striking passion inspired me in two profound ways. Firstly, it raised hope in me that life might be more than I had experienced and thus far imagined; these fervent people seemed so certain that life was worth living and worth fighting for. And, secondly, their vivacious presence and breath-taking courage created a space for me to hesitantly whisper, "I might be…I wonder if…," and eventually, "I am…queer."

So began the process by which I came out and claimed my identity and life as a lesbian. Coming out, of course, involved deep, serious examination of Georgia O'Keefe's art, secretive, tentative searches for queer literature and art, and lonely and awkward trips to Toronto's Church Street in desperate search of instructions on coming out and being queer. (While I knew I was a lesbian, I had no idea how to be a lesbian.) Coming out also involved careful, isolated, confused, agonizing study of queer struggles on issues including HIV and AIDS, discrimination, harassment, the place of queers in the church and queer parenting—if that was even possible. As I grew more confident, my engagement with these issues and activists intensified. Initially, I was more curious and eager to know real queers than I was interested in their causes. But it was not long before I was swept up in their activism.

I watched activists writhe with pain and fury as they fought against discrimination, pleaded for access to drugs, demanded safety, and asserted their humanity. In the streets, in the courts, in families, in communities, and in all of our institutions, these activists were fighting big, public, bloody fights. From where I stood, it seemed to me the activists were not only losing many of the battles, but they were also losing their dignity, their privacy, and even each other along the way. And yet they refused to be overcome by their anguish. *How could they not be?* I wondered. How could they not be? I was fascinated by their capacity to face such grotesque and cruel injustice and remain unwavering in their conviction that life was worth living. As I watched, mesmerized, I began to realize how wrong my perceptions of their losses were. Quite to the contrary, it was through struggle that they maintained their dignity and each other—and built the momentum that would eventually lead to so many other victories.

I finally began to see that their anger was fuelled by the joy they experienced loving each other. I became seduced by the magic and passion of these ferocious souls and overcome by the realization that the most intense and immense ways one can experience joy is through human interaction, through the tangling of lives and dreams and collaborating in the pursuit of others' joy and well-being. Coming out, for me, was about becoming queer. And in becoming queer, I was able to realize that joy is a means and an end. Put simply, what I found was not just the joy of being queer, of being myself, but a joyous way of being; I found that living one's life in pursuit of social justice, so we may all know joy and well-being, is immensely joyous.

GRATITUDE

I am often overcome with gratitude when I consider the life I have because of the brazen, beautiful activism of queers who were active long before me. Their love and their activism made my life possible. I've drafted so many love notes to these activists whose work allowed me to crush out, to come out, to stay out. I am awestruck when I consider the security and well-being that marks my life (which is enhanced by class and race privilege), but was near impossible just a few decades ago. Living in downtown Toronto, I am out in every part of my life. I have a partnership with a brilliant woman. We have two children together—and, at this point and place in their lives, our children are secure and safe and comfortable in being "queer spawn." My life is full of joy—joy I imagined because of those queer activists, joy I have realized because of those queer activists.

How can I possibly thank these generous, fierce queer activists who changed my world and created the one which I now inhabit? Of course, the only answer is to live the life they made possible with joy—and with determination and commitment to help others live with similar joy and security. And so I try. I start my days dancing with my children and partner, and give much of my heart and mind to social justice work. I march in the streets when called upon and have even "been to jail for justice," as the song says, more than once. I have the honour of working with dogged anti-poverty organizations and women's organizations with whom I have won a few battles and, with whom, I am certain, I will win many more.

Of course, there are moments of despair. The injustices and the inhumanity can be overwhelming. The need can seem insurmountable. And there are more battles lost than won. And yet, we are tenacious because it is by persisting that we find and create joy in each other, thereby diminishing some of the injustice and cruelty we seek to end. And of course, when we do win, there is great joy.

THERE IS NO BETTER WAY TO LIVE

There are moments in which I have had the impulse to take what's mine, namely the security and the prosperity, and go off and live solely for my family and myself. As a parent, the urge to protect my children is strong. And the uncomfortable truth is that I am sometimes overwhelmed by the near impossibility of living in a world that is so complex and wicked. There are moments in which I am distraught and nearly paralyzed by the challenge of trying to help my children not just navigate this world, but thrive in it. Can it not just be enough to live our lives for ourselves? Being queer has allowed me to find the answer to this question. No

What really makes my queer heart throb is when I reach out and open up. Being queer has fostered and nurtured in me a certainty that love and creativity is greater than all of the hatred. And it is this queer optimism that I seek to pass onto my children so that they may confront that complexity and wickedness with determination and joy. There is no better way to live. The fact that so many queers are social justice activists is an expression of our victory. Through profound personal and political struggle, we have created amazing lives for ourselves. We know how glorious life can be—and so we fight, with fierce love, for others to know and live that joy. There is no better way to live.

"You read about these monumental
teachable moments in education publications,
but the authors always leave out this part:
that to reach the hearts of your students,
a teacher must sometimes bare her own."

HOW I CAME OUT TO MY
CLASS OF TWELVE-YEAR-OLDS

Laurie Townshend

Out of a class of twenty-five, seven and a half hands shot up while everyone else stared at me with wide, earnest eyes suggesting a Benjamin-Button-like reversal of the puberty process. It was near the end of the period, and I had an unusual problem for a middle-school teacher. A first, in a sixteen-year career in public education: a class full of engaged twelve- and thirteen-year-olds oblivious to the beckoning dismissal bell because they had just put all the clues together and learned that their teacher is gay.

The usual suspects spoke out of course and had to be asked to wait their turn. The class clown was in perfect form with his follow-up to the marriage question, "If you ever *do* get married, can I be your flower girl?" The remaining questions contained that perfect mix of childlike spontaneity held down by carefully thought out words. No sentence fragments. Not one "like" or "um." Just coherent interrogative phrases spoken with the sole purpose of understanding, satisfying curiosity, and as I learned, confirming suspicions.

EARLY CLUES

I had always tried to imagine how this day would go. Since beginning my teaching career in the late 1990s and homing in on my sexual truth around the same time, I had fretfully envisioned that uncovering my sexuality would result in bathroom stall etchings, schoolyard gossip, and (more recently) mean-spirited Tweets. Yes, it's true, no matter how seasoned a teacher you may be—the threat of bullying and isolation is real. I was certain that however it came out, my *coming out* would relegate me to the back of the line in the minds of my students and their mostly new immigrant and working-class families.

It would be fair to characterize my fear of coming out as silencing, but I wouldn't say that it rendered me immobile or *completely* ineffective as an educator. I may have taken up residence in the proverbial closet, but from time to time, I could be heard rustling around, rearranging hangers, singing to myself; I am certain that some of my students picked up on my restlessness, even if it was behind closed doors. Due to my transparent politics around sexual freedom and social justice (which came through my teaching assignment of Phys. Ed and Health at the time), several students identified me as a *safe* adult within the school. As early as my second year of teaching, I had an eighth grade boy confide in me that he was ready "*really ready*" for a boyfriend. I remember feeling honoured that he would trust me with his secret. I also recall the hot lump that sat just beneath my rib cage as I held back from telling him exactly *how much* I could identify with his struggle of telling his parents. In the end, he was referred to the guidance counsellor. He moved on to high school, and I never heard from him again. But there were others. Several, in fact. Boys for the most part who, if they found themselves suffering through uncertainty, felt they could approach me for a compassionate, nonjudgmental ear. I am strangely proud of those days, for when I look back, I was present for those kids, if not present for myself.

WHO DONE IT?

So who eventually pried that closet door wide open earlier this week?

As far as my students were concerned, it was the plumber.

We were having a discussion about tradespeople and their importance in society. It just so happened that that very morning my household awoke to a leaking pipe originating somewhere behind the walls of our kitchen. On my commute to work, my partner called and assured me that she could work from home to oversee the repair. She even sent me an iPhoto later that morning of the two rectangular holes decorating our kitchen walls. As our classroom conversation about the skilled trades continued, I did what I often do—I took a page out of real life to illustrate a point. To make the learning real. To ensure that my students were *really* listening.

Well, were they ever.

Student 1: "So like there's a plumber in your house, *right* now?"

Me: "Uh…yeah." (Downplaying as I can sense where this is going.)

Student 2: "Does he have a key to your house?" (Yup, exactly where I thought this was going.)

Student 1: "You let a stranger in your house?!"

Me: Of course not.…. So governments want to ensure that there's a balance of workers in all sectors…" (Pretending to not hear the question and simultaneously wishing I hadn't worn such a clingy blouse.)

Student 1: "Then who's at your house?"

Me: "Umm.…."

And that was it. The flurry of wordless surprising glances and knowing smiles eventually gave way to your typical question and answer period. They *needed* to know the answers to simple and predictable things like my partner's name, how long we've been together, where and how we met, if we want to get married.

"If you get married can I be your flower girl?"

If an out of body experience is one that serves up your life in distorted vignettes, leaving you feeling like a physically removed viewer watching a slow motion montage, then this was the complete opposite of that. Perched at the edge of my desk in front of my humming Smart Board, amidst the frenetic buzz of teenaged curiosity, I lived every high-def frame of the discomfort and excitement in real time. Any teacher worth her expertly managed pension fund will tell you that the greatest classroom rush is when your kids *get it*. When their faces typically contorted in some bizarre combination of confusion and pain, light up with complete unadulterated comprehension. Well, as I sat there surveying the faces of the teens whom I've witnessed in just about every state of *mis*comprehension, I noticed something new. Rarefied. Exhilarating. Collective understanding of something really, really big. You read about these monumental teachable moments in education publications, but the authors always leave out this part: that to reach the hearts of your students, a teacher must sometimes bare her own. In those heady moments of vulnerable dialogue about my road to self-acceptance, in the precious relieved tone of one student's, "I thought you were alone," I concluded that on this day each of my students would earn an A+. As far as I was concerned they had earned their doctorates in compassion.

There were other moments during question period when I felt like I was meeting my twenty-five Ph.C. candidates for the first time. The serious girl who sits in a group of four on my left? There was something different in the way she looked at me. It felt like she was…proud of me? The self-professed ladies man, who usually has something sarcastic or self-aggrandizing to say, shook my hand as I thanked him for asking his question so respectfully. He quipped, "Ms., I'm a respectful guy." Perfect. Then he smiled what he'd call his "swaggerific" smile and strutted away.

When the last of my students finally exited the classroom, I looked around in silence at the relics of adolescent learning splayed across the walls. Descriptive paragraphs dreaming of what it might be like to one day contain purely relevant details. Mathematical word problems still yearning for their algebraic solutions. My mind flashed on a looming deadline for report card completion. I winced knowing that a report card, designed as a snapshot in time of my students' progress, would fall shamefully short in capturing the magic that took place in class today. For my new graduates of the School of Life, there would be no room on their reports for the only comment that should matter:

> "This term, [your child's name] shifted the universe
> ever so slightly toward a greater understanding of
> human compassion by exhibiting empathy,
> understanding, and acceptance for another human
> being who happens to be his/her teacher."

Who was I kidding? No reports would be written this evening. Instead I wanted to linger in the euphoria of this milestone of my career. I wanted to go home and announce to the people I love that, "We became a family today!" in the imaginations and, more importantly, the hearts of my students.

Before closing up shop, I stood at the threshold of my classroom. I thought something hokey like "Today, we slayed dragons!" Tomorrow we would tackle square roots and Pythagoras. Anxiously, I wondered if everything would return to normal? Maybe room 109 would just go back to being a regular grade eight classroom and feel less like the sacred space of the Bikram yoga studios I frequented in the early 2000s.

In the end, I decided to take a page out of my now defunct yoga practice. I flicked off the lights, remembered to trust in love's presence, and released the breath that was caught somewhere between my speechless mouth and my full heart.

"It will never change unless
we start being vocal about our
experiences and stop hiding
behind the rainbow curtain."

I USED TO BE ALONE

Kaylie Sorrenti

It began when I was passed out on the lawn; I don't remember for how long. I flinched when I awoke to a paramedic stomping out the cigarette that had fallen mere centimetres from my head upon fainting. Soon enough, I was being lifted onto a stretcher while simultaneously being bombarded with questions: "What medications do you take? Where is your health card? Why are you taking estrogen?" The paramedic lifted me into the back of an ambulance.

We took off to the hospital, the sirens blaring, as fast as ambulances are legally allowed to travel in Ontario. It should have been unnerving that I didn't know what lay ahead of me. Instead, I felt like a fish caught by a fishing line. When we finally arrived and I was rushed into the children's emergency ward of the hospital, I couldn't help but start laughing. I knew then that the next day, month, or even year my life was going to be miserable. I knew this because I was now in the hands of the psychiatric system. When the paramedics heard me cackling while pushing my stretcher down a vast hallway of teddy bear and butterfly decor, one of them said to me in a condescending tone, "You're getting some sort of sick pleasure out of this, aren't you?" Indeed, I was. I knew that they were about to make my life a living hell, and I had no way of stopping them; there is humour to be found in tragedy.

When the paramedics arrived at their destination, I was set up in a sort of "patient waiting room" where patients were to be seen, assessed, and moved to different wards. I immediately noticed the security guard they posted just outside my room. Soon after, a nurse came over to stick an IV in my arm in order to flush the paroxetine and whiskey out of my system. Unexpectedly, I had a visitor. It was my friend, Brad. Upon seeing me, he immediately started tearing up. "It took me awhile to find you. I was so used to Kaylie I didn't think to ask to see Lucas," he said with a grin. I gave a faint smile, but wasn't able to have much of a conversation with him. "Thanks for coming to see me," I said. Brad acknowledged what I said with a nod. "After what happened it was obligatory." I didn't really know how to respond. I didn't expect to be alive much less be talking to my best friend in a hospital while under watch by security. After another ten minutes or so of conversation, Brad departed as he saw my parents entering the room from the other end of the corridor.

My mother and father walked over to my hospital bed. They didn't make a sound, but by the look of their faces, they made it obvious they had been crying prior to coming to see me. Soon after their arrival, my brother and sister-in-law also joined in the circle of teary-eyed people surrounding my hospital bed. My mother finally broke the silence. In the sniffy voice of a fifty-year-old woman trying to hold back her tears, she said, "Why did you do it?" I took a while to respond while pondering what response she was hoping for. "I want to die, Mom," I said. The silence lingered except for the sound of sniffles. It was broken by a resident psychiatrist who came into our room to see me.

"Those are some pretty bad tremors," he said, gesturing towards my trembling jaw. My brother acknowledged what he said and asked him if it was a symptom of antidepressant overdose. In the seriousness and passion that can still be seen by newly trained medical students, he went off on a tangent explaining to my family all the symptoms I was currently suffering from. Soon enough, the resident left the room never to be seen by any of us ever again and was replaced by the chief psychiatrist of the adolescent ward. He came to inform my family that I was to be in the adolescent ward involuntarily for the next two weeks, called for a porter to show us to the ward, and left.

My family seemed to be less upset after talking to the medical staff, and soon enough, the porter arrived to take me to the adolescent ward. The porter was quite the character. He was a man in his early sixties named Dave with long flowing gray hair, a pair of tinted purple sunglasses, and a tone of voice that suggested he was the calmest person to work in the emergency ward of Victoria Hospital. I believe Dave was the embodiment of the hippy era about to take me on my magical mystery tour to the ward I would be forced to stay in for the next two weeks.

Upon arrival at the ward, my family and I were sat down in a private room with a long rectangular table, six chairs, a fridge, and a small kitchen area and discussed with one of the ward nurses things such as visiting hours, rules, and other expectations we needed to know about. Things ended on a high note for my parents, them leaving the ward knowing that I would be "safe," but I soon realised the implications of being a transsexual woman in a psychiatric ward. Soon after my parents departed from the ward, a nurse approached me to fasten a white semi-transparent band on my arm. It read, "Lucas—Kaylie—Roberts Adol. Psych." Reading it immediately put me in a state of anger. "Why can't you make it just say Kaylie?" I proclaimed. The nurse gave me an apathetic look and said, "It's hospital policy. I'm sorry." After that, there was no argument as there was no one single person I could fight to change it. I would have to take on an entire system that has deemed me too unstable to take care of myself.

The next morning when I asked one of the nurses if I could shave my beard, they informed me that razors weren't allowed in the ward due to the self-harming nature of the majority of the patients. I'm not sure they were aware how humiliating it was for me that I couldn't shave. I also wondered if they would treat a cisgender woman who could grow a full beard with the same sentiment. As much as I wanted a razor, even if I were to sneak one in for my own use, the facility was brand new and had heat detectors and cameras wired into both the bathroom and bedroom of each patient's room. Of course, I didn't let this go. I fought them for a week over it. The collective consciousness that was the psychiatrists and nurses of the adolescent ward came to an impasse in their irrational arguments and allowed me to use a battery powered electric shaver. For the moment, I felt I had made some headway on the awful uphill battle to preserve my dignity.

It wasn't always bad times in the ward. I frequently had a visitor named Sarah. Sarah was a woman in her early forties with long curly brown hair, brown eyes, and a bubbly nature that has made her amazing at the advocacy work she does. She'd play games with me, talk to me, but most importantly, advocated for my release.

I wanted nothing more than to be released from the ward. I wanted to be able to use a razor. I wanted to be able to feel safe from the transphobia that encapsulated my experience within psychiatric institutions. After Sarah and I finally sat down and talked to the chief psychiatrist of the ward, he released me from custody.

Upon my release, I was confronted with the fact that my parents had already left for vacation. I didn't get to spend a day with them outside the ward before they took off to camp in the wilderness of South Africa; I was alone. Worse yet, I was unable to shake the unbearable agony that overdosing on antidepressants had on my emotional state. Within a week of my release, I was institutionalized again and stayed at a long-term care facility for the next two months.

It's been two years now since this all happened to me. In the months after the incident, I learned that paroxetine has a rare side effect that has the potential to increase suicidal tendencies in youth who take it. Despite that knowledge, the psychiatrists still saw fit to diagnose me with Adjustment Disorder and Gender Identity Disorder. I never believed in either of those titles. They just served to pathologize and catalogue the experiences I had that were unique to me. I used to believe I was alone during those times, but I found out that there are dozens—if not hundreds of transgender people just like me, who were forced to go through similar if not worse circumstances. It saddens me to think of the others, who weren't as fortunate as me, who were forced into electroshock therapy.

A year after the incident, I became a facilitator for a youth group that catered to trans* identified youth in London. Through my time there, I witnessed a handful of youth who attempted to take their own lives. Some of them were institutionalized and, upon release, had their own stories of injustice. It will never change unless we start being vocal about our experiences and stop hiding behind the rainbow curtain.

Since then, it had always been comforting to me knowing how many of us there are. We're your friends, your neighbours, your classmates, your family, and although all of us are different and have different experiences, we have one thing in common—we're all human.

"The only way I could survive
in a world where I am discriminated against
because I am a trans person is if I fight
discrimination against trans people."

NOT YOUR TYPICAL MINING TOWN EXPERIENCE:
MY LIFE AS A QUEER TRANS MAN IN SUDBURY, ONTARIO

Vincent Bolt

I have lived in Sudbury, Ontario, my entire life. I have visited other Canadian cities and heard criticism of Sudbury from the outside. In 2008, I went to the Youth Line Awards Gala and met some of the other guests. Some had lived in Sudbury, some had only visited. I met some who lived and fled Northern Ontario and made Toronto a home, away from the Nickel City experience. I was asked why I chose to stay in Sudbury for university (I was in my final year of high school and had accepted Laurentian University's offer). I said to them, "If I leave Sudbury, and every other LGBT person leaves Sudbury, then there will be no one left to change the city." The only way I could survive in a world where I am discriminated against because I am a trans person is if I fight discrimination against trans people.

I first discovered that I was trans halfway through the ninth grade in 2004. I was absolutely devastated to be inflicted with such a thing (or so I thought). I thought that being trans made me a freak, and I would not want to live the rest of my life that way. That night I had tried to kill myself. I understood that trying to convince myself that I am female was not getting me anywhere. I knew I could not keep lying to myself. I also knew that I am terrible at committing suicide, so I had better learn how to live with myself (this was not my first attempt). The next day I told my girlfriend what was going on and that started my transition process. I slowly started replacing my clothes with male clothing. I stopped wearing makeup, and started thinking of a new name for myself. At the time I was very fond of Impressionism and vintage horror movies, also Vincent comes from the Latin word *vincit*, which means to conquer. My teenage megalomania was a sign that I had to fight transphobia right from the start. In the eleventh grade, I came out to my teachers. I came out to my classmates by doing projects and presentations on transgender rights as often as I could. I was invited to another local high school and even to speak for students from the Northern Ontario School of Medicine. Somewhere during these formative years I heard the quote: "Be the change you want to see in the world," and it has never left me.

It was far from easy being trans here in Sudbury. I lived full time as Vincent for over a year before meeting another trans person. I felt tremendously lonesome. It is an isolating experience feeling like there is no one else like you in the world. When I did finally meet a second trans person in Sudbury, we decided to start a trans support group. At first it was the two of us, and as moral support my girlfriend at the time would join us (cisgender allies were also welcome). Over the weeks, a few more people started showing up. Sadly the meeting space in a local not-for-profit office was no longer working for us, and we had to move our meeting to a local bar. I was eighteen, and even though I was never asked to leave by staff, I felt uncomfortable being there and decided to stop attending.

Eventually the group disappeared. I continued doing presentations and had given up on starting a support group again until the summer of 2010. There was a women's group that opened its doors to trans women but that left nothing for trans men. Even though the numbers were not large enough to support male and female segregated groups, I decided to try an all men's group. I came up with the name Double X Men, and this group ran the duration of two semesters. There were about three to four regulars who would attend. Sadly, with the commitments of work and university, I could not keep the group going.

I graduated from Laurentian University with an Honours Degree in English Literature the same month I was laid off from my job as a store clerk. I quickly learned that there is a very marginal job market for someone with a literature degree in Sudbury. This gave me some spare time to reconnect with people within the trans community. I found out that a few of the members from the trans group had continued to stay in touch and meetings had started up again with a group called TGInnerselves. I saw many new faces, and it was a beacon of hope. It meant that the new generation of trans youth do not have to struggle alone with their identity. This means that we can become more visible and create a larger movement in the city. We had a noticeable presence at the Pride march that year. I left for Europe for three months, and during that time I received an email from Jennifer Norwell at CBC Radio to see if I would take part in a special called *Trans North*. I explained I was overseas, so we arranged for a telephone interview. My interview happened in an eighteen bed dorm room in Malmo, Sweden, where I spoke about my refusal to accept gender norms while complete strangers I would be sleeping among walked past me. To my delight, not a single person even looked at me strangely. It was a couple months later when I listened to the special online in a hostel in Pisa.

I was relieved to see the same level of attendance at these meetings when I returned from Europe. This gave me confidence that the momentum of the group would remain strong, and things did pick up very quickly. In May, I was working at a local social-services centre called N.O.A.H.'s S.P.A.C.E, and we were asked to watch a police training video about strip search policies for transgender people. This video was from 1999 and was outdated. We explained what our concerns were regarding this video. There was nothing in this video about respecting the person and their identity, only on how to conduct a strip search. TGInnerselves was then invited to work with the Greater Sudbury Police Services to make a new video. The new training video contained personal stories from several members of the trans community. We talked about our own struggles as trans people in Sudbury, why some of us were afraid of the police, and what kind of relationship we want to have with the police.

Our work with the police does not end there. Four of us, Rita, Darlyn, Catherine, and I were invited to conduct training sessions for all employees with the GSPS. Over thirteen training sessions, we trained 400 plus staff: a mixture of officers and civilians. We started each session with our own personal stories. Catherine, who is a very strong cisgender ally, spoke about the person who inspired her to study trans issues for her Master's thesis and work with the community. For her it started with another university student who is a trans woman. This woman had a very difficult time at university. Her locker would always end up vandalized, and when she would go to the campus smoking section, everyone else would leave. Catherine and her became friends at the time, but as the years passed, they lost touch. She tried to get in touch with her just before the training started this year only to discover that the person who inspired her was no longer with us. She had committed suicide. Rita, who is in her fififties now, spoke about the struggles of having a family that are not able to fully accept her as a trans person, forcing her to live a blended life. She took on the most masculine persona she could to hide her desire to be female. She worked in a dangerous career and hid her identity as long as she could. There comes a point though where you cannot hide anymore. She would say in her personal story, "The only difference between a coffin and a closet is that one is standing and one is lying down." Darlyn is seventy-four years old and describes herself as feeling more like she is forty-seven. She grew up in Denmark and was inspired by the story of Kristen Jorgensen. She stumbled across her story in the 1950s before she immigrated to Canada. She describes the past several years, the years she finally started living as her identified self, to be the happiest years of her life. I spoke about my struggles trying to fit in at an all girls' Catholic school while struggling with my gender identity and sexual orientation. I came out as being queer at this school and faced harassment by my principal and teachers. My high-school years were better. However, while at work as a trans person, I faced harassment by customers and coworkers. I spoke about my depression and suicide attempts. Our stories alone are only the voice of one person and can be easily dismissed as just one person's experience. The four of us together took hardened police officers, with over twenty years of experience, from crossed arms and contempt to the brink of tears. We would then provide a trans 101 and discuss the amendment to include gender identity and gender expression in the Ontario Human Rights Code, and trans statistics.

These training sessions became a golden ticket for us to bring our stories and lessons about trans rights to the schools. We started our first training session for high-school students and staff in November 2013. The movement for trans awareness is happening in Sudbury. TGInnerselves is now incorporated as a not-for-profit organization dedicated to helping trans people and educating people on the rights and needs of trans people. I would have never imagined training every police officer in Sudbury when I was a teenager. This is the kind of support that I would like to see across the country. To have a police service approach the trans community because they want to make sure we are being respected and our rights are recognized not only breaks down the negative stereotypes of police services, but creates a very large and powerful group of allies for our community. This past summer we had police officers ask us if they could march with the trans community during our Pride march, not just as security. Next year, I hope to be asked by teachers and other members of the school boards after their training. Our visibility is increasing. There is no longer a reason for any trans youth in Sudbury to feel that they are alone.

> "I do this work because
> I finally have a voice."

WHY?

Iona Sky

"Why do you do this for work, Maimai?" my son asks me. He wants to know why I teach others about "gay people and how to be kind, caring and accepting of everyone." He doesn't quite understand why some people might not be ok with gay people and why I work at being an educator and advocate on LGTBQ issues.

How do I explain to him that I do this to hopefully spare someone the hurt that I have felt—the pain of being seen as "different" from the norm, and so I try to live my life in ways that push for change and acceptance through advocacy and education. Understanding, acceptance, and compassion—those are also things I have had to learn along my own journey being an East-Indian lesbian immigrant to Canada. How to show all those things to the people who have hurt me and other LGBTQ people through their lack of understanding and sometimes hatred.

My son looks at me in confusion as he does not understand why there would be a need for people to do the work that I do.

"Why would anyone not like someone because of who they love? Isn't love just love?"

All good questions coming from my eight-year-old, as this all seems like such a foreign concept to him. Just as loving someone of the same sex was a foreign concept to me growing up as a racialized girl in the Middle East. As I played in the desert and watched the waves of the ocean, the young person in me did not know there was anything possible outside of the heterosexual relationship norm with which I was inundated. As a teenager trying to figure things out, love seemed so restricted and caged within the confines of "acceptability" and "decency." All actions or life events seemed to revolve around making good choices for the future. Your family honour was tied into reputation, marital connections, and hierarchy.

Firmly rooted in this boxed sense of love and relationships, I moved to Canada at seventeen. Immediately, I was awash with the multitudinous stimuli of sex, bodies, and love all around me…from the commercials on television to the huge malls filled with images of scantily clad people. That didn't happen where I came from, so a new world of possibilities opened up for me. Possibilities that led to me coming out in university, the first real place where I saw real queer people. Other people like me really existed in the world, and finally, I felt like I had found a place to belong.

I talk to my son about how our home is one of acceptance, and will always be a place where he belongs and will be loved unconditionally. I hope he learns that social justice, and pushing for change, is not about who you value because of your beliefs, but about fighting for all, regardless of your beliefs. We are all human beings worthy of dignity, respect, and rights, regardless of the colour of our skin or whom we chose to love. I do not tell him that I had to learn this in many ways in life, one being in the very place where I thought I had finally belonged. Although I embraced the queer scene, I was saddened and surprised to find that racism exists there too. I thought that an oppressed community would not in turn be oppressive—hard lesson to learn that I was wrong, to be seen as *different* yet again, but I learned to adapt. The coping mechanisms to deal with racism kicked in even though I had put those guards down when I entered the queer community. I did not think I would need that armour.

But where do you find the armour to wear to deal with the hurts of homophobia? I do not go into this with my son as he is too young to understand, but one day I will tell him the depths of why I do this work. I do this because I did not learn how to deal with homophobia like I had learned how to deal with racism from my family and community. There was no LGBTQ community for me to learn from. I did not know whom to ask about how to deal with being disowned. Instead, I learned to exist with the pain through the passage of time. Through time, the pain did not get better, it just got different. For seven years, I learned to live without the people who birthed and raised me. I do not tell my son these parts of our story yet, but he will learn the truth one day.

I tell my son that I do this work to help fight for rights for all groups of people. I explain to him that before he was born, two people of the same sex could not get married because some people believe we should only marry those of the opposite sex. I tell him stories about how his other mother and I were big advocates for same-sex marriage, and that we were the first same-sex couple in our small Ontario town to get a marriage license. I do not tell him that, ten years after our marriage, my lawyer tells me we are not the first same-sex couple to get a divorce. I am glad to not have that "claim to fame" as I struggled against the shame of letting "my community down" because our marriage did not work. Instead, I tell him that although his mommies' marriage did not work, some people's do, and what is important is that people have the same rights regardless of whom they love. I tell him that no matter who you love there should be spaces of support and safety for anyone who has to walk away, without shame and fear, from a marriage that did not strengthen their heart and soul.

I try to explain to my eight-year-old that I do this work because I finally have a voice. A voice that was often silenced is now being given spaces and places to be listened to. The voice of mother, lesbian, social worker, activist, advocate, and educator. All voices that I never thought would come out of me.

But most of all, as my son looks at me with his soulfully beautiful brown eyes, I tell him that "I do this work because in Canada *I can.* And more importantly, *I must,* not only for us here, but also for all the people around the world who cannot."

FORGING FAMILIES

"Visibility was my mantra.
Visibility was the key to unlocking the cages
straights had shoved us into.
Visibility would throw open the doors."

ON THE PIANO

Jane Eaton Hamilton

When the neighbours spit my way over the fence, I just kept carrying the sandwiches out to Joy, raised my voice and said, "Darling, how did it go at the *lesbian* library this morning? Did you put *lesbian* gas in the car? Come and sit down on your *lesbian* chair. Put down your lesbian spade and eat some *lesbian* food. Honey, here's your *lesbian* tomato and cheese sandwich. May I have a sip of your *lesbian* Coke?"

I could have been worse, really. I'd let the 'phobes off lightly. I could have said sex things.

Joy and I had talked about how it might go being two of the thirty-six litigant public faces in a court case against the federal government for same-sex marriage in Canada. Our pro bono lawyers, barb findlay and Kathleen Lahey, estimated it would take us about seven years, start to finish, for the cases, which they felt we had a good chance of winning thanks to Canada's living tree constitution, the Charter of Rights and Freedoms—there were three cases, one each in Quebec, Ontario, and BC. Did we have that kind of tenacity? Did our kids? Would our kids, now cuspal adults, get pulled in, and would they feel safe, at all times safe? Joy and I talked about the kinds of things that had happened to queer activists around the world—the loss of homes and jobs and custody, the beatings, the murders.

We could be killed. Anyone could be killed, any one of the women or men stepping forward to insist that it was our time.

But I had advancing heart disease, and Joy had had breast cancer, so death figured differently for us. Personally, I'd seen death's face so many times that every time the scythe swung my way I just stepped aside. *Grim Reaper calling? Go suck lemons, Hoodie-Hat.*

Being in the case meant being a professional queer, and being a professional queer meant being out in a whole new way. This was not just being out at school with your kid's teacher or at work with your supportive colleagues or out with your family members— this was everybody, not just queers and allies, but prudes and know-it-alls and right-wing zealots and thugs who thought they oughta knock or rape a little straight into lezzies knowing who we were. At a restaurant? Walking on the street? Using a public washroom? At the supermarket? In the dentist's chair? At the car wash? At a client's house? Taking out your garbage?

We could be targets.

In 2000, it wasn't a friendly world for queers. It was only three years since Ellen had come out on the Oprah Winfrey Show, two years since Matthew Shepard had been tied to a Wyoming fence and tortured. Here in Vancouver, a gay man named Aaron Webster was still to be beaten to his death in Stanley Park. In Iran, in those days, queers had the choice of death by stoning or jumping off a cliff.

All over the world, we heard repetitive messages: *You are bad.*

You deserve to die. You are pedophiles. You are abominations. You are going to Hell.

Queers assimilated other, subtler messages, too, from the things said around us:

We don't invite you to family events (because you embarrass us).

When we talk about our husbands, don't chime in with stories about your partner; it's just not the same.

No, you can't be at her bedside. You're not family.

Our photo was not on the piano at my not-in-law's house.

To think there is not a caustic backlash to being treated as invisible, as embarrassments, as second-class is as absurd as thinking that spaghetti is not food. This treatment erodes couples. This treatment is acid poured on a queer family, slowly and steadily consuming its health and stability.

It is hard to stand up tall when your own people continually cut you down. It is hard to assert the loveliness and glow of your relationship when people everywhere are telling you your partnership is filthy and hazardous to your children.

It's hard, but queers did it. We developed a fuck-you, bite-me, we-don't-give-a-frig-about-straights swagger. And we really didn't. Sod straights anyway. We had our own community where our heads, when we weren't actually giving head, were held up high and proud, where we could love our own ways, where we could be the outlaws we'd always been told we were.

Still, there was bullying. Family rejection. Trouble at school. Foster homes. Homelessness. Drop-outs. Low self-esteem. Stereotyping. Discrimination. Sketchy relationships. Instability. Poor housing. Poor mental health. More stress. Poor physical health. Time spent in mental institutions, in reclamation camps, in sad hetero marriages. Often someone lost their job, or their apartment, when someone found out they were gay. Sometimes someone got beaten on the street. Sometimes someone killed themselves. Sometimes someone was murdered.

Sometimes a "gay panic" defense was used. *I killed him, but only because he came on to me.* And mostly, in those years, a gay panic defense worked to set murderers free.

In those days, most straights didn't even realize they knew any queers. They didn't know a lesbian personned the mammography machine. They didn't know three of their letter carriers were queer. They didn't know two out of eight tellers went home to same-sex partners every night, and two more partied till dawn in gay clubs three nights out of seven.

We had Pride, in 2000, but we didn't have visibility.

Visibility was my mantra. Visibility was the key to unlocking the cages straights had shoved us into. Visibility would throw open the doors.

It had once been illegal to be gay in Canada, and punishable by death (though this had not been enforced). This law was repealed in the late 1800s, replaced with an act forbidding "gross indecency between men," which stuck until PM Pierre Trudeau turfed it in 1969. In 1984, after Trudeau pushed through the new Charter, thanks to activists and their lawyers, equality rights blossomed. It was contentious— some queers wanted to keep our outlaw community intact; some thought gaining rights meant selling out, aping hets. Some just thought it meant safety. Some rights stole money from queer pockets, as when lovers, newly considered a couple, got only one benefit cheque instead of two. But ultimately, every Canadian citizen, and every Canadian couple, needed to be governed by the same laws.

I didn't believe benefits that accrued to married couples should exclude single people (why on earth could a single person not pass along their pension to their kid, or their friend, the way married people could their spouse?) but I thought that whatever was enshrined had to be enshrined across the board. I didn't think marriage was without its problems—among them its origins as an institution where women were property—but, thanks mostly to feminists, Canadians had altered marriage to suit modern times. The mothballs were gone, the webs dusted off. Despite its problems, marriage remained a potent institution. It was, among other things, a family-maker, and a scaffolding under which to raise children. Some of the power disparities common in het marriages wouldn't be issues in queer marriages, since no one went in with a predetermined role.

In Sept, 2000, Joy and I and bill bissett went to Vital Stats in Vancouver and applied for a marriage license, which was denied. Other couples across the country were doing the same. The cases launched. BC's was heard first, in Justice Ian Pittfield's courtroom. It lasted two weeks. Joy and I heard every nasty bit of business the right wing had to say about queers: *We would ruin marriage. Marriage had been one man and one woman since time immemorial. If we were able to marry, we would so sully the institution that no straights would ever be able to wed in Canada again. Next, we'd be asking to marry animals. Next, we'd be demanding to marry corporations.*

It was the sort of thing we needed support to tolerate. We needed to be able to feel the groundswell of our community shoring us up as the right wing ripped off our skin. But the eight couples from BC didn't have our queer communities behind us; our queer communities hung us in the harsh winds of homo-hate.

We'd rubbed some people wrong, and editorials were published against us in vitriolic diatribes week after drubbing week. Jane Rule, lesbian author, came out against equality.

It became cool to be against marriage. For us, it felt like a big schoolyard pile-up. Vancouver queers leaped on top to squash us like bugs.

Our spirits flagged. Was a quickie really as meaningful as a long relationship? Were we actually ruining queer culture forever?

Were we really *those* fags and dykes, assimilationist and boring and living in suburban homes with 2.5 kids? Our vibrant out queer histories were scrubbed with a magic eraser.

We sat around my living room together, the Vancouver couples, and we pulled questions we were likely to be asked from a jar, and we practiced over and over and over again, cobbling together reasoned responses. Not just to the hets who would be asking, but, alas, to the queers.

And then we set ourselves loose into the questioning hands of reporters, into the fray of the rainbow community, into the jagged het community.

I saw you in the newspaper, people said. Or they said nothing, but just stared, recognizing us from a newspaper or magazine or TV spot, their cheeks turning rage-blue. Guys in vans shouted hate as they pushed down their gas pedals.

And then we not only lost our case, we lost badly.

Meantime, Joy's mom died suddenly, fracturing the family, and we celebrated Thanksgivings and Christmases alone.

The pain was like crunching razor blades.

Ontario's lower case won in 2002, and the government was given two years to change the law. Our appeal was heard in the spring of 2003, in front of three justices, a shorter hearing, and this time when the verdict was rendered, we'd also won. The federal law holding that marriage was between one man and a woman fell.

But wait.

We won, sort of, but we didn't, exactly. What the court called "the remedy," marriage, was put on hold for fifteen months.

Joy and I considered flying to Belgium, which had just enacted same-sex marriage, the first country in the world, but my mom had just died, and I was too wrecked.

In the middle of May, we celebrated our tenth anniversary.

A scant three weeks later, on June 8, 2003, Ontario's appellate court issued their ruling. The federal law was changed effective immediately. Marriage performed by religious banns became retroactively legal, and marriages began in a gay frenzy.

We re-applied for licenses in BC, twice, figuring if there was only a federal impediment to marriage, and it had fallen, same-sex marriage ought to be legal everywhere.

But BC, absent the feds forcing them, would not issue licenses.

We got together with our friends Tanya Chambers and Melinda Roy, another litigant couple, and decided, all four of us, to travel to Ontario.

So we did, hopped a red eye to city hall and were given a bona fide marriage license; after our prior rejections, Joy and I, Melinda and Tanya all wore shit-eating grins. A Tokyo TV reporter bought us flowers from the corner store, stiff dyed mums; our friend Maggie divvied them up as only a lesbian could do, still plastic-wrapped, and thrust them into our shaking hands. Five in a row with our daughter Meghann at our side, in front of a gay judge, we spoke our legal vows.

I know of no legal impediment why I, Jane, may not be married to you, Joy—

I know of no legal impediment.

> "I am a deeply spiritual person
> and would never presume to stand
> between another person and
> their relationship with their Creator."

A MARRIAGE TO PERFORM

Sassimint Grace

Sally and I found each other on August 2, 2008. Although I had been openly bi for many years, I was the person she came *out* for. In the first few months, we both continued to attend our individual spiritual homes, with the occasional visit to each other's church

We both grew up in this small town, but there were fundamental differences in our background as well as where we were in our lives. I was brought up by a liberal family while she had been raised in a strict conservative home. We were both university educated but in different schools and fields. I took liberal arts and she took physical education. I had been twice married to men while she had never taken the plunge. Sally still had both parents living, but mine were deceased. I had raised a child and was a grandmother. The first time I had been introduced to her seventeen years ago, I assumed she was a lesbian, yet she seemed to be unaware of it at that time. I often said to our mutual friends, "Sally would be much happier if she came out." True it was, but my sweetheart's coming out to church and community wasn't easy.

It is difficult for me to imagine how traumatic this whole situation had been for my sweetheart, as I had been immediately accepted and affirmed by my family when I came out. I had attended a lesbian honouring ceremony of a friend in the late 1980s facilitated by a Unitarian chaplain. When I joined the Unitarian church eight years ago, I knew I was becoming a part of a welcoming congregation, so I was sure that community was safe. Everyone is welcome there, including LGBTTIQQ2SA, regardless of culture, religion, or political belief.

Sally grew up in a Christian church, and she never felt comfortable at the Unitarian church. Ironically, the Unitarians had hired a retired United church minister for pastoral care. During this crisis, on my request, he came and visited us and was able to help Sally accept herself, even though her own spiritual family had treated her like a leper. She was struggling under the shame from a mix of societal taboo and parental teaching, and the rejection from her church community was the last straw. This minister provided us with plenty of support for the belief that Christ did not hate homosexuals. So ultimately, those who called themselves Christians probably shouldn't either.

Sally proposed to me that Christmas. The following spring we planned on embracing both my spiritual beliefs and hers by having a hand-fasting rather than a legal marriage and a traditional wedding. Her mother was really upset by this as she had the strange notion we were practicing witchcraft at the Unitarian church. The pressure of that planning caused us great stress. On Easter Monday morning, Sally called with the news that she wanted to break up. I was devastated. She had returned to her church and claimed that the relationship with me had been a mistake. All I could do for the next weeks was cry.

I was to have major surgery the following month. That day, I knocked on her door and asked if I could come in. She said yes. I went in her apartment and wrapped my arms around her and held on for two minutes at least. We talked and cried. I told her I had to go, as I was being picked up for my surgery. She said she'd call me at the hospital later to see how I was. She did call, and we spoke for a short time, and then she said, "Just hold on. I'll call you back in a bit." The next thing I knew, she was at my bedside and almost never left. She was supposed to go away that weekend with the church, but she stayed with me instead and never went back.

With time, prayer, and support from loving friends and some of her family, we were able to heal the hurt she had experienced from the episode with her church. It took longer for me to get over the fear that she would leave me again. I worried she may again feel the conviction that God wanted her to return to her earlier church. I am a deeply spiritual person and would never presume to stand between another person and their relationship with their Creator, so I suggested we end each day by praying together before we went to bed. I hoped that this would keep our love sealed with God's touch.

When we said we were getting legally married, one person said, "Why can't you stay the way you are. Why do you need to do this?"

I said, "You want us to pass as straight, live a double life, deny who we really are." Then I asked her, "Why did you marry your husband? And why should I not be allowed to have a public ceremony and celebration with the person I love and wish to spend the rest of my life with, simply because I have the same equipment in my underwear as my bride?"

Since I've had relationships with men, I have often been asked to definitively declare one sexuality or the other (as though there are only two). My answer has been consistent. I don't fall in love with a person's sex organs. I fall in love with their personality—their heart and soul. The anatomy is tertiary to me.

Because Sally was not attracted to the Unitarians and she had no church of her own, a friend recommended we visit a United church in our area where we were assured we'd be welcome. We did. And we were completely accepted there. Homosexuals led groups and even managed the Sunday school program. So we had found a spiritual home we both could embrace.

That was over four years ago. Our government allows same-sex marriage in this province, our church accepts this, but what a time we had trying to find someone to perform the ceremony.

The first one we approached was our new church's minister. Months before, she had booked off the whole month of August for holidays. We had already set the day and told people, so we had to find someone else.

We approached a member of our church we knew was open to same-sex marriage, who was ministering at a nearby United Church. We knew that congregation rejected homosexuality but asked if he could perform the ceremony at our church. A few days later he called and explained, with deep regret, that as long as he was under contract to that church, even off site, he could not perform a same-sex marriage.

I approached an unemployed ordained minister I knew for over twenty years. She said no. We heard about a same-sex couple who were both ministers in a neighbouring community. I called and inquired. She also had to give me no for an answer. Not because she did not want to perform this ceremony, but once again, because she was employed by a congregation who disapproved of same-sex marriage. I was most affected by her no because I knew how it must have hurt her, that in order to feed her family, she had to refuse me the same rights as she enjoyed.

As a member to the Unitarian church for years, I knew we had the option of a chaplain from there, but we wanted a Christian service performed by a minister. After sharing my woes in a group I belonged to in our church, one spoke up with some helpful information. Apparently, the performer of the ceremony doesn't need to be a licensed minister, but the person who signs the legal documents does. It so happened that a woman we had become friends with there was in the process of becoming ordained. She would not be legal in time to sign our documents, but we asked our church's octogenarian Minister Emeritus to do the legalities. He was delighted to participate, and our friend who was still in training was overjoyed that we would be her first wedding. She used our time together in pre-marital counselling as training hours for her education. She is also married to a woman.

Our wedding on a shoestring budget went off without a hitch. After that rough beginning, everything fell into place beautifully, and we enjoyed a picture perfect, classical church wedding. Although my mother-in-law struggled with the idea and originally planned on being on another continent during our nuptials, she did come around and at least attended the ceremony.

We live in a small town in the Maritimes, and by chance, our wedding fell on Gay Pride day. Unfortunately, we were a little too busy to attend the parade that year. I wore a white gown with a long train, and my daughter walked me down the aisle as my three granddaughters aged two, eight, and thirteen, managed my train. My daughter sang a beautiful song, and our dearest friends did readings and stood up with us. There were probably close to one hundred in attendance, including one transvestite, and two transsexuals, gay, straight, bi folks, and people from both families and our adoptive families, (the Twelve Step Program communities), from the Unitarian church and our new church. Our reception was an alcohol free, hot and cold potluck feast, serviced by our friends. The decorations were borrowed and homemade.

There were reports from those in attendance that there was a feeling of love in the room they had never felt before in a Christian sanctuary. And that day, the bell rang and told the downtown area of the joyful union of lovers, just as it had in that old bell tower over seventy years earlier, on the day my grandparents were married there.

"The expectations we give to each other,
and put ourselves through,
are a lot like living in a shell."

3

COVERBOY

David Le

"Are you going to find another husband?" asked my aunts. My grandmother, who was dying from liver cancer, sat upright on her hospital bed. White sheets lingered over her like vultures, held back by her laughter.

"No, he will only get under my foot!"

She was plump for her condition, and her wrinkled skin shone with the intensity of a tortoise's shell. She had made no efforts to reconcile with her diabetes and took measures to spite it instead. Her body jiggled because of her giggling, and I couldn't help but think of her as the chocolate mousse she ate daily since she was diagnosed with diabetes.

Her scorn was not just directed towards food she wasn't allowed to eat, but towards men as well, an attitude which seems to be shared amongst all of her daughters and their daughters thereafter; an attitude borne from what my mother would call a "legacy of shitty fathers."

The women in my family had always looked up to my grand-mother, which was peculiar because she was rarely in their lives. My mother, along with her three sisters, had to abandon grandmother and their home in the Laotian countryside. Having only reached adolescence by the time they arrived in Canada, as refugees, they endured suitors hoping to take advantage of their tiny frames and vocabulary. Without my grandmother's calloused-toed guidance, the women in my family experienced Canadian "hospitality" which has led to their restlessness and each of their divorces, an attempt to reject the "fantasies" imposed on them.

Since my grandmother's sudden death, my mother has begun to exhibit the same disdain for authority with the same ferocity as my grandmother, who'd aggressively down pudding cups like shots of tequila. However, unlike my grandmother's new addiction to chocolate, my mother spent her time watching soap operas and reading Harlequin novels. My home was thrown into disarray, and my father began to sleep on the couch because of the lack of romance, and within months, my mom and her sisters moved into a large house together. Each of them inhabited a floor of their own, and would congregate at supper where they would have a show-and-tell of their broken utensils and talk about their newfound feminism. The males in the family protested to the move, demanding tradition, family values, and human rights, but it ended promptly when they learned that the women had no problem beating with, or throwing at them, whatever items were in their hands. At first, these would be small, hand-held items: ladles, vacuum handles, and if the men were lucky, vegetables, but eventually the women threw items proportionate of their rage, such as a chair when my mother found out I lost my younger brother.

My mother preferred to have a daughter as her first child, which may explain my innate fascination with the boys at school. Unfor-tunately for her, however, I was born male. She'd try multiple times, but after three sons with no success with females, she finally gave up.

Frustrated at my father for producing only the Y chromosome, she vowed that she'd raise her children romantically inclined and proper, just as in her books. This had proved to be problematic for my brothers who would often ask for a woman's point of view, to which my mother would reply, "She is always right!" and then continue to burrow herself into her Harlequin novel.

My father eventually left the house, much to the dismay of my mother; to pursue a life he envisioned consisted of true family values. Although I had predicted a separation, I did not foresee my mother's reaction against my father's firm illusion of a family unit. She insisted the family was fine as it was and the expectations she endured in life, and from him, were unrealistic, yet the sounds of my father's footsteps continued to prevail over their weeks of intense arguing.

Although my mother brushed us off, she had influenced my brothers and I in her own way by leaving around the house, on counter tops and empty couches, romance novels with dog-eared pages that my brothers and I would occupy ourselves with while growing up. We, as a result, have become, as our father had alluded, "Animals." Though my brothers and I would never contemplate harming a lady, and would, instead, offer our own blood in place of a woman's tears, I couldn't help but admire the way my father left, dragging and slow, with the light against his large backpack, like a tortoise in the sun.

As a result of the novels my mother would leave around the house, I have a lot of expectations for romance, but I've yet to experience it. In my mind, not only am I slouching on a throne, but men are also feeding me grapes with nothing but velvet around their waists. I swipe my finger across my phone, scrolling through, with increasing disappointment, profile after profile, picture after picture, of men in washrooms with their arms outstretched, not holding grapes, but holding up their phones for the selfie, a self-taken photo. Of course, seeing people through a screen automatically opens them up to judgement. It's the nature of things; celebrities, models—they are all perfect—so growing up exposed to the television, it is within my reasoning that anyone behind the screen must appear perfect, and if less than that, at least appear interesting. While that makes me completely shallow, I should also point out that I am one thousand times more forgiving towards those in person; however, being the hermit I consider myself to be, no one would be able to confirm that. So instead of meeting people and giving myself a chance to show the world the glory of my personality, I sit here in front of my computer screen mumbling, "Next, next, next," while feeling as lonely and ugly as everyone else.

Being modelled after the men in romance novels, failing to meet the physical requirements, and being the first-born son of immigrants, has resulted in two conflicting identities. There have been several times I have been fetishized because of my appearance, which is very unlike the men of the covers of romance novels. These men, Caucasian, burly, and stocky in stature, all have scruff on their faces, a chiselled jaw, and forearms made for catching, fanning, and of course, feeding beautiful dames. I, on the other hand, have a feminine and childish appearance, which I've gathered from messages from men expressing their desire to "fill that Asian boy-pussy." Feelings of inadequacy arose, and the realization that I could not live up to the fantasies that my mother and her sisters have been able to employ when they arrived in Canada, left me feeling marginalized. Yet, despite the frequent offensive messages, I still click on the bright illuminated circle above the profiles because, to me, it still felt nice to be wanted.

There was hope, however, as I had a date with a guy who didn't describe me as some foreign import with hard-to-read instructions. Indeed, I was looking forward to finally meeting this person, someone who saw past my ethnicity and my boy-like appearance, and above all, a guy that delivers pizza for a living. When he rang my doorbell, I sent him a text explaining that the door was unlocked. I sifted my way onto my rose petal-covered bed and posed as Rose did in Titanic. I placed the petals over my pale body like pepperoni on raw dough and waited. It had already been fifteen minutes since I sent him the text, and I was beginning to feel entitled to whatever he could offer me: love, romance, and pizza. Stuffed with impatience, I put on my clothes, walked past my roommates' bedrooms, and headed towards the front door where I found my date—a greasy blond with a Hawaiian t-shirt. His back was hunched, his eyes were disinterested, and I could see the smell emanating from the stains on his shorts. I was excited to live the movies for even one night! I set aside my disappointment of his tardiness and lack of food, and instead found my mood rising into a golden brown as he raised his pale arms and offered me some marijuana.

We drove on the highway that evening and made an unexpected stop on the side of the dark road. I could determine that the delivery boy was trying to be spontaneous and suggested we sit in the back seat of the car. I rolled my eyes in the darkness and told him that we shouldn't because of the risk of getting caught, yet there I was two minutes later in the back seat with my pants unfastened and a flashlight directed at me. I relied on the childhood logic that if I didn't see them, they didn't see me either, and pulled my clothes over my face. In the videos, the officer would then ask the girl, "Is everything alright here?" to which the flustered and embarrassed girl would reply, "Yes, officer." In hindsight, I should have shook my head, but instead I just thought, "Even now, in this situation, I am still seen as the feminine one," and so I nodded.

It wasn't until we drove home that I learned I was as shallow as the men I'd reject daily on the Internet, and that, like the adults in my family, the expectations we give to each other, and put ourselves through, are a lot like living in a shell—they are of no comfort to anyone but ourselves. I realized I was no better than anyone else and would choose to, thereafter, enjoy the fantasy while it lasted.

"My siblings and I learned more
about my mother from images
than words. Our home shifted to
the cadence of her dreams."

THE COST OF LIVING

Valérie Bah

It was only at age twenty-seven that I fully realised I'd grown up on welfare. On a late July afternoon, as my mother and I rushed downtown to pay for a parking ticket in my sister's rent-to-own Nissan, we bypassed the highway and detoured through an inner city artery bordered by Dairy Queen and McDonald's plazas.

"That, is Ottawa Housing," said my mother nonchalantly nodding toward an avenue that led to one of our old neighbourhoods.

She initially kissed her teeth, but I insisted that we cruise through Carver Place, a crescent-shaped plot of attached housing, like a rundown ski village. Around this horseshoe lived other Haitian and African families, a first-generation cultural checkerboard or whatever my grade ten civics teacher taught us about Canadian immigration.

As we rolled away past the concrete and primary-coloured park where I'd once flung a used condom at my friend with a stick, my mother said, "If only you knew how far we've come."

I had some idea. When my mother, the family's usual sole income provider, packed her five children into the Dodge Caravan for grocery trips, we *whoop whooped*, then held our breaths with her at the checkout counter, hoping the scanner wouldn't beep an overpriced total. The no-name cereals that imitate their brand-name counterparts were always cut first. In winter, sometimes our un-settled hydropower bills cut central heating and kept us clustered in the kitchen around the stove or puttering around in comforters like walking marshmallows. Weeks later, we would also receive a food-drive package of a frozen turkey, powdered mashed potatoes, fruit cake, most of which would stretch out for at least two weeks. What didn't fit into our usual rotation of rice, beans, and Kraft Dinner—the ever-mysterious box of turkey stuffing and tin of cranberry sauce—accumulated at the back of the pantry until next year.

Moments of relative plenty came with summer visits from my paternal grandparents when the pantry stayed stocked with sweetened condensed milk, the ambrosia of Haitian cuisine. This sugar-rush-for-breakfast was just as gratifying drizzled on one-dollar French baguettes as it was pilfered by the spoonful before bed. I was gifted at sneaking it.

But the trade-off with these summer visits was the tightening of house rules. Suddenly, we were to take regular baths and sit dutifully in the living room instead of stealing scrap wood from the green bins of construction sites to build tree forts in the shallow urban woods with the neighbourhood kids. I'd survey the trajectory of mosquitoes and pinch the segment of skin they were biting until they burst while listening to my parents use the voices they reserved for Sunday morning phone calls to relatives in Africa—smiling and deferential.

My father had left Cotonou, Benin, at age eighteen to pursue an

IT degree in Canada, but twelve years later was prone to brooding silently in the living room. As a sometimes construction worker, sometimes security guard, mostly unemployed young father of five children, our grandparents' stays provoked him to fits of housecleaning that made us afraid to leave our room.

My parents and their in-laws would gather in the living room around a plate of Maria biscuits and orange juice, making jokes with no punch lines and laughing a little too long at them. The only moments that prompted me to follow the conversation came when they brought up things they mutually hated or loved. They would cheer when someone quoted the Eddy Murphy film *Coming to America* or do a send-up of Jean Chrétien. Michael Jackson, they loathed. The cosiest moment I ever saw between them was when they exchanged anecdotes about how disgusting they thought it was for two men to be in love. I kept my face neutral, confused about whether they were so angry or just trying to bond over another topic.

A few summers later, I settled on an answer. It was Canada Day, one of the rare times we left the house as a family, and I was trailing behind my mother in the Byward market when she swivelled her head and saw the men first. Ahead of us, a couple held hands, one of them Black, wearing jean cut-offs and a confident smile. She didn't say much, but her furrowed eyebrows related everything.

My siblings and I learned more about my mother from images than words. Our home shifted to the cadence of her dreams. She would mention an early morning vision, and if it didn't predict the future, it expressed her latest intuition. The time she dreamed of spirits disguised in sheets scurrying from our basement's legendary dirty laundry piles initiated a deep cleaning of our house. When she visualized Jesus's return and saw our family among the damned, she was re-baptized in the Seventh Day Adventist after a seventeen-year hiatus.

Dreams. One morning at age twelve, I woke up sour and drenched, having pissed the bed again. In that night's dream, I recalled hugging Francine, the puffy-haired French Canadian girl who sat across from me in homeroom. The invisible balm on my damp mattress was remembering how the dream version of her smiled at me so broadly that the clear elastics fastening her braces stretched to their limit. Also, she was naked. I usually kept quiet about my dreams.

It wasn't until I started my freshman year at an evangelical boarding school implanted in Oshawa, a car-manufacturing city, that I learned to control my bladder. Joy, a coquettish Filipina and one of my first roommates, would tease me for the new sleeping position I adopted when we'd decided to move our beds together—that of a mummy, arms immovable at my side or sometimes crossed on my chest. I flinched over my cereal, one Saturday morning in the cafeteria, when she and a friend playfully announced that they'd prompted me to talk in my sleep the night before. If I'd said anything at all, they never told me what it was.

The late Friday afternoon before my parents enrolled me in that school, they beckoned me into their bedroom.

"We need to warn you about how *not* to be with boys," they said gravely.

"You must not giggle with them,"

"Don't go off alone with them."

"In fact, avoid them."

And so went the list of maxims. By the time the talk ended, we were a trio of outlines on their queen-sized bed. The sun had set and all three of us were sitting in shadows because no one had bothered to flip the light switch. Incidentally, my mother had started a campaign against unnecessarily wasting energy in the house that year. Semi-distracted that they'd bought me new pyjamas, my first brand-new set that I determined to keep urine-free. I also felt responsible for the fact that the school tuition would be another expense clawing into grocery money.

I was not only eager to obey my parents' wishes regarding the opposite sex, but also smug that I could bewilder them with my chastity. To my delight, there was safety in the scrutiny the school administration maintained when it came to dating. Couples who were caught pawing at each other or loitering unsupervised in the school chapel were chastised with a two-way restraining order. "Social Bound," they called it. The risk was nil for me; I was the goofy side-kick to the pretty girls and I rolled my eyes whenever conversations turned to boys.

But I felt a pang of guilt at the beginning of my sophomore year. On an impulse, I reached out to a solitary freshman I had noticed sitting defiant and alone at Friday night vespers. Back in the dormitory that night, shortly after room check, I knocked at her room door and introduced myself. She invited me in and I sat cross-legged on her spare single bed and oohed and aahed exaggeratedly at the family photos she showed me, intent on showing interest. At one point, imperceptibly, there was a lull in the conversation and suddenly I was afraid to make eye contact. That was when she asked me:

"You like massages?"

"Um, what?"

"You know, massages!"

My eyes flitted to her as she slid off her sweater, unhooked her bra, and belly flopped on her bed, motioning me to approach. Suddenly, I was persuaded that the school dean was on the other side of the door.

"Go ahead, you do me and then I'll return the favour."

At that, I left and speed walked down the hall to the dorm phone booths, even though calling hours were over. I woke my mother with a collect call during which I whispered nonsensical phrases about making new friends, and when she interrupted me, asking if everything was okay, I nodded in response, even though she couldn't see me.

Sometime during that school year, I boarded the choir tour bus on a weekday to attend a political rally in a mall parking lot. Rumour had it that the finance officer of my church high school had an up and coming politician cousin—a ruddy greying Ken doll. I chanted his name timidly along with the rest of my classmates, grateful for an hour off from classes. Reeling from the sugar high of the cookies and juice the teachers passed out afterward, I commented to a friend that I thought Stockwell Day was a catchy name.

The giddiness I felt from participating in the student council and social activities at school contrasted with the gloom I felt when returning home for holidays. I can't forget the thud of The Slap. The summer before my senior year of high school, I clipped my hair short, stunned by the shape of my small Afro, squinting from all angles at my mirror image. Before I decided how I felt about my new hair, my father, who had come home from an errand, saw me and silently backhanded me, hard, across the face. I weaved hair extensions into my hair as soon as it grew long enough, but also, it was the last summer I would ever spend at home.

The first time I went abroad as an adult and someone asked me to describe life in Canada, I answered, "Well, it's kind of unsophisticated, and people are a bit closed-minded." I didn't understand it then, but my words were naive projections of my insular sliver of experience in my country.

The second time someone asked me that question, I flippantly mumbled a summary of the country profile entry I'd read that day on *The Economist* website. "Separated historically by an economic East-West divide," I sputtered at a Russian exchange student, four glasses of wine into a house party.

By that time, I was well-versed in the inanity of the fourth-season plot line of the L Word and aware that in the year 2000, Stockwell Day, former leader of the Canadian Alliance, a short-lived conservative party, acknowledged that he would block a Supreme Court decision legalizing same-sex marriage. I also knew, from tremulous experience, that no one would "Social Bound" me for sneaking off to the bathroom with a girlfriend in a crowded bar. I knew that, if anything, a surly waitress just rapped at the door.

It makes sense that weeks short of receiving my first long-term job offer, I came out to my mother via a terse filibuster of an email in which I avoided filling in gaps about fabricated boyfriends or why I seldom visited them. Rather, I curtly reminded her that gay marriage was legalized in our province. She never addressed the political content of the email but replied within seconds, with three lines about how she loved me no matter what. Following that, there was a month of awkward phone calls during which she would strictly inquire if I was eating enough and whether I wanted to say a prayer with her before we hung up. At long last, it's very fitting that our next truly intimate conversation started with, "Last night, I dreamed that..."

"I hid who I was from everyone,
even myself.
I created a whole new persona
in an attempt to convince myself
that I was straight."

WHO I AM: THE STORY OF A SECOND GENERATION LESBIAN

Nicole MacFarlane

Growing up in the 1990s in a small town, I knew my family was different from other families in my town. My mother and father split before I was even born as I was a product of a week long relationship. Between the ages of two and nineteen, I had no contact with my father. My biological mom is also a lesbian, but she has not always been comfortable with that fact due to the area she grew up and also negative personal experiences. My mom began dating women when I was just over a year old, and stayed with the first woman for about five or six years. I was in elementary school when they split up. I understood that most kids have a mom and dad, not a mom and a mom, and the kids I went to school with made sure I knew that I was different.

When my mom and this first woman broke up, my mom started dating another woman shortly after. This woman is now her wife, and they've been together for over fifteen years. My stepmom used to work at the daycare I was enrolled in, and this is where they met. My stepmom's stories and struggles had a huge impact on me because I realized the enormous impact that being LGBT, and out, can have on an individual in all areas of their life.

Halfway through elementary school was when my mom and my stepmom started dating. My stepmom has two kids from a previous marriage, and they moved all three of us kids in together, under the guise of two single mothers helping each other out. Again, they hid their relationship to protect us kids from any more harm. They set up individual bedrooms and attempted to hide their relationship from us and from any friends we had over. However, at least to me as the oldest child, it was obvious that they were dating. This added to my confusion, and I became convinced for the longest time that being LGBT was a thing a person had to hide.

My parents tried hiding their relationship to protect my step siblings and I from further bullying, but in a small town, rumours spread fast. The invisible scars from the bullying and the taunts that I too would be gay haunted me growing up. I was in elementary school, grade one, when an older student told me that I was going to be gay because my mom was. As a grade one student, that took me for a loop. I was highly confused as "gay" was not yet in my vocabulary, but I quickly learned that this was something bad, something that had to be hidden. I filed that fact away, and each time I heard it while in elementary school, I became increasingly confused. I was also told in elementary school that my mom was a fag/dyke, and numerous other derogatory terms. Parents were hesitant to send my classmates over for sleepovers, and teachers called my mom's partner my aunt, which added to my confusion. All I knew was that my mom was living with another woman, and that that woman was like a parent to me.

It was in middle school that I realized I was attracted to girls, not boys. However, because of the experiences of my mother and my stepmother and also the words from other classmates, I hid who I was from everyone, even myself. I created a whole new persona in an attempt to convince myself that I was straight. I listened to the latest boy bands and faked a crush on one of the members. I pretended to be interested in the boys in my grade, and I feminized myself. Despite these attempts, I was still bullied because I was overweight, I acted differently from the other girls, and I had two female parents. Middle school became a living nightmare for me, and I was removed from school for a week because of the problems. Even after I returned, the bullying continued.

In high school, things slowly evened out, at least until grade eleven. It was in grade eleven that my best friend and I started exploring our feelings for each other. We never officially started dating, but it must have been obvious to other students that we were both LGBT. I began hearing the words fag/dyke, and other such terms directed at me, not my parents. Students who knew about my parents told me that I "was gay because my mom is," or "it was only a matter of time." I began to question my own sexuality, wondering if they were right. In grade twelve, couples started planning for the prom, and then new barriers were introduced to me. Friends of mine who were openly gay and dating were not allowed to bring their same-sex partner as a prom date. The face of inequality was introduced again, and I understood on a different level the changes that had to be made to introduce equality to everyone.

Even after I finally realized I was gay, it took me years to accept that I am not a lesbian because of my mom. I am a lesbian because that's who I am. I would not change my life, my family, or my relationship for anything. Being raised by same-sex parents did not influence my sexual orientation because same-sex parenting does not have any impact on a child's sexual orientation. I had to bury the words of former classmates and realize that nothing could have changed my sexual orientation as it was encoded in me from birth. This was a huge realization for me, and some days I still struggle with understanding my sexual orientation.

The first time I came out to my mother she denied that I was a lesbian. She told me it was "just a phase." This hurt to a deep extent, and it was not until years down the road that I realized why she said this. It took a deep conversation with my stepmom for me to understand that "no parent *wants* their child to be gay, especially a gay parent." I finally understand all the emotional turmoil my mother went through in accepting the fact that I was also a lesbian, but it was not her fault I was. Although I struggled with who I was, it must have been a larger struggle for her to accept me. She grew up in the 1980s, in the era of AIDS, of extreme prejudice, and in a town that still does not recognize LGBT community members. She moved me to a little bit larger town when I was a baby, but experienced the burning of a gay bar, prejudice from employers, and shunning from family members. I finally realized that she was trying to protect me from other people, and from pain and suffering. She was not trying to deny me who I truly was; she was trying to deny me pain.

Although I have only focused on the negative aspects so far in this narrative, there have been some phenomenal moments growing up. These moments enforced the fact that my parents are just like any other set of heterosexual parents. Birthday parties, family trips, family jokes, Christmas mornings around the Christmas tree, holiday dinners, graduations, anniversaries, and sports events to name a few. We laughed, we fought, we cried, and we loved like a "normal" family. My parents raised my step siblings and I like any other parents, except for the fact that they had to hide who they truly were for the longest time. If I can be half the parent my mother was for me when I have kids, I know for a fact I will have done good for them. Watching my biological mom finally accept who she was, and tell me herself that she is a lesbian, has been some of the happiest moments of my life. Having my fiancée and I as their witnesses at their wedding was an incredible moment for me, as I never thought that my parents could get legally married.

I am currently studying for the LSAT as I want to go to law school to study human rights law and family law. My experiences growing up fueled my passion for equality for all families, no matter their makeup. The moments that I have mentioned in this narrative are moments that changed me, for the better and for the worse. They have fueled my passion and desire to fight for the rights of all families.

"You can't choose to be heterosexual
or homosexual. Those are matters
of pathways, hormones, and genes."

COURAGE, A CASTLE, AND THE *CUNT COLOURING BOOK*

Andrea Hayward

There are people who stand up, wave flags, and are arrested as they cry for fairness and justice. There are others who live in countries where being gay comes with a mandatory life sentence, corrective rape, or execution. I am fortunate because I am living in a place where it is, mostly, ok to be gay. Even so, coming out changed my life. I am writing this because I believe that the only way things will get better is if people like us speak out and show that we are humans who have as much value as do our straight neighbours—despite what the rest of the world says. Courage and pride can come in the smallest of actions, and the unlikeliest of places. This is my story.

I came out in a castle. The gray stone walls, lead paned windows, and Hogwartsian dining hall of my university residence still haunt my dreams. The building was a seminary, with towers and turrets, located smack in the middle of the University of Toronto. Built to house theology students, a gradual reduction in the number of aspiring ministers left room for oddballs like me—a random U of T genetics graduate student from out of province. We read in a sunny paned-glass library, ate in a grand dining hall, and dodged film crews who regularly turned our home into medieval bedrooms or ancient tombs.

I had lived in this residence for three years while I worked on my research degree. When I graduated, I continued to live in the residence for a while, while I figured out what to do with my life. During that time, I was employed as a science writer, and I spent long periods in the library, pouring over scientific papers for a book chapter on blood vessel growth in the early mouse embryo. (Not exactly a riveting topic!) As I worked, my mind drifted, and I couldn't stop thinking about someone from my program. We knew each other a little from work, but all I could think of was how much I enjoyed spending time with her, and how much I wanted to be with her. I had never felt this way about anyone before. In fact I didn't think that I *could* feel that way about someone. And she was female. But there it was. All of a sudden, I was no longer asexual, but...lesbian?

This was unexpected, so I did what any self-respecting scientist would do. I thought. And wrote. And thought. And wrote some more. I filled thirty journals with writing and analysis. I looked at nude art and analyzed my responses. I read research articles on the genetics of LGBT individuals. I critically analyzed every significant relationship in my life to that point. In short, I handled the question pretty much the way I would tackle any scientific problem. The answer was always the same. It is true. I am gay.

That was the easy part.

It is funny how words can be acts of courage. The first time I came out, I spoke to a good friend. Even so, during that conversation, I couldn't bring myself to say "gay," let alone "lesbian." There, in the privacy of her room, over a cup of tea, I stammered that "I... might...not...maybe...kind of...possibly...be...quite...straight."

I was lucky. Though my friend followed a non-gay-positive religious denomination, she didn't react in horror. In fact, she supported me as I struggled to come out to myself, and to those about whom I cared. A person with a good sense of humor, she left a fresh bunch of pussy willows outside my door the next day—as they too were just starting to come out.

Coming out. It's amazing how two words can tear your soul apart. Being gay is a choice, but not a biological one. You can't choose who you love or to what body type you are attracted. You can't choose to be heterosexual or homosexual. Those are matters of pathways, hormones, and genes. The choice is one of integrity, and it is quite simple. Be true to who you are, and risk *everything*, or create a straight persona over your true self and hope that you aren't forced to come out later.

But this is a tale of courage, and there is little that takes more courage than being honest, especially when the stakes are high. Realizing who I was, and accepting it was like being flayed alive. Strip after strip of my flesh was torn off, until nothing remained. I felt it physically, mentally, spiritually—everything was pain and fear and grief. Pure anguish. Everything you know is wrong, and those things that have supported you in the past—identity, faith, love, and family—all of them are taken away. It is being burned alive, plunged again and again and again into boiling water. Your blisters get blisters. You are horrendously alone, and more than alone because the world itself is against you. You can't go for a walk without being slapped in the face by the sight of a hetero couple holding hands. You try to escape into TV and movies, but they are all about straights. Ads on the radio, billboards, magazines? All straight, or (worse) have gay people played for laughs. Even in my castle, some of the religious students were more than happy to talk about their discomfort around "evil" gay people. Some helpful soul deliberately tore up the residence posters about it being a "gay-safe space." You are utterly vulnerable, and everywhere you turn, something new is rubbing salt into your torn and burnt flesh. There is no escape.

And yet this external vulnerability is nothing compared to the hell that is tearing apart your own mind. Everything you thought you knew about yourself. Everything you hoped. Everything you dreamed. All of it ends at once. You hate yourself. And then you hate yourself for hating yourself.

In the end, it boils down to courage. It takes courage to look at yourself, and decide that—at least for now—perhaps there is something in you somewhere that is still worthwhile. It takes courage to look at the pillars of your faith and to realize that though the "infallible" holy book says that you are an abomination, that perhaps that book is wrong. (And what else is wrong in it?) Finally, it is courage that, when you are eventually standing on the edge of a seventh-floor apartment balcony, perfectly calm, and ready to put an end to the pain, that you step back and keep going.

It is all courage. But it is courage in small steps.

Shortly after I came out to myself I decided to check out the local gay bookstore. I walked down Yonge Street one night and passed by it twice before I allowed myself to consider going in. The rainbow flag above the door might as well have been a glowing neon sign saying "Look at the dyke over here!" On my final pass, I pretended to check out the science fiction bookstore below it, while eyeing all of the passersby. I felt like some kind of debased criminal, wanting to go to a "gay" store. When the street was clear, I opened the door and scuttled up the staircase, desperately hoping that no one would see me. The shop keeper acknowledged me—himself a flamboyant character—and I scurried to hide in the darkest corner I could find, trying to stay low to avoid some outsider's glance revealing me through the tiny crack of window not covered by lesbian mysteries. I was amazed—and a bit terrified—at all of the books. There was porn of course, and lots of it, but also a huge collection of non-porn items. Still a little scared, I browsed something innocuous.

The door opened, and I heard a new customer speak to the shop clerk. He was trying to buy a present for his lesbian daughter, and wasn't sure what to get. The shopkeeper wasn't sure either, so he yelled over to me, "Hey, you're a dyke aren't you? What do you think of the *Cunt Colouring Book*?"

The...what? They *make* those? And...what do I think? Umm...I don't...

The ground sadly did not swallow me at that point, though I fervently wished it would.

"Do you have any ideas? Do you dykes go for the pussy shots?"

I stammered something like, "Gottagogoingtobelatefor something...," and fled like a bat out of hell. You could have seen a trail of fire left behind me.

It is funny how quickly things change. A few weeks later, I turned to that bookstore as a safe place after coming out to my parents. I suppose you can get used to anything if you have to. Though for the record, I can't say that the *Cunt Colouring Book* does much for me.

Flash forward to today. It has been a decade since I came out, and I can say that it did get better. Many people that I told already knew. One person in my residence knew I was gay two years before I figured it out, and had been inviting me to LGBT-friendly events, just in case I finally clued in. Some people were surprised. Most didn't care. Canada allows gay marriage, and though I've had many conversations with people who don't support it, I have only had gay slurs flung at me once. No one has come at me with a broken bottle yet, even though I now live in one of the most conservative provinces in the country.

Parents who struggled over potentially family-destroying news have begun to come to terms with it. Our relationship is actually stronger now than it was before, and while they aren't ever going to leap down the street waving rainbow flags, it could be a lot worse. There are still people whom I have been asked explicitly not to tell, but I work in a place where boss and co-workers alike know, and don't care that I am gay. Not everything has a happy ending. The woman I fell in love with turned out to be straight, and what friendship we had fell apart because of my unrequited feelings for her. Still, there are many other fish in the sea, and I've found that some of those fish even have rainbow scales!

In the end, life goes on. I am gay. I am worthwhile.

And I am courageous.

> "My family gradually caught on that my sudden interest in gay rights was personal. I think they figured there couldn't be anything threatening or fascinating about gay people if I was a part of that crowd."

COME OUT COME OUT WHOEVER YOU ARE

Joanne Brigden

Like most of the gay people I've met who were born in the 1950s, I grew up thinking I was the only person who was attracted to their own gender. There were exceptions, like the girl in high school who looked and dressed like a boy and even carried a black comb in her back pocket. I could never figure out where she got her courage, and I'm certain that, at the time, I saw it as stupidity. Did she want people to shun her? But they didn't. They liked her. I couldn't figure it out because I knew absolutely how homophobic my own friends and family were. As a coping mechanism, I created a third sex in my mind's fantasies. But more about that later.

When she graduated high school, my older sister went to work as a secretary at the local women's prison. It was a minimum-security place, so she and the inmates got to see each other every day. My sister was only seventeen and quite attractive, and I'm sure the women took great delight in teasing her with catcalls. She would come home with tales of women who had short, slicked-back hair, danced with each other, and ordered men's shoes out of the Eaton's catalogue. I was appalled and scared at her description of her idea of a lesbian. Was this my future? I knew I wasn't a femme, but I didn't fit this butch role she described either.

Apparently, a lot of the women were overweight, and at the time I weighed in at about 200 pounds or 90 kilos. I vowed to lose weight and keep my hair long lest anyone suspect I was one of "them." To give myself some credit, I also decided I would have the decency not to date men because it wouldn't be fair to either of us. I had three unmarried aunts who were fine with being single. Of course they were also staunch Roman Catholics who thought we were sinners for listening to Rolling Stones records so their version of the swinging single life had its drawbacks.

I did take a few stabs at entering the gay community. I lived with my family in the suburbs, so I would go to Toronto a few times a month to pick up a few copies of the gay newspaper, *Xtra!* I would always leave a copy on the bus home for the next passenger. How kind and risqué of me. Back in my room, I would pore through it for any listings for non-bar events, since I was always dieting and never wasted my precious calories on alcohol. My idea of the bar scene was that it was loud and hard to have a meaningful exchange with another person. In other words, it was accurate. In the 1970s, the kind of events I was looking for were few and far between. The very first lesbians' meeting was one I unwisely got from a general announcements board at the University of Toronto. It was at a house and run by a couple of very radical women. The welcoming announcement by one of them was, "Lesbians cannot be monogamous!" Oh. There was one girl in particular who was very amused that I had come in from suburbia, and she got my phone number from some petition we had all signed. For weeks, she would make crank calls to our house until one time, suspecting it was her again, I lowered my voice and answered, "Police Sergeant Stewart, who is this!?" Problem solved but back into the closet for another decade for me.

I had zero self-confidence, no courage, and I had no intention of testing my parents' and siblings' love for me by coming out of the closet. What I did have was an imagination that got me through years of solitude. I would get a crush on some TV star, and we would have a beautiful life together inside my head. However, while I truly believe these fantastic relationships kept me going, after awhile "this way lies madness," and I knew it.

Finally, after years of therapy and several moves to and from Toronto, I began to regularly attend lesbians' coming-out meetings at the 519 Community Centre. At thirty-seven, I joined the social group Out and Out, and got to know some real live homosexuals.

My family gradually caught on that my sudden interest in gay rights was personal. I think they figured there couldn't be anything threatening or fascinating about gay people if I was a part of that crowd. Luckily, this was around the time Ellen Degeneres came out. At the time, I didn't see it as a big deal, but it was a societal game-changer. Oprah Winfrey gave Ellen her seal of approval. In the mainstream 1990s, that mattered big time.

I said to my half-deaf father while he was driving me somewhere, "I'm gay."

"What? You want me to drop you at the Bay?"

To his credit, when we got our wires uncrossed, he said, "Oh, well there's nothing wrong with that." The only thing my mother, best friend, and two of my three sisters never forgave me for was my conversion to cat lover. I had been so smug that I didn't fit into the "cat-loving dyke" stereotype, and then I moved into a house that had two cats living in it; two cats who weren't about to cede their room to me just because I'd moved a bed and a dresser into it. I not only bonded with them, but now I even have a dog!

Now that we have gay marriage, better awareness of human rights, and many anti-bullying programs, I would like to believe it is much easier to come out today, but, in my heart, I don't think it is.

> "A well-dressed woman asked us
> which one of us was the mother,
> and we replied, 'We both are.'"

CHOSEN FAMILY

Jane Byers

Our family was conceived on a backpacking trip in the Canadian Rockies. We walked up and down mountains, quickly past grizzly bears feeding on roots, slowly past views of the massive Mount Assiniboine. Like most important questions, the "kid" question percolated in the back of our brains. Towards the end of the trip, after many days of quiet walking, we both agreed that, yes, we wanted a child. It seemed as natural as donning our packs and hiking boots by then.

Neither one of us had a strong desire to be pregnant/give birth; hence, adoption emerged as the best fit for our own values. This was around the time that borders were closing to international adoption for same-sex couples. There were thousands of Canadian kids that needed homes and here we were, a couple who wanted kids, so we opted for domestic adoption through the Ministry of Child and Family Services.

"My partner and I would like to start the adoption process," I managed to speak into the phone calmly during my initial phone call with the adoption worker.

"Please give me your and your husband's name," responded the government worker. After I stated that my partner is a woman, she backpedalled to correct her mistake and explained that they did not discriminate on the basis of sexual orientation. Throughout the adoption process, we were consistently told it would likely take longer to find a match for us because we were not the ideal family that many social workers or birth families imagine for adoptive children. This was always followed by an awkward explanation that the ministry was not homophobic but wanted what was best for the children in care and that it was easier to get buy-in from all parties involved with mom/dad adoptive parents.

Thankfully, our social worker saw beyond our sexuality. We were considered for twins she was trying to place. We were skeptical given the systemic biases, so we were pleased to hear from our social workers that we were one of two families still in the running after their deliberations. We had to write an essay outlining how we would raise a boy and ensure positive male role models. The process seemed to drag on, and when we pressed them on why, we were finally told it was because of the concerns raised by the evangelical Christian foster parents. We were requested by the social workers to meet the foster parents in person to reassure them and to help them tolerate the thought of us as the adoptive parents. While this was a healthy step for developing a working relationship, it further delayed things for more than a month.

Eventually, we made the long, snowy drive to Kelowna to show the foster family we didn't have snakes for hair and to answer any questions they had about us. All I wanted to do was see the little girl and boy we'd heard so much about, and whom we wanted to adopt. I wanted to witness their every movement and gesture, knowing that at fourteen months they were becoming more mobile and changing so much every day. In the meeting we were asked, "How will you feel if your kids turn out to be heterosexual?" I swallowed my disbelief and answered the question as best I could: "I'm not a ballet dancer, but if one of my kids turns out to be, I'd be happy for them. Chances are they will be straight. That's totally fine. We just want our kids to be happy." Despite the questions from left field, it was clear they loved the twins, whom they'd fostered since shortly after birth. We ate up every detail—the foster mother told us that the girl was Ms Energy and the boy, Mr. Energy Efficient. That she stole his bottle, but she also took care of her brother.

While we thought the meeting went well, it wasn't made clear to us who was the decision-maker and we had no idea where we stood. Days passed during which we busied ourselves with distractions, held back from hounding the social worker, and tried to be subtle in our baby-proofing efforts. When the phone call finally came, I was standing in the kitchen staring at the call display, scared and excited. The news we received set in motion two weeks of frenzy, what most couples have nine months to do: buying and assembling cribs, strollers, decorating their room, stocking up on baby supplies.

Next we spent fourteen days of "hard labour" at the foster parents' home, getting to know the twins' routines, personalities, and gradually taking over all aspects of care for the twins. We felt particularly under the microscope even more than just anyone would have been because we are a same-sex couple. The most difficult moment came in the kitchen one day when the foster mom said, "So how does it feel knowing you will go to hell because of your lifestyle choice?" I chose not to engage and instead focused on cleaning the sippy cups, while thinking up rebuttals (Hell will be more fun). The foster mother continued her questions from the other room as I tried to breathe and contain my reaction. Thankfully we debriefed and got support with our social worker after that.

The foster parents' began to swap their beliefs steeped in stereotypes for ones based on first-hand experience. They saw us caring for the children. They saw the children gradually coming to us for their needs to be met, and us meeting those needs at every opportunity. During the last meal we ate together in this transition, they said that they believed the children were well placed.

We were bleary-eyed mothers. Our friends dropped off meals and clothes. We hunkered in and held them a lot those first months. The first year was a blur. The irony that our sexual orientation was an obstacle in adoption and the post-adoptive reality of life with twin toddlers was not lost on us. Never had I felt less like a lesbian in all my life. Too tired for sex, too frazzled to finish any conversations with friends about what rights were being won or lost in the world. We would remark that our lesbian "membership cards" would be revoked any day.

At home in the small, progressive city we live in, we are easy to spot coming down the street—two moms with twins of colour. It feels like everyone knows us or knows of us. I feel our differences most acutely when travelling to Bible belts: the Okanagan or the US mid-west. Pre-kids, we only caught the eye of other lesbian couples when travelling. We are so clearly a unit now, kids yelling "Look Mama. Look Mom," we get stared at. Sometimes it's amusing, but mostly it's tiring. We answer questions such as what do they call each of you? Do you have male role models? My personal favourite happened in an elevator in Florida. A well-dressed woman asked us which one of us was the mother, and we replied, "We both are." She turned her back and urgently pushed the elevator buttons.

My four-year-old daughter came home from daycare recently and said, "My friend at school says that boys can only marry girls and that girls can't marry girls and boys can't marry boys."

I looked at her and said, "Well, I'm a girl and I'm married to mama, who is also a girl, so girls can definitely marry girls and boys can marry boys, too." She marched back to childcare the next day and found her friend right away, "You are wrong! Girls can marry girls and boys can marry boys, too." I stood there watching, waiting. The little girl looked at me confused. I shrugged and said, "I'm a girl and I'm married to another girl." The friend seemed satisfied and asked, "Okay, do you want to play with the blocks?" Off they went.

It was a relief to be able to state as a fact that girls can marry girls. Most of our friends in the US don't have that option, and their relationships are de-legitimized as a result. In Canada, it is simply a fact that same-sex marriage is legal.

We are one of two lesbian parent families in our children's kindergarten class. We are not pioneers. When we were picking a kindergarten, we were immediately put at ease by the teacher who let us know that she had seen my partner's documentary about same-sex couples adopting (including our story). Whew, no explanation needed. We have already dealt with homophobia in kindergarten and are now the "diversity" curriculum experts. We have no worries that our kids will rise to the challenges with the same panache as my daughter did at daycare or as my son models for his classmates by playing 'house' with a mom and a mama.

Of all the labels we get assigned, e.g. transracial family with lesbian moms, most of all we are a family with young children, tired in the way heterosexual couples are, bemused with our children and the delightful and brilliant things they say, juggling jobs, family life, house repairs, how to each fit in a workout, how to have some quality couple time.

It took me a long time to believe I was worthy of having a family. I am happy to be a mother of young children in my forties. I know myself well and know what I have to give to kids. The process of starting a family was so much more grounded and positive than the process of coming out, twenty years before. Devoid of role models, split in two, my very private lesbian life and the rest of me. I had a fear of being caught by roommates during private displays of affection, for there were no public displays of affection then. With each telling, I wondered if I'd be completely rejected and lose someone in my life. It was an emotional roller coaster. I didn't realize then that I was becoming more resilient to deal with future challenges. I see many adoptive parents treading in the unfamiliar territory of being excluded because of their differences. As lesbians, we are well equipped to give our children tools to meet these challenges head-on.

We continue to keep in touch and visit the foster family so our kids can maintain that essential connection. When we visit, we are given a room with a double bed, which would have been unimaginable after our initial meeting. Once they even babysat our twins and let us stay in their honeymoon suite that they normally rent out for romantic getaways. We happily took them up on this offer, all the while laughing at the irony and marveling at how far we'd all come. They told us they thought we were the best parents for our kids. They said we were doing a great job and that it was challenging their worldview that kids need a mom and a dad to be well adjusted. They said it was liberating to see us being such great parents and to see us committing to love and behaving "as Christians," without identifying as such, while others who say they are Christians kill each other in the name of religion.

There is much more work to be done with laws south of the border and with heterosexist and homophobic attitudes on both sides of the border. As people witness their gay and lesbian family members marrying and raising children, perspectives change. As gays and lesbians themselves refuse the closet, demand equal rights, and ask for acceptance rather than tolerance within their families, attitudes change.

Perhaps as you read this, somewhere in the BC interior, there is a lesbian couple and an evangelical Christian couple that calls each other family and considers each other friends, sharing a birthday cake and celebrating the twins that they have all had a hand in raising.

"I have had many ups and downs with friends
and family members who are trying to
understand my decision but want to support me.
There were some awkward questions or
stereotypes that needed to be discussed, especially
about bisexuality and my feelings towards men."

REDISCOVERING MYSELF
IN THE LGBT COMMUNITY

Jaclyn Haynes

Before it happened this time, I recall another time in high school. I was in grade nine and in between boyfriends at the time. I do not remember much, but this is what I do remember—there was this skinny girl, very tall, with long light brown hair and a great big smile. She was a close friend with whom I used to hang out with every weekend, having sleepovers, and going to parties with a larger group of friends. The moment I knew for sure popped into my head, we were at a mutual friend's house. A group of us were hanging out; more girls and the guys were coming later. We were both single. All of a sudden, I was drawn to her lips and wanted to kiss her right then and there. They were full, red lips and I stared at them. She started giving me a weird look. I was drawn to her, and she had asked me a question. I quickly blamed it on being distracted to get out of the awkwardness, and she re-asked the question, "What movie do you want to watch?" I didn't want to watch a movie. After that, I just wanted to get the hell out of there.

I stayed and went home with all the others. I put it all behind me and moved forward, flirting with guys, and being pursued by the manly persona that I wanted to be my partner. I had many happy relations with guys in high school and post-secondary. But there came a time when I was no longer interested in looking and wanted to give up dating. I stopped and left my love life to chance—letting it figure itself out. Occasionally, I went out on dates, but these relationships did not last much more than a few dates.

This time was completely different. I was the one being pursued, but I was not quite sure in the beginning. Over five years ago, Lizzie and I met through a mutual friend. We slowly started hanging out more often and became friends. In December 2011, Lizzie told me how she felt about me and that she wanted to be something more. When she told me, I was actually seeing a guy, and I was trying to figure out if we should continue dating or break up based on personality challenges and his job. I was waffling. With Lizzie, I was surprised, but I knew in my gut that something had changed during the summer. I recall Lizzie being really excited to do up the zipper of my dress I was planning to wear out to dance. There were lots of other "incidents" that made me question her intentions; though it did not concern me.

In summer 2011, I was curious about her background, why she did certain things or said something, so I talked to our mutual friend for advice. Over the summer, I talked to my mom a few times about Lizzie and that Lizzie might be interested in a relationship. Mom and I discussed our thoughts on same-sex relationships and the possible impacts on my career.

In order to figure out what I wanted, what she wanted, and what we wanted, Lizzie and I had many talks. I was not sure what to do.

I was nervous about stereotypes and the reactions of family and friends. After several talks, on February 9, 2012, I took a leap of faith and tried something that felt right to me. It was hard at times, but it has only brought our loved ones and us closer together. I have had many ups and downs with friends and family members who are trying to understand my decision but want to support me. There were some awkward questions or stereotypes that needed to be discussed, especially about bisexuality and my feelings towards men. On my path to accepting who I am now, I received mixed reactions from individuals in the LGBT community. I have felt alone and unsure about myself in the community, with LGBT individuals and their family and friends. Though the most surprising reaction I received was from my grandmother.

Over the August long weekend in 2013, I was a scaredy cat and couldn't come out to my grandparents during lunch with Lizzie. After my grandparents dropped us off at the mall to meet up with my dad, I asked Lizzie to help me come out to them. She went back to their car and explained that she is actually my girlfriend. Lizzie slowly walked back to where I was, on the phone, and told me the news. It felt like it took several minutes for her to reach my spot. She shared that when my grandmother heard the news, her face lit up and she had a big smile on her face. Lizzie told me that grandma was happy for us and was glad that she was making me happy. My grandfather drove back around to go where Lizzie and I had walked. My grandmother gestured for us to come to her door, then opened it. She told me she was happy for me and that she just wanted me to be happy. Happy, teary-eyed hugs were shared all around.

A week later on August 9, 2013, Lizzie and I had plans to go out for dinner to celebrate our year and a half together. After a long week at work, I was reluctant to go out and get dressed up. I suggested that we stay in, get take out, and watch a movie together. Lizzie convinced me that we should go out; we hadn't gone out for a while. We got all dressed up and headed downtown. Before dinner, Lizzie said she wanted to make a quick stop; it felt like we were walking forever, especially in heels. We sat on a bench in Major Hill Park, and while the sun was setting, she told me to open a very large gift bag. It was a scrapbook filled of things we had done together over the past year and a half. On the last page, it said "Jaclyn, will you marry me?" I was in shock and didn't know what to say. She was down on one knee with an amazing ring. I kissed her and said, "Yes." She put the beautiful ring on my finger. Afterwards, we celebrated at a downtown restaurant that we both wanted to try. It was a fantastic evening celebrating our love that continues to grow.

There are still certain points of views that concern me as we move into our life together as a couple, getting married and building a life together. However, the support we provide each other and from our friends and family will make the journey and adventures worthwhile.

"An odd thing can happen when you parent a child. Sometimes you forget that they are individuals, not just extensions of you."

INCORRIGIBLE MEETS INCONGRUENCE

Noelle Bickle

My youngest child was born with bright blue eyes and pudgy cheeks perpetually tinged pink. I swaddled her in blankets the colour of cotton candy. Throughout the years, her closet was crammed with delicate dresses, shoes that glittered, and rhinestone encrusted cowgirl boots stamped with southern girl boldness. The boots suited my spirited child. With her, you were always in store for a push to your pull, opposition rather than surrender.

Faced with a strong-willed and argumentative child, we put on the Pollyanna Sunshine hat in order to see future potential. We told ourselves, "This little scrapper is going to grow up and be a force to be reckoned with! She'll probably become an activist and change the world!"

It was a better alternative than oppositional defiance disorder, as had been suggested by a psychologist. I sat in his office desperate for advice—my now nine-year-old child struggled with constant anxiety, OCD like tendencies, and social isolation from peers. Despite raising my third child the same way with the same rules as my older two children, my youngest was in a constant state of depression that was terrifying to witness. I was mentally preparing myself for a future tragedy that somehow seemed inevitable and beyond my control. I second guessed my instincts and felt like I didn't know how to parent. I'd always been sure of my mothering, but with this child, I felt helpless and lost. "Supportive" suggestions from family members, friends, and random strangers implied it was all behavioural, that we had indulged her or hadn't been consistent or disciplined enough.

We tried behavioral therapy but didn't get very far. Nothing was changing. During sessions, our child was polite and reserved—similar to behaviours seen at school. The message was always the same—she was socially awkward, yes. But we should try to be consistent, register for more afterschool activities, and try to arrange playdates with friends. It all sounded so simple. But it was hard to arrange playdates for a kid who had no friends. And at home, we were dealing with temper tantrums that lasted four to five hours and included violent behaviors and self-harm. It was as if a switch turned off during these episodes—one that blocked pain and all reason. There was no comforting, no amount of reassurance, negotiating, or reprimand that made a difference.

After years of struggling, we decided a full psychological would provide a solution. Spending ten weeks and almost $2000, it was a wasted effort. In hindsight, the whole thing was quite appalling. Most astoundingly, he didn't make note of, or report in the assessment, a crucial comment my child made on the first appointment with the psychologist and the entire family sitting around the room, "I'm not a girl, I'm a boy."

Maybe it was the chuckle of her then thirteen-year-old brother,

the look of embarrassment on her father's face, or my reaction—
an endless stream of ramblings trying to smooth over the austerity
of her statement. This was something that had been happening
for the last few years. Our daughter's proclamations of self had
graduated from "I'm a tomboy" to "I'm more like a boy than a girl"
to this newest and clear declaration: "I'm not a girl. I'm a boy."

We didn't know what to do with it, and apparently, neither did
the psychologist. He simply moved on and didn't discuss it further.
After all was said and done, he reluctantly handed over a report
that stated there were signs of anxiety, social angst, and severe
depression. It wasn't news to us, and the confirmation was void of
any silver lining. He told me to call if I needed anything further from
him. I didn't.

With seemingly no support on the home front, my little spitfire took
to the schoolyard to be heard. Not the easiest route—convincing
thirty other fourth graders that things aren't always as they appear—
perhaps that the grass isn't green, the sky isn't blue, or that she was
actually a he.

We were clueless and didn't recognize the depth of our child's
discontent related to birth gender. We didn't understand the daily
battle with non-believers at recess, with endless pleading for
them to stop using the name on the class list. She wanted to be called
Shadow. Her best friend complied, along with a handful of kids
humouring the request. I received a note from the teacher complaining
that my child refused to use any name other than Shadow on tests,
book reports, and class folders. He wanted the situation resolved. Out
of the mouths of babes came a compromise—she suggested writing
Shadow followed by the given name. It seemed fair to me. I felt like
it allowed self-expression without disrespecting the teacher and the
rules of the classroom. The teacher was unimpressed. I chalked it up
to one more person who felt we over-indulged our child. Parts of me

weren't sure if everyone was right. My efforts were in keeping my child somewhat content. It didn't seem permissive; it felt like middle ground to me.

Shadow was a self-nominated nickname—one she was called at the Taekwondo studio and which was engraved into the trophies and medals won at competitions. Shadow was strong and confident, while our child had begun to associate her given name as unlikable. Unlovable even. So Shadow it was.

Aside from the informal name change, things went on as they had been for years. Sadly, the renaming of Shadow hadn't made her more peaceful, less anxious, or suddenly socially confident. There was still a torrid battle with depression, which was lending to isolation from everyone. Even family events posed a problem. Shadow didn't want to participate in celebrations or attend events. Things took a turn when my sister planned to marry and asked that all my kids be in her wedding party and assumed—along with all of us— that Shadow would feel special to be included. We assumed wrong. The endless fight was the attire. My sister, in all her feminine glory, had picked out peach chiffon dresses for the girls. For months, Shadow complained about the feel of it, the colour, the fit, and the general issue of it being a dress. The constant demand was a t-shirt and shorts instead. We thought this was more of the usual: resistance, stubbornness, irritability. In the end, it was agreed that Shadow would wear the dress for the ceremony with a stipulation of no pictures allowed, and that a t-shirt and shorts would be within arm's reach the minute the "I dos" were done.

That damn peach chiffon was the straw that broke the camel's back, though I suppose I should be thankful for it. My heart is weighted with shame when I think about the look on my child's face having to suck it up and walk down the aisle in that dress. Though we had suffered years of tantrums and tears, I don't know that I ever saw my youngest looking so dejected. In hindsight, I can't believe how blind I was, how little compassion I had.

An odd thing can happen when you parent a child. Sometimes you forget that they are individuals, not just extensions of you. That kind of self-importance can render you ignorant, even to the most obvious things and to people that need the most consideration and care.

Six months later, I finally heard what my child was trying to tell me. It took endless torment on the school bus, and schoolyard arguments that left wounds far greater than black eyes or swollen noses. There were many months of hearing Shadow complain about the teasing and unkind remarks. I understood that kids could be cruel, but I thought her anxiety was getting the best of the situation, making it seem worse than it actually was. The teacher and other staff thought things were relatively normal. After all, not every kid is part of the in-crowd. I purchased a journal and told Shadow to carry it all day long. My advice—every time someone said some-thing unkind, to write it in the journal and then let it go. Not to fret about it, not to let it swirl around or fester for the day. Write it in the book and afterschool we could read it, discuss it, tear up, burn or bury the pages—whatever worked. It was simply a method to cope and get through the day. The first day the journal came home, Shadow had hand-written six full pages.

> "You're not a boy, you're a girl."
> "Your name is not Chad. And you're a girl."
> "If you're a boy, why do you have long hair?"
> "I saw you use the girl's bathroom,
>   so we both know you're a girl."
> "You don't have nuts; you'll never have nuts,
>   so you'll never be a guy."
> "You're crazy."
> "You're not a boy, you're a girl."
> "You're not a boy, you're a girl."
> "You're not a boy, you're a girl."

Those words scrawled in large print made it clear to me. I had not supported, comforted, or protected my child from a full school year of pain and suffering. I had neglected every maternal instinct due to fear and shame and internalized phobias of many colours. I had left him to fend for himself.

Then things kicked into high gear. School ended weeks later, and the first thing Shadow wanted to do was cut off his waist-length hair. We started using male pronouns in and outside of the home. I spoke or sent letters to family and friends, explaining what was going on, and asked for their support. Some of which we got wholeheartedly, some not so much. I enrolled him in summer camp as a boy—now renamed, after much laboured thought by our once Lainey, once Shadow, now Chad. He went to a PFLAG teen camping weekend, and Camp Ten Oakes, a week-long LGBTQ camp, where he bunked in junior cabins with four others who happened to be ten and transgendered. For the first time in his life, he felt he fit.

That fall, he returned to school as a fifth grade boy named Chad. We decided to stay at our rural school with only two-hundred and fifty students, made up of generations of farm families and country Christians. Though not a diverse urban mecca or worldly school, we expected the administration would rise to the challenge and support our family. They waded through new territory, and surprisingly didn't disappoint. Egale worked with our family and the school to make the transition for Chad a little easier.

On the first day of school, Chad delivered a speech. He stood tall and explained why he was returning to school as the same person, but different too. It was his appeal to accept him for who he was. He stood up for himself and for every child whose birth gender is incongruent from how they feel they are as a person. There are multitudes of courageous people standing up for what they believe in, but I've never met anyone braver than my son. My Polly-anna hat firmly in place—he will indeed move mountains.

It would be wonderful to simply end this story on a happily-ever-after note. No more depression or anxiety, all things calm in our home and at school. The truth though is Chad may likely have a lifetime of challenge, so his courage will serve him well. He is living honestly and authentically, which is impressive for any person, let alone a child just starting his journey. I wish the road for him could be easier. I wish the path for me as his parent, witnessing his struggle, would be gentler on my heart. But resilience through adversity is always a beautiful thing.

INTERSECTING IDENTITIES

"Thank you for smelling like smoke and earth.

I want you to know I love your laugh lines,

your toughness, your shyness, your uncertainty,

your too-tight jeans, your worn and tattered

hoodie, your bound chest, your peach fuzz,

your underarm hair and your sternum."

A CURTSEY TO HANDSOME BUTCHES, BOYS, AND TRANS GUYS

Shannon Webb-Campbell

To all of the handsome, boyish, charming butches and trans guys out there, I would like to extend my thanks to you.

It is to you that I bat my mascara-clad lashes and pout my lip gloss-coated lips. It is for you that I sometimes don't wear underwear and push up my bra just so. It is to you that I smile, flirtatiously, with a twinkle in my eye. It is for you that I walk with a sway in my step.

I know that sometimes you feel the world is too much, that you are in need of a soft place to fall. My body is land and my heart is ocean. These strong femme arms long to hold you, to cradle you.

You make me feel visible in a world that sees me as just another girl—deemed not quite up to snuff. I know that you see me, the real me, all of me. You never question why I am not dieting or wonder if I am, in fact, someone's trophy wife. You know the wiser. I see you watching me on the bus, at the gym, in the bar, and at the park. Your shy grin and eyes glued to the floor give it all away. I won't stop looking at you.

There is an understanding that transpires when your eyes meet mine, a language without words. You are my desire, pure and embodied. All of my life I have been told that I have a pretty face. I'd be beautiful if only I could lose my belly flab, grow a little taller, get a nose job, and have bigger boobs. I have lived my life never quite measuring up until you came along. You look at me with intention, longing, and admiration.

Please don't stop looking at me. No one else sees me the way you do.

To the world, I am just a girl, not pretty enough to be noticed, yet curvy enough to be heckled. To a community, I am not queer enough, orbiting somewhere between the lands of lesbianism and bisexuality, not quite straight, not quite gay.

Thank you for asking about my mother, my grandmother, and my grandmother's mother, for listening to the stories of the way life used to be, how the women I've come from formed the woman I've become. How I found myself daughter, little girl, young woman, and inevitably, femme.

How I learned the curves of my spine come from a lineage of trailblazers—a Mik'Maq elder, who wasn't only a hunter, trapper, and bootlegger, but a midwife to 700 babies in rural western Newfoundland. A grandmother who caught a shark when out fishing with her brothers, could play cards all night, and drink tea with the best of them. A mother who held an entire family tree of trauma together, keeping us reaching for our branches, seeing the colours of our potential, and reminding us we are all love.

Thank you for listening to the stories of family, loss, and giving me time to unravel. To heal. To travel, inwards and outwards. To understand the lands I came from, the landscape I've chosen, and the native spirit in my soul. To let me go when I needed to and to welcome my return when I came back. Thank you.

Life is difficult for us both. Some days I can hide and you can't. I know this is hard. It's hard for me, too. When you feel invisible, as if you don't exist, as if you are nothing, no one. We charter the terrain of no man's land.

You are always visible, always seen, most often for what you lack rather than who you are. You are my kind of man—boyish, s/he, butch, hir, trans, genderqueer.

I love the way you polish your boots, even if they are heavy and offer no support. I want you to know that I appreciate that you are wearing them. You look so hot. I love you in them. They look great with your ripped jeans, dress pants, and boxer shorts. If it makes you feel any better, my feet are killing me, too. I know you are noticing my cleavage. I like it. I can see you looking into my eyes, occasionally dropping your gaze to the locket dangling between my breasts. I placed it there to distract you—tricky, I know.

It's cute that you talk about the colour of my eyes when you want to kiss me. Please kiss me.

I want to thank you for being butch, boyish, androgynous, and trans. I want to thank you for being visibly queer all day long despite the guff society gives you. I know it's hard. I know you had no choice. You are brave. You are safe. You are sexy. You are loved. It is within you that I recognize myself. I feel beautiful and whole. We are our own fanciful version of *The Great Gatsby*, without all of the wrongdoings, cheating, and stealing.

Sometimes you want to play Daisy and I get to be Gatsby. I like how we can blur traditional plot lines and keep a romantic narrative despite the odds. Neither of us have to die for our love, we can let go, if and when, we need to.

Thank you for escorting me to my door to make sure I get home alright. I like that you linger every time, careful not to assume that I'll invite you in even though I always do. Thank you for respecting me, and my need for space, to explore and nest.

Thank you for putting your arm around the small of my back when we're in line at the movies. Thank you for holding me before I delve into the lagoon of depression. You recognize my triggers before I see them myself.

Thank you for embracing me when I need an extra hour to get ready in the morning, steal the blankets, or leave lipstick marks on your cheek. Thank you for loving me for me, for seeing all that I am and all that I desire. Thank you for letting me in, allowing room for me to love you. Thank you for loving me, every last inch.

Thank you for smelling like smoke and earth. I want you to know I love your laugh lines, your toughness, your shyness, your uncertainty, your too-tight jeans, your worn and tattered hoodie, your bound chest, your peach fuzz, your underarm hair and your sternum. I love it all.

I want you to know that I love you even when you don't love yourself. I'm learning to love myself, too. It's not easy. Sometimes history threatens to consume the present, trauma enters and doesn't want to leave the room. Despite being asked to please exit, the past presents itself in the body, and yet your strong hands only soften to its touch.

The ocean you once called forth from within me hasn't dried up forever; it's just a momentary gulch. This is merely a lapse in time to recover, recoil, and remember. My body is a vessel; I love to feel you move through me. When we're together, it feels like wildfire, all wilderness and heat.

Thank you for asking what colour my dress is and for showing up in a matching shirt and tie, with a pair of earrings to go with my outfit. You look so handsome, with your sparkling eyes and inquisitive grin.

Together, we are life force. When seen through your eyes, I am a whole person, gorgeous and transformed. Turns out, I am the belle of the ball after all.

> "I've always thought of myself
> as a Martian, someone who has somehow ended
> up on a beautiful but often baffling and
> sometimes threatening planet called Earth."

CHICKEN SOUP FOR THE MARTIAN SOUL: ONE MAN'S QUEST FOR MASCULINE IDENTITY

Paul Nathanson

I'm a Martian. Well, I've always thought of myself as a Martian, someone who has somehow ended up on a beautiful but often baffling and sometimes threatening planet called Earth. I felt no sense of belonging here as a child, except with my own family or in my own room, and I still don't in some ways. But that fact, I now realize, doesn't matter. The search for "home" has made me who I am. After decades of turbulence and a few lingering neuroses, I like who I am.

First, I'm gay. That makes me neither proud nor ashamed. It's simply part of who I am and not necessarily the most important part. Which is the most important? My answer has changed over the years because I keep discovering new things about myself. But by now, after sixty-six years of hard living, I know that being a man—a male human being—is more important to me than being a gay man, a Jewish man, a middle-class man, a highly educated man or whatever. It's true that being a gay man, in particular, forced me to think about being a man. But that was the means to another end. As a little boy, I didn't always like the fact that I was going to become a man. Later on, I set out to find at least something about being a man that I could like—that is, value and respect. This quest eventually led me to academic research. I'll come back to that. But first, let's go back to the beginning.

Like all children in school, I wanted to be like the others. But I wasn't. In one particular way, which baffled me for many years, I was different. So different that other children ridiculed me relentlessly and with increasing hostility from late elementary school to the end of high school. No one ever hit me, but many children, both boys and girls, called me names. First, it was "sissy," then "fairy." No one knew precisely what those words meant, but everyone understood that they had something to do with what adults would have called "gender-inappropriate" behavior. At summer camp, I developed an intense crush on one of the counsellors. (Fortunately, he wasn't my counsellor.) The same thing happened in grade ten. I was infatuated with one teacher. (Fortunately, he wasn't my teacher.)

Meanwhile, my favorite movie stars were always men. I liked some female stars, too, but they lacked something that male stars had. On a trip to Boston, when I was about ten years old, my father took me to see *South Pacific*. I was aware of my intense preoccupation, both emotional and physical, with Lt. Cable (the one who sings "Younger than Springtime" and dies in the end). Without quite knowing why, I didn't tell my father about this. And yet I felt excited, not guilty. Being attracted to men would be very inconvenient, I gradually realized, but I saw nothing wrong with my feelings and had no desire to change them. Only one thing did trouble me morally about my interest in male stars: being fascinated now and then by the "wrong" ones. This happened to me while watching *Ben Hur*. I didn't care about the protagonist. I cared only about the villain.

Censors had cut the scene in which Messala visits a bathhouse, I later learned, but not the one where he dies in the blood-drenched arena, agonizingly but somehow erotically.

By the end of high school, I began to realize that I was "homosexual," although I still knew very little about what that meant. In one issue of *Life*, I read about homosexual street life in New York. It must have been a very progressive article simply for recording the subjects as real people and doing so in a matter-of-fact way. For me, though, the article was far from reassuring. These folks liked to have sex in public toilets. God, I had no urge to do anything in those filthy and disgusting places—not even to use them for their intended purpose. A few years later, I found the courage to buy a psychology book on homosexuality. The author went on and on about symbolic dreams that I had never had. He went on and on, moreover, about "seductive mothers" and "absent fathers," which had nothing to do with my family life. (My parents were happily married, and home was the one place where I felt truly happy.) For a while, I just forgot about homosexuality—but not, of course, about handsome young men.

I had always been unhappy in school. I liked reading and learning, it's true, and I did well in some subjects: history, geography, and art. In grade five or six, I won an art contest. But I didn't like the social environment. For me, hell was other children. Nonetheless, I had always had several very important resources and cultivated them carefully.

Being Jewish was one of these. From grades one to seven, I went to a Jewish day school. (It was run by an Orthodox synagogue, which my family never joined, but it was funded by the Jewish community as a whole. We learned about Judaism, but no one assumed that our families were Orthodox.) We spent a lot of time studying biblical stories in Hebrew and learning how the rabbis had traditionally interpreted them. The overwhelming impression that my teachers left with me was that Judaism was about holiness but also about justice, compassion, and learning. As for Jewish history, which we studied every day, it was about being persecuted but also about enduring. Much later, in college, I discovered that the rabbis had classified homosexuality as a vice. Worse, I discovered they had not classified tolerance as a virtue. (I read up on this and discovered something that surprised me. The Romans had classified tolerance as a virtue but not compassion, although they allowed pity and mercy; the Israelites had classified compassion as a virtue but not tolerance.) But the rabbinic position on homosexuality didn't matter to me. What did matter was the rabbinic preoccupation with both justice and compassion. Whether or not I agreed with the rabbis about this or that interpretation of scripture didn't trouble me. I could take this attitude because the tradition relies on learned debate, not passive obedience. Present a good enough argument, using rabbinic methods, and you could, at least in theory, reverse centuries of tradition. I never thought about all of that consciously, of course, until I became an adult.

Another resource was my own mind. I had a good mind, and I used it even in elementary school to think about my condition. Why did children persecute me? After all, many of them had parents or grandparents who had suffered under Nazi persecution. Whatever I was doing wrong, and I must have been doing something wrong, I understood that it could never have justified their way of treating me. Their behavior lacked compassion or, at the very least, common decency. As a human being, I deserved better than malice and ridicule.

Yet another resource was my imagination. In spite of my lowly position at school, I could experience joy. I relied on an active fantasy life to make everyday life tolerable, daydreaming about an ideal world in which justice and compassion would prevail. This fantasy world—I made up stories, based partly on old wartime dramas, which I staged in my mind as a movie director would on film—wasn't entirely naïve. To maintain their way of life, my characters had not only to struggle against those who would destroy it but also to sacrifice themselves if necessary.

I was in college when I told my parents that I was gay. And guess what. It was easy. They already knew, without anyone saying anything, and I knew that they knew. My mother worried that I wouldn't give them any grandchildren (although my sister would do that). My father worried that the family name would die with me. He worried also about some practical matters. What would happen, for instance, if I had an erection in some public washroom? Both worried mainly, though, about the prejudice that I'd have to face. After a discussion that lasted fifteen or twenty minutes, we sat down for supper. Why were they so blasé? It was probably because of their attitude toward sex in general. Both were modest but not prudish. They didn't talk about sex, but they did indicate in many indirect ways that they enjoyed it. One day, for instance, I opened the kitchen door and found them standing there, alone, holding hands and smiling at each other. But having a gay son? They would have preferred me to be a straight son, of course, but they didn't stop loving me and therefore wanting me to experience the deeply satisfying kind of pleasure that they experienced.

In 1968, I went to Columbia University for a master's degree in art history. I couldn't have chosen a worse time. The Vietnam War was raging everywhere, symbolically, especially on the campus. Frankly, I was neither a hawk nor a dove. I couldn't have cared less about some Geneva Convention or the "domino theory." What troubled me profoundly was the connection between war and manhood. Today, in the United States, young men (but not women) must register for the draft at age eighteen. Just in case. In those days, young men (but not women) were actually drafted for combat. I found it hard to understand how a country that officially valued "life, liberty, and the pursuit of happiness" could deny some citizens (but not others) the right to life itself. Being Canadian, I shouldn't have worried very much about being drafted, although some foreign residents had indeed been drafted. But I did feel deeply troubled by this new threat to my identity (let alone my body). I tried to discuss this with other male students at the dorm, but no one was willing to do so. Well, they were willing to talk about why they opposed the war on moral or political grounds, yes, but not about what it meant to them specifically as young men whose lives were considered expendable. That was going too far. Not for another generation were even a few men willing to think about their own vulnerability. That left me, once again, a lonely Martian. I disliked myself for many reasons, some of them legitimate. But I hated myself merely for having a male body (although I had no particular desire for a female body). I bolted for home, at any rate, feeling confused and angry and defeated.

Back in Montreal, I could "forget" about the war but not about the need to find a career or at least to get a job. Plan B was going to library school at McGill University and getting a professional degree. After that, I spent several dismal years as a librarian. Nothing could have been less suited to me. I liked books, sure, but that didn't make me a good librarian. My jobs were all managerial, but I disliked managing people and had no managerial skill at all. I had no interest, moreover, in cataloguing or reference or anything else that went on in libraries. (I probably would have liked selecting books and thus building collections, but I never found an opening for that kind of job.) I couldn't wait to get out of library work. Being a Martian, I was ready to bolt once more. But two questions troubled me. First, what should I do, if anything, about being gay? Second, what could I do about earning a living?

I wasn't into the bar scene. At bars, I couldn't see anyone through the smoke and couldn't hear anyone over the noise. I worried that no one would find me attractive, moreover, and with good reason. (I wasn't deformed, but I certainly didn't look like a movie star, much less a porn star.) After some very "disaffirming" experiences, I decided to join a gay discussion group instead. The atmosphere was better, from my point of view, but even this didn't work out for me. I was losing interest in the gay scene. Some members of this group told me that the most important feature of their identity was being gay. But that made no sense to me. I found them boring (and knew that they found me equally boring). Other members were extremely handsome, and I didn't find them boring at all. But they obviously found me boring and were usually unwilling to give me the time of day. Sitting there, week after week, I could feel those Martian antennae popping out of my brow.

After dithering for a while about what to do for a living, I decided on a radical experiment: joining a church and becoming a priest. It wasn't quite as surprising as you might think. There were many things about Christianity that I admired. And I'm not referring only to the art and music. The most important thing was Jesus. Okay, I didn't suddenly come to believe that he was the Messiah or the son of God or the ticket to salvation in another world (and I never stopped thinking of myself as a Jew, no matter how odd a Jew). But I did find his story compelling as the ultimate paradigm for living in this world. As much as I loathed the idea of a nation sacrificing its young men in war (but pretending that these young men sacrificed themselves), I valued the idea of *self*-sacrifice.

I chose the Anglican Church of Canada. It was liberal enough to accept me but conservative enough to maintain a distinctive intellectual and aesthetic tradition—or so I thought—and lucky enough to have avoided the historical stain of anti-Semitic persecution. But my sojourn in the church didn't last long. After three or four years, it was over. Not because the church was anti-Semitic. On the contrary, it wanted to stress its roots in Judaism through me. Not, moreover, because the church insisted on doctrinal conformity. On the contrary, no one really cared what I believed or didn't believe. And *that* made me bolt. (As Groucho Marx once said, "I wouldn't join a club that would have me as a member.") See, I had risked a lot to join, even hurting people to do so. My father didn't care that

I happened to be gay, for instance, but he did care that I had chosen to be Christian. The church offered me nothing that I couldn't have had without joining. Evocative rituals and theological jargon notwithstanding, I found that the church had become profoundly secular (despite a few traditionalist congregations that continued to exist in a kind of ecclesiastical ghetto).

As usual, I resorted to analysis. And my analysis, several years later, revealed what I found so inadequate about the church. Masquerading as theology for many leaders and laypeople (though not all of them) was pop psychology about "healing" and "community." New ideas had been pressed, as it were, into old wineskins. And I discovered that the same was true of other churches, although some reduced Christianity to pop sociology or political activism instead of, or in addition to, pop psychology. In fact, I discovered that the same was true of many Jewish communities. For them, I observed, Judaism was reducible not so much to morality and political activism (although it had been in earlier Reform Judaism) but to ethnocentrism, nationalism, and (in many Orthodox communities) to business—that is, to religion as the fulfillment of a contract with God, not as something that nourishes the soul. At one time, the Jewish people had existed in order to propagate Torah and holiness; now, Torah existed to propagate the Jewish people (by giving them a distinctive identity, discouraging intermarriage and so forth). My point in saying all this, however, is merely to note that what had once been the central focus of my identity, religion, gradually ceased to be that central focus. I didn't abandon religion, but institutional religion had abandoned me. Whoever I was, ultimately, it wasn't Paul the Jew and certainly not Paul the Christian.

Next, I tried to find an identity, a "home," in the academic world. I'd be a scholar and belong to an institution that prized critical and independent thinking. That should work even for me, right? Back I went, therefore, to do a doctorate in religious studies at McGill

University and then post-doctoral research.

I began my academic career with an interest in the surprisingly ambiguous relation between religion and secularity. My first book was *Over the Rainbow: The Wizard of Oz as a Secular Myth of America* (1991). It soon became clear, though, that I could no longer put off my own questions about manhood. That topic chose me, in other words, as much as I eventually chose it. By this time, I was working on a research grant with my former dissertation advisor, Katherine Young. Our grant, held at the McGill Centre for Medicine, Ethics and Law, was for research on public attitudes toward—and the moral implications of—new reproductive technologies, mainly in vitro fertilization and surrogacy. It didn't take us long to realize that all of the research so far had been done on implications for only one sex: What did these technologies say about women and motherhood? We began to write about these technologies from another perspective: What did these technologies say about men and fatherhood? Should women have complete "reproduction autonomy" (which is what some feminist groups were indeed demanding) and therefore exclude men not only from full participation in family life but also prevent them from feeling any stake in the next generation or making any investment in the future of society?

That led us to a series of books on men and the effects on men of misandry (the sexist counterpart of misogyny). *Spreading Misandry: The Teaching of Contempt for Men in Popular Culture* (2001) originated as the first chapter of a single book on men. We ended up with a whole book on the avalanche of misandry that became pervasive in popular culture during the 1980s and 1990s and remains pervasive. Misogyny, too, is pervasive, but many people have written about that. A host of government and private watchdogs monitor it very carefully, moreover, and protest very loudly whenever it appears. Misandry, by contrast, is seldom even acknowledged. And those who do acknowledge it often try to excuse or even condone it. Our point is to challenge the double standard. Misandry and misogyny, we argue, are two sides of the same sexist coin. We can't eliminate one form of hatred without also eliminating the other. In one chapter, moreover, we show how sexist ideologies, like all other ideologies of both the right and the left, can undermine the fundamental principles of any liberal democracy. Several volumes followed, first *Legalizing Misandry: From Public Shame to Systemic Discrimination against Men* (2006) and then *Sanctifying Misandry: Goddess Ideology and the Fall of Man* (2010). Still in the works are *Replacing Misandry: A Revolutionary Theory* (about the effects on masculine identity of technological change since the Agricultural Revolution) and *Transcending Misandry: From Ideological Feminism to Inter-Sexual Dialogue* (about the possibility of creating a new society, one that takes seriously the needs and problems of both men and women).

I don't regret being an academic and certainly don't regret my research on men, but I've long since ceased to believe in any necessary correlation between academic research and the search for truth. Academic fashions keep changing, and the current fashion repels me. Post-modernism, in my opinion, is a clever disguise for cynicism, at best, and a clever front for ideology, at worst. Subtleties aside, its advocates deny not merely our ability to know objective truth perfectly but the very existence of objective truth. In that case, there's only "our" perception of truth versus "their" perception of truth. And the solution is to "deconstruct," or undermine, the latter, leaving room in the public square only for the former. Even cynicism wouldn't be so bad, actually, if it were applied consistently. But it isn't, because "our" truth is almost always some political ideology. At one time, that was Marxism. Now, it's feminism (ideological feminism, that is, as distinct from egalitarian feminism). As a result, post-modernism serves primarily as an umbrella that protects ideologues from attack. They feel free to undermine other ways of thinking but draw the line at anyone undermining their own. By now, it's difficult even to raise questions about this or that feminist doctrine without being attacked in response as a defender of "the Patriarchy" and therefore a "misogynist." Universities declare that teachers who make students "feel uncomfortable" merely by challenging conventional wisdom—including the ideas on which ideologies depend—face disciplinary action. Some universities rely on "surveillance" to ensure that no one studies or teaches anything about men except from the perspective of feminism.

My personal identity now focuses directly on manhood, not on gay (or any other version of) manhood. It's true that being a gay man means loving men. But loving men, for me, doesn't mean merely loving male bodies. It means caring for all men as fully human beings. Among the many communities that have somewhat disappointed me, therefore, are those of gay people. I do appreciate the effort to fight against prejudice. I could hardly be who I am had it not been for the gay movement. But this doesn't mean that I automatically accept whatever gay leaders say or do. Here's an example of what I mean. Instead of bringing gay men and straight men together, let alone bringing men and women together, the gay movement has allied itself politically with an ideological version of feminism that neither does nor can help men find a healthy collective identity on their own terms. They can see themselves through the eyes of women, in short, or not see themselves at all.

If being cautious makes me a conservative, then I plead guilty. Ultimately, though, neither liberals nor conservatives can ever own justice. Nelson Mandela, along with Martin Luther King Jr. and Mahatma Gandhi, followed the biblical prophets by making a clear distinction between justice and revenge. There can be no justice, in fact, without reconciliation. And this is what my life, so far, has taught me. Oh, and I no longer worry about being a Martian, because I now realize that we're all Martians in one way or another.

"Two-spiritedness isn't a sexual identity
the way that gay, lesbian, bisexual, and
queer are, nor is it a gender identity
the way that trans and genderqueer are."

TWO-SPIRITED SEXUALITY & RESISTING ASSIMILATION

Margaret Robinson

The addition of a T or a 2 for "two-spirited" to acronyms such as LGBTQ has become common in Canada. Yet this inclusion is not simple or easy. Like a Boba Fett action figure in a Star Trek play set, two-spirited identity is the odd man out. The closer we examine it, the less it fits. Two-spiritedness isn't a sexual identity the way that gay, lesbian, bisexual, and queer are, nor is it a gender identity the way that trans and genderqueer are. The fact is, Aboriginal cultures understand sexuality and gender differently than settler cultures do, and uncritically incorporating two-spirited into LGBTQ is a form of cultural assimilation we must resist.

As an Aboriginal woman with white skin, I am often pressured to deny my Aboriginality. Resisting racial and cultural assimilation is difficult for people like me, who grew up without Indian status, since we can't live, own, or inherit property on reserves, vote for our chiefs or councils, or access band resources. Without access to native language speakers, many find it difficult to learn or preserve our traditional language. For some of us, colonial culture is the only culture we've ever known. I am what some people call a "white Indian." I know only a few words of Mi'kmaq. I haven't spent more than twenty minutes on reserve. I pass as White everywhere, even among other Mi'kmaq.

An example: I am at a Mi'kmaq event. I am not dressed appropriately, but don't know it yet. I only sense people looking at me with disappointment. I don't know the protocols, so I watch what others do and mimic them. When people speak an opening prayer (what I assume is a prayer) in Mi'kmaq, I understand none of the words. When my grandmother was a child, she was beaten for speaking Mi'kmaq at her English-only school, so she forgot her language. An elder (someone I assume is an elder) walks around the circle with a seashell filled with burning sweet grass. The smell reminds me of my grandmother's house. I say "wela'lin," which means "thank-you" in Mi'kmaq. I learned it online through an mp3. Later I will look up "smudging" to find out what it was we did, and what it means.

Pressure to assimilate into the privileged category is also familiar to me as a bisexual, since people often treat us as if we are, or ought to be, heterosexually aligned. Perhaps it is because of this stereotype that my attempt to integrate into the queer community has been unsuccessful. No matter how much history I know, how much activism I do, or how many events I attend, I am treated as an outsider. Some people are openly hostile. But I have found strength and security in bisexual culture, bisexual politics, and bisexual activism. I use my experience coming into my own as a bisexual woman as a template for building up my Mi'kmaq identity. The alternative, that I am lost before I even begin my journey, feels intolerable.

Living in Toronto, I am surrounded by Aboriginal cultures that are not my own. I learn Ojibwe terms and practices through osmosis. I long for Mi'kmaq traditions but make due with pan-Indian practices, which are locally accessible. I attend two-spirited gatherings, counting on our common queerness to smooth over the rough spots of my cultural ignorance. The events are welcoming, and the people recognize and understand the effects of assimilation. The organizers are generous with their cultural knowledge. Sitting in a room at Anishnaabe Health Centre with other two-spirited people, one of whom is a fellow Mi'kmaw, I learn an Ojibwe song about an eagle as it pours rain outside. None of us can keep time on our hand drums, and we have to look at the whiteboard to remember the words. We are all beginners, but our mood is one of joyful discovery. A song is a prayer. A drum is a heartbeat. I walk home, soaked to the skin, but feeling washed clean.

Two-spirited identity enables people like me to claim an Aboriginal cultural significance for our same-sex attraction or gender nonconformity. When you're under heavy pressure to assimilate, anything that bonds you closer to your culture is good. Just as importantly, two-spirited identity allows us to distance ourselves from LGBTQ identity and the assumptions those identities carry. It is difficult for White LGBTQ audiences to hear about this distancing without framing it as internalized homophobia. But my reasons have nothing to do with homophobia.

My first reason for wanting some distance is that LGBTQ identity claims can erase or override other ways of understanding our sexuality. Too often, identities such as straight, gay/lesbian, and bisexual are presented as if they exist apart from history, written into our DNA, the same across every time and place. Yet in reality, how we view sexuality is shaped by our cultures and our place within them. This is true even if you believe that same-sex attraction has a biological basis. How our attraction manifests and what it means—to us and to others—depends on our social context. And it is the cultural meaning of our sexuality, not our genetic makeup, which is the essence of identity. So what my same-sex and other-sex attractions mean is different depending on whether I'm looking at Mi'kmaq culture or White culture.

The White colonial model of sexuality categorizes me based on my sex assigned at birth (female), and the assigned sex of my potential partner(s). I am bisexual because I have both same-sex and other-sex attractions. Yet rather than connecting me with others, the bisexual label has been a barrier to community belonging. When bisexuals get together, the one thing we often have in common is our experience of rejection, by both the straight world and by gays and lesbians. So while I do identify as bisexual, it is not the only way of understanding my sexuality, and it is not an Aboriginal way of doing so.

One doesn't have to read many books to encounter alternatives to the White colonial model. Systems of sexuality that attach identity to sexual roles—active or passive, for example—have been well documented. Some Aboriginal cultures recognize multiple genders and have a sexuality system that focuses on social gender rather than sexual identity. Identifying as two-spirited connects me with other two-spirited people across North America, but it also connects me with my Mi'qmaq culture, and with traditions of female masculinity, sexual freedom, and sexual and gender fluidity.

The existence of same-sex partnerships in pre-contact Aboriginal nations has been used to argue that same-sex attractions occur everywhere. Yet such discussions often assume that Aboriginal models of sexuality are inferior to the LGBT model. White scholars sometimes re-label two-spirited people as trans, bisexual, lesbian, or gay, portray them as closeted, as suffering from internalized homophobia, or as having an under-developed sexual identity. When White models of sexuality are presented as if they are true for all times, all cultures, and all places, then Aboriginal models are viewed as wrong inasmuch as they fail to reflect the White model.

A second reason I am suspicious of the universalization of LGBTQ identity is its erasure of spirit. Unlike LGBTQ identities, two-spiritedness assumes that attraction and love are connections of spirit as well as flesh. In First Nations across Canada, spirituality grounds our understanding of the world and our place within it. Spirit makes up one fourth of our medicine wheel, and animates all life. Our model of gender is a circle in which ends of the spectrum meet. While we may not literally have two spirits, each of us contains a fluid mix of masculinity and femininity, and our roles in community and in relationships may reflect this. First Nations may include female husbands or warriors, male wives and basket weavers, or shamans whose particular mix of masculinity and femininity enabled them to perform sacred functions. My twenty-first-century understanding of spirit may not be the same as that of my Ancestors, but I feel that something important is lost when our sexuality is reduced to an effect of chromosomes, hormones, pheromones, or the size of various regions of our brain. Love is not determined by biology.

My third reason for being suspicious of the universalization of White sexuality is that it erases power differences between those of us who are racialized as White and those of us who are not. Many LGBTQ people are alienated or expelled from our families of origin, and LGBTQ communities have taken up the language of family to describe the bonds we form in our communities (e.g., drag family, family of choice). Escaping to urban LGBTQ communities is often presented as the solution to homophobia in our families and communities of origin. Yet for Aboriginal people, the migration solution ignores our need for solidarity with Aboriginal and other racialized people against racism, White supremacy, or colonialism. It also ignores the fact that, due to racism, colonialism, and white supremacy within the LGBTQ community itself, participating can feel more like work than like family. For people like me, whose culture has been the target of government mandates of eradication, assimilating into a racist and colonialist LGBTQ community is not a positive experience. Two-spirited identity recognizes my sexual or gender differences while also asserting my Aboriginal cultural belonging, and taking my experiences of assimilation, racism, and colonialism seriously.

Non-White, non-colonial sexual identity systems open new avenues of truth that have been denied or ignored. As a person with a foot in both Aboriginal and settler cultures, I hold truths from each community in tension with one another. The bisexual label, with all its cultural baggage, does capture a truth about myself and my experience. Yet I am also two-spirited, even if the entirety of what that might mean is not always (or perhaps not yet) clear to me. While affirming that both these identities say something true about who I am at my core, they do not capture the same truth. Their truth may not even be complimentary or compatible with one another. They may tell contradictory stories, and that's okay too, because contradictions are part of the human experience. While my Boba Fett figure might coexist with the crew of the Enterprise, I must not make the mistake of assuming that their universes are the same.

> "Liberation must be done collectively.
> Anti-oppression means no one is left behind."

ALTERNATIVE: MOVING TOWARDS LIBERATION & ANTI-OPPRESSION

Lukayo F.C. Estrella

So many beginnings, but when asked to pinpoint it, most times I choose that summer. Twilight had begun to creep along the edges of the park I was in, the kind of grassy expanse on the edge of Scarborough and East York typically littered with late night drug deals and roving bands of prepubescent figures that bristled with the stream-lined, lateral violence of generations. A Torontonian childhood spent in these kinds of places should have prepared me for what happened, but at that moment, life had taken a grey pallor that drained my expectations into listless stares.

I guess it was because tonight, it was hard for me to care about anything.

So I didn't notice the kid circling the playground or a posse clumped several feet away, watching the unfolding drama. I was sitting alone, on a swing, staring off into the sky, trying to sort out all the feelings that surged within me. Well-meaning friends of my parents had taken my brother and I to a house party, showering us with pork, rice, and *pancit* as if to landfill the recent loss with food. I'd silently slid away from them, off to the nearby park, a tendency everyone was familiar with.

"Hey!"

This time I registered the group of youths. I also noticed the one who had called out to me, a scruffy, light-skinned, masculine teen with a wide grin and malicious dark eyes. For lack of a better noun and pronoun, this person is indelibly stamped in my mind as a "boy" and "he." At the time, I never thought to ask. Possibly because he was the one asking questions.

Once he saw my eyes return his gaze, he launched into his barrage.

"Are you a *girl* or a *boy*? Huh? Huh, *freak*? What *are* you? Hey! What's *wrong* with you, you freak?"

I froze. I could only assume he and the group behind him were there for one reason and one reason only—to beat the living daylights out of me.

I was fourteen years old when this incident happened, and even though I'm more than twice that age now, I can't stop going over this memory in my mind. The moment has become an old favourite novel to me, this movie I re-watch weekly because every replay teaches me something new, something important about this world and the kind of people that are in it.

In one version of the story, I get up and run. I bolt from the park, fleeing their taunts. Questions about my gender, my ethnicity, my sexual orientation—all of it thud against my back as I retreat too fast for them to catch up.

This move will ripple throughout my life.

It echoes the curled-up ball I morphed into many times in

elementary school, my mind flying through clouds as I waited for the kicking and punching to stop. It echoes my legion of favourite books, anime, comics, shows, websites, video games; these constructed landscapes I lost myself to get away from contact. It echoes the moment I got on the plane to leave my beloved sun-drenched islands for this land of ice and snow, without knowing if I would ever return.

The future is riddled with highlighter marks on every leave-taking and back turned. Some are personal, such as my first girlfriend's refusal to hold my hand in public and acknowledge our relationship or my poetic mentor and boyfriend's death. The others involve communities—movements that would sweep me up and become an endless array of closed doors. Queer parties that can only be reached by long flights of stairs. The T after GLB or LGB standing more for "token" than for the needs and rights of trans women, trans folks, and those with trans histories. Conferences lacking interpretation, translation, and attendant care. No acknowledgement of the land we are on or outreach to their Two Spirit descendants. Posters and pamphlets dominated by smiling, white, masculine bodies but insisting their events and spaces are open to all. Human beings deemed "illegal," like goods that can be shipped back to a land that would erase them for being born "that way." Dwindling support for organizations and campaigns because the holy grail of marriage has been achieved.

In the end, I burn out and live out the rest of my days in a one-bedroom apartment. Justice and liberation for our diverse bodies, minds, expressions, ways of loving—all of it thud against my back as I retreat too fast for them to catch up.

In another version of the story, I stand up and fight. I beat the kid into a bloody pulp, a primal scream ripping from my throat as every injustice explodes out from my lips and fists in an incoherent barrage. The others pull me off of him, and I get scratched from a knife before they drag him away and go, promises of retribution hurled over their shoulder but terror at my berserker rage in their eyes.

This move will ripple throughout my life.

Backwards, the rumblings in my schoolyard past are precursors for this eruption. Shoving my brother in the hallway after a bad day at school because nobody ever taught me to talk about my feelings. Being thrown across the yard because I lunged at a girl for trash talking me at lunch time. Throwing the first punch when a boy stares me down at recess. Every micro-aggression and outright aggression that has been met with my raised chin, my cocked fist, my defiant snarl, is a prelude.

Forwards, I charge through life, dominating all those that get in my way, prepared to do whatever it takes for justice and retribution. The tactics employed are similar to those who bullied or oppressed me, but I am filled with a righteous rage, and it's not hard to find others who burn with the same magma-hot desires. Harsh call-outs of problematic language and behaviour in public spaces and social media, regardless of past work or present alliances. Backdoor gossip to circulate behind closed doors and private emails. Funding grabs for single organization goals instead of working with other agencies and resource-sharing. Trying to get people fired or to boycott their direct action campaigns immediately without an attempt at private discussion or mediation. Pushing an objective through without community consultation.

In the end, I live out the rest of my days working in an office tower, alienated from large portions of the community who promise retribution but cannot touch me because I've achieved so much of what other parts of the community have demanded, no one ever admitting their terror of the berserker rage in my eyes that I hide with a handshake and a smooth grin.

These two tales, of flight and fight, twine themselves through my being and my life—neither completely true nor false. But in the end, the version that happened in the park that night in the summer of my fourteenth year was neither of these things.

I must have sat there for only a few minutes, but it felt like hours stretched on, my heart racing and hands shaking from the tidal waves that crashed inside me. I stared at the group of youth in front of me and picked out a feminine-looking person wearing a white bomber jacket and long, brown ponytail, who looked old enough to be finishing high school.

My legs carried me towards this person, the one I labelled "teenaged girl" and "she" in my mind. The others around her stared at me, a mixture of curious and guarded. I had no plan, no inkling of what I was going to do, whether fear or rage would win out inside me. Clearly, from the look on the girl's face, neither did she.

I surprised them all; I surprised myself.

Words spilled out of my mouth and I told her about the boy, who stood at the edge of her crowd, about how it didn't seem fair to me, about my life, about my gender, about how I just wanted some peace and quiet to think, my parents had left the country for the funeral, that I didn't want to cause any trouble and why were they coming after me?

One sentence, though, rang through the air, changed her face: "My grandfather just died."

She called the boy roughly over and he apologized, face staring at the ground, shoulders hunched in remorse. And then, unexpectedly and suddenly, as abrupt as my decision to speak with her, she wrapped her arms around me, the rest following suit. I was pressed under the weight of strange bodies in fall coats, the sense of loss emanating out from all of us mingled with comfort and hope. In that moment, inside the precious seconds of stillness as we stood connected by something we all understood, it dawned on me. There is another way.

This move will ripple throughout my life.

Everything I've ever been proud of in the movements I continue to be a part of is because at some crucial point, some crucial decision-making moment, we found another way. Flight and fight have their place in our daily lives, collectives, and organizations because they are still legitimate strategies in certain situations of oppression and injustice. Yet they cannot be our only strategies.

I see this in my past, from the nonviolent Philippine People Power Revolution of 1986, of which my parents were a part of. I see this in the personally influential work of Andrea Smith, Harsha Walia, Eddie Ndopu, and Leah Lakshmi-Piepzna Samarasinha. I see this in the intersectionality of the collectives and organizations that I work with, from No One Is Illegal to Project Acorn to Jer's Vision. My courage and pride comes from this work and the work of all those who have gone before, from the First People of this section of Turtle Island known as the Dominion of Canada, to the first group of youth who started a school alliance between different sexualities within Coast Salish Territories (Coquitlam, BC) in 1998.

I am proud of and gain courage from the growth of healing justice and empowerment in the work we do to resist the constant degradation of violence and internalized hatred in our lives.

What does this look like? Transformative justice based mediations between individuals and between organizations. Community care plans and check-ins so folks aren't left behind, and community agreements so folks start to become accountable to each other. A broader understanding of how emotions and justice interact, and how we incorporate that into our work.

I am proud of and gain courage from how we call each other in and connect with each other in the work we do to resist the alienating forces and isolating tendencies from the systems and norms we are steeped in.

What does this look like? Consent culture pervading all we do, from the way we build romance with each other to the way we build solidarity within our movements. Taking leadership and guidance from those most impacted by the injustices we swear to be against. Sharing resources, skills, and roles between people and collectives so that we can be more effective and foster greater capacity.

Mostly, I am proud of and gain courage from all those who have faith in me, all those who work with me, all those who will continue to work with me and the future we are building together from the ripples of choices we are making now.

What will that future look like?

Though this essay is from my perspective, that future is not going to look like me. My face will be lost in the sea of community members, all of us working together, healing together, resisting together. It will not look like celebrity activists and superstar spokespeople. Liberation must be done collectively. Anti-oppression means no one is left behind.

This is a movement that will ripple throughout our lives.

*"That beautiful bouncing boy
was only a boy on the inside.
Outside he had the body of a girl."*

ON BECOMING ALEX

Alex P. Whey

A little over thirty-five years ago, my wonderful mother gave birth to a beautiful bouncing baby boy.

She named her Angela. That beautiful bouncing boy was only a boy on the inside. Outside he had the body of a girl, and he would spend over thirty years coming to terms and struggling with the mental turmoil and exhaustion of having a body that didn't match his brain.

By the time I was four years old I knew I was different. I knew I wasn't quite the same as the rest of the little girls in the neighborhood. I hated, with a passion, the frilly dresses and pretty shoes and cutesy hair clips.

I wanted jeans and a t-shirt.

I wanted sneakers.

I wanted hair that didn't have to be long and combed and pinned back and fussed over.

I might have been four or five when I took the scissors to my own hair and just tried to rid myself of it. I don't remember for sure if there was forethought there, telling me to cut my hair off so I could be like a boy. It was more a severe dislike for that fuss and muss that was atop my head. The bows and buckles and hair bands and combing and prettiness. I was rougher than that. I was the one out digging the holes in the garden alongside the dog, flipping the rocks to look for bugs, riding my brothers BMX down the dirt hill and wiping out at the bottom, but all the while thinking how cool it had been because I had that pretty girly bike with the crossbar that slanted down and you just didn't look as awesome or feel as good clunking along at 40 km/hr with the wind in your hair and the bugs in your teeth while riding a girly bike with the slanted crossbar.

I knew I was different, but I didn't really understand what it was all about. There was no name for it in my vocabulary, and I probably didn't even think too much about it until grade four or so when all the pretty girls were putting on the makeup and trying to impress the boys. I barely remembered to brush my hair most days, let alone put on makeup. As a small child my parents never really dissuaded me from doing so-called boy things. My dad loved it because my brother was not really the most masculine boy on the planet, so he took what he could get from his little girl. Mom, of course as most moms do, fussed over my hair and my clothes and tried desperately to get me do girly things but she never got too mad when I disputed. She didn't want to see me hurting and I guess just chalked it up to me being a tomboy.

And that's when I learned there was a term for me after all. A word that I could associate in my brain with how I felt inside.

So I felt a little less alone. Now when the kids at school or on the playground would say, "Why do you act like a boy?" I had a response: "Why, I'm a tomboy of course."

And it all starting making sense to me, in its own weird and convoluted way. It was as clear as mud, but it was a reason. It was a word I could speak—like a security blanket of sorts. It was an alibi or a motive—why did you do it? Well this is why I did it! And if you don't have words to explain, words to define, there is fear and confusion and doubt and such a huge plethora of finely tuned adjectives for the way the brain reacts when there are no words.

The innocence of children is a fine gift, but sadly something that doesn't last very long. They lose it somewhere along the way, or they are raped of it by society, or it just plain fades like a flower that has been sitting in a vase for a little too long.

Though I feel a little less abnormal as a child, that too fades, and of course puberty hits and just rams through my body like a freight train going a hundred miles an hour—unsupervised, unrecognized, and not the least bit understanding of what it is doing to my brain.

I start to get these…things, sprouting from my chest, and there is talk of bras and all I can think is, *OMG. WTF!*

It totally destroyed the image of myself that, up until that point, I had honed to perfection. And then of course, low and behold, by the time I am eleven, "aunt flow" decides to rear her ugly head and not only do I have "boobs and bras," but then I have "periods and pads!"

Not only do I have to worry about covering myself up, now I have to worry about how I move when I jump down from that tree so as to not dislodge a disgusting, soggy thing from between my legs, or heaven forbid have an incident where one of those…things…might get lose from the holster I have them strapped into.

I departed further and further into myself. Developing shame over my body. Developing a self worth that didn't seem worth very much. I fell into a depression that haunted and followed me far into my life. I would secretly strap my breasts down, usually in the privacy of my own bedroom, and I would stare at myself in the mirror, imagining myself without them. I would tuck socks into my underpants and stare at myself in the mirror and imagine what I would look like with a penis. I wanted a penis so badly, and I wanted these things on my chest to disappear.

I spent a lot of my childhood alone, playing by myself in my bedroom, pretending to be a garbage man or a police man or a rock star. I would take baths and pretend to shave my face with my dad's shaving cream, a mirror, and a comb. I remember thinking very often, *I just wish I was a boy.* The thing was, I felt like a boy. Everything inside of me told me I was.

My brain screamed *boy*! Yet my body kept shouting, "Shut up, you're a girl! Can't you see these lovely breasts, and you have a vagina for Christ's sake. Boys don't have those things!"

And I would cry and cry because my body was betraying me; my body was my prison, and it had locked me away and destroyed the key. By the time I was fourteen, I was on a host of different meds. Anti-depressants, anti-anxiety, anti this and anti that. Anti for everything, but they had yet to come up with the "anti-self-hatred drug." There wasn't a pill for that or a cream or a rinse or a syrup. So you get diagnosed with depression, and no one ever finds out the real reason you're so depressed to begin with. I couldn't tell anyone. I couldn't speak it. I didn't have the words for it. The thoughts within my own self would send my brain into a frenzy. Searching high and low, sending out electrical responses—a brain-sized Mayday or SOS.

"Mayday, mayday, there are no words stored in the central processing unit to describe the feeling this body is giving me. We're going down, Captain!"

So you get diagnosed with depression, and you dutifully take your meds, and you slip further into that distress call, and the captain goes down with his ship.

As I grew from child to teen, I tried to not think about the reasons why I felt the way I did, but it always seemed inevitable. I would sleep and dream, and in my dreams I was the guy that I had seen myself as on the inside, and I would awake and everything would feel fine, until I realized, "Oh, right, that's not me. This is me, here in this suit. This suit that I can't take off." And reality floods in, and darkness falls on the brightest days, and I send the thoughts to the back of my brain, and I get up out of that bed, a place I love so much because in my dreams I am who I am supposed to be, and I go about life as if this is the life it is supposed to be. Pretending, masquerading, faking, acting, lying, forgetting, convincing, existing...

Time passed. Life passed. In the blink of an eye. As an adult, identifying as a lesbian (a place that became safe for me) I met my very first transgender person. I was in awe. I had read a little bit about "them" but had never seen any in person. Her name was Felicia. I can't remember now how old she was, but I am sure late forties-ish. She had spent her life struggling with her identity. She had been in and out of mental care facilities where they treated her as though she was insane, highly medicated her, refused to allow her to live as the woman she was, electro-shock treatment sessions to try and "cure" her, and as she sat there across from me, in her female wig and beautiful dress, I could see just how well that had worked. She hid her identity for years and struggled and denied and pretended, I guess until she could pretend no more.

Years later, after meeting her, I happened upon a posting of a letter to some support group on Felicia's behalf, saying how she had pleaded for hormones and she was outright refused treatment. I read this years after meeting Felicia for the first time, years after she had come out and lost her family so she could be who she needed to be, years after she took her car to an open area out by her family cabin and set herself on fire, years after I attended her funeral and cried for a woman I barely knew, a woman buried as a man, under a headstone marked with the name of the man she hated being, the essence of herself left burned and alone in that old pit in the middle of the woods. Years later I was reminded of Felicia though I have never really forgotten her. She was my first insight to real life. She was my first glimmer that I was not actually alone, that there are people out there who feel the same way I do, and sadly she was also the sickening truth behind the inner turmoil and the destruction of life that being trans* can bring forth in one's life. She would never get to learn what I have come to learn: that it is ok to be who you are, and sometimes in order to be truly happy with yourself, others will have to experience hurt. But they will get over that hurt a lot faster than we will get over the torture of not being true to ourselves.

Felicia died a horrible self-loathing death, her life lost in vain. However, it shall be through her memory that I will move forward and take what I have learned and live my life the way I am supposed to live it, as the person I was supposed to live it as.

I am proud to be a Transman; I am grateful for the experiences I have experienced and blessed by the lessons I have learned in my life. Every butterfly has to start as a caterpillar, creeping along through its short life, knowing that it is living as something it is not meant to be, yet surviving until that one moment—that butterfly moment— when the little fuzzy and sometimes awkward caterpillar will burst victorious from its cocoon, spread its beautiful wings, shake off the dust of transition, and fly with utter splendor, into the sunset of a glorious day.

"I have been left single, orphaned,
and nearly thirty years living with HIV.
But, what really changes?"

MORNING HAS BROKEN:
LEAVING HIV!

Francisco Ibáñez-Carrasco

My physician gave me one pill a day, one little jewel, a Sierra Leone diamond. Having drunk the dreaded HIV cocktail from vile vials; having been acupunctured with the needles of chemotherapeutic alchemy, being one left from the lost generation of GRID and AZT, I have become an insectariums queer coleopteran, another poster bug for another pharmaceutical Pyrrhic victory. Drug users, people living with HIV are that, a pill for this, a pill for that, our licit and illicit consumption of promised felicity, a gain here, and a trimming there, emotional Botox, gateway to gleeful dependency. Basked in the early lullaby of pharma names and letters that deliver new Alice in Wonderland, one Pristiq, some T, some G, and Interferon or special K—not a morning cereal, but the perfect breakfast. The trivial and titanic, the mundane and the miraculous are compressed intimately into a time-release capsule, better than Twitter at communicating joy and distress, at glorifying life expressly. Standing barefoot in my kitchen, I fill a glass of cold water. It is six a.m., and it is cold outside.

My soul and my dick hang like puppets taking a rest from the performance of the city outside. I can hear the DVP from where I am living, Toronto cars like rivers, screeching, and sometimes piling up. I raise my hand with the pill, I open my supple lips to it, firm, incoming, and I pause to think….

I turned fifty years old at the beginning of 2013, and it has been a year of celebration of its own kind and of taking stock. I have been left single, orphaned, and nearly thirty years living with HIV. But, what really changes? Our skin becomes more invisible to many but hardened to the touch of a few. The skin misses those who touched it as cute, desirable, terse, taut, and festive and receives the clinical touch that nothing gives, the touch that measures and charts and decodes symptoms of illness. The skin becomes damaged goods, used currency, not a renewable resource. The child in me, still hiding, still curious, a glimpse inside the pupils, craves the validation, the warmth of the palms saying I belong, come here, and take pause and praise. We all have our little grand traumas from childhood, "realities" they call them, reassembled to tell ourselves that we have lived, we have not passed unnoticed, composites made with the debris from the fallout of what the others did, their easy love, their vulgar romance, their disdain, their most pedestrian abuse—we never think twice about abusing others subtly! I am very resilient and courageous, they say, and this "asset-based" turn of phrase is flattering for a moment, while in the intimate quarters of my own community, gay men of my generation, young queers, still recoil in fear or disgust at the sight of this HIV coleopteran, the drag queen insect and its queer throbbing, or they think about me—us—twice, and respectfully calligraphy "I'm clean and disease free" in our odious little hook-up sites.

My kitchen floor is cold. I must have left a window open last night to remind myself that I'm not in a hospital or a hotel or an airport, the hermetic places of goodbyes, that I can still open a window and jump. I think of courage and I think of war. My own private Hiroshima exploded in my skin in the 1990s, Kaposi's sarcoma, unease, discontented my body at the assault of risk, opportunistic disease of too much precocious sex and too many little vices, betrayed by my body, by the death of others, by the neglect of our hypocritical societies in the 1980s and good part of the 1990s. But who is keeping tab on social neglect? Isn't all AIDS discontent over? And who is around mumbling disgruntlement anyway? Who would listen? The KS bombs mushroomed in lesions all over my body, and its rages are tattooed in my skin for the rest of my life, like memory, like rock songs. I turned fifty and something magical happened, the intention of the touch of others changes, this, if they touch me at all, becomes distant. And I wait for the touch of strangers—promiscuity they call it, we judge it. I sit in the evening sunset, like a constant Penelope waiting for Ulysses....

Pride, courage, and social justice for all queers and misfits in Canada—oh yes, this is what I wish when I get up. I stand in my kitchen unable to turn the radio on, the pill pregnancy in my belly, unaware of my nakedness. I think of how lonely and long was the night, and how the little blue Imovane and some tokes of weed helped me get through it. I think, I should use my glasses when I distractedly grab a blue pill from my night table and do not grab a piece of blue Viagra and eat it and spend the night alone with my lonely priapism. Intimacy, whatever that is, after fifty, is becoming scarce, pixilated, a far-flung rustling in my bedroom linen. Even though I have left my Hiroshima behind, and worked twice as hard as the others to join my contemporaries, and today my body is stronger, my skin thicker, my voice lower, my animus purer, my manner conventionally attractive, our gay culture of overselling and buying image reminds me that this is not viable, everything is production, competition, and outcome, and money, yes, an eternal money shot.

The world in billboards, magazines, the dentifrice smiles of others, their payments to therapies, skin tugs, and clothes, and gym memberships and towel service. Our little but over exposed and over-researched queer minority demands designers' clean surfaces, shiny, skinny, cynical to the cycles, bodies that do not age, that laugh through every orifice with equine teeth. Solitaire, my body disproves the dream, my gut grumbles. I fart toxic. I chuckle, unable to move. I nervously scratch a dry patch on my left buttock. Feeling the hangover, my body roars insolently, combustible. I see my peers encrusted, encroached, or too demoralized to have fun much less to love, and that we favour habit over vengeance, they have covered the mirrors sitting Shiva for too long, denying the pleasure of para-philia, of loving what is broken and patched together, loving ourselves, self-compassion. Queers, an angry and self-castigating minority. The cliché, "time takes care of everything," becomes a physics law, my faithful responsorial. And those who seemed my enemies: the "racists," the "homophobes," the "heterosexuals," the "police" of this or that, now seem like aggravating family members. I tend to find justice and equality in everyone but "my own." They still tell me I am too much (jovially, he he) and censor my writing when they can (it is too blunt, or too intricate, they say).

I must stop consulting the oracles of the Internet, the patient's discussion boards, the blog, the incessant chattering of the AIDS patient or any illness patient autopathography. Who the fuck cares what you are dying of? Just die with dignity all right! I lay on the floor—not sure how I got to it—and the kitchen linoleum on my back feels like a cold infinity pool. I have come to live with prudence and resilience and compassion and intent; and cunningly and with a sonorous timbre. I have come to celebrate my own gains, throw my own parties, because other queers and medics will rarely give you an inch, not the inch you want anyway—ain't it your full individual unique responsibility to be alive and well and happy, happy, happy? My survival began to lose cache in the late 1990s, the sunset of AIDS exceptionalism.

I breathe the morning air that recombines the dust and smithereens and loneliness of the previous evening, the aging pets of my petty peccadilloes, the fatuous attempts at connecting over the Internet with a rarefied community of distant Stepford wives. Safe sex is a reality, finally. We won—victory! Isn't this what we fought for? Safer sex and all the other metaphors that have been lessoned into us, to replace our language with epidemiological and medicalized talk, psychometrics, rough and rugged and handsome language that comes from behind, filled with warts, procedures, eczemas, dysfunctions of the body, viral loads (which are collectibles, it turns out!), CD counts, hemograms telegraphing doom, your constellation of private symptoms interpreted by specialists, one per organ—they know what each of your isolated organs feels and means, you don't. The anxiety, depressions, short breath, the diligent immunology, the near diabetes, the near liver cirrhosis, heart palpitations, the scars, an Andromeda of labels titillating in each corner of your body, every inch of colonized membrane, the biopsy that digs deeper than the best penetration you ever had. I am a cyborg database, a wiki-leak of conditions and half-truths determined and spoken by others, and I am made to be fluid and polyglot, to speak medical properly, or else…

Mental note in my lips, never discuss *barebacking* (that is to say unprotected sex between queers) in presence of lawyers, doctors, policy makers, and scientists. They get so discombobulated, poor things, hearing about the very motions and motives that keep them in business.

I must have fallen asleep for a while. A tremor reverberates all through my spine, a feeling Kafkaesque, a memory adolescent, waiting to be loved by men, practicing what priests taught me about sex behind the school doors, needing a father figure, safekeeping, and loving. I have had sex with hundreds of men, not bad men, just keeping their closeted commitment, their shame and fear, who left me with my hind legs up, filled with their shame, with my arms begging, with my mouth engorged, with my swollen necessity. And here I am in the kitchen naked and on my back again. Got to laugh. How glamorous or pathetic. What Pride are you talking about when queers still can't resolve our need for disdain and humiliation, for falling in love with the boot that kicks blunt, the smirk that bites deeper, and the rejection that makes me want it harder, thicker, and juicier. What Pride really is to be found outside the jingoistic hooray of many queers that still do not face HIV, our sceptic tolerance for our brothers in blood and spirit. How does this Pride help me peel myself off the kitchen floor? I need a clapper. I have fallen and I can't get up!

I will eventually get up; I am not paralytic, muted, I am not fully hologrammed yet. And now ageing with HIV is a new trendy topic for journalists and scientists and social workers. Here is to hope, comrades, that age will help me make it back to the social marquee I inhabited as a dying young gay man, the prime time. I will get up and take a shower, hot to remind me I burn outside too, not only in my cavities, and I will dress up the day like Mary Tyler Moore and will face the day with a beret thrown in the air, opiates, platform shoes, kaleidoscopic prints, silicone hair products, everything that was trendy becomes "retro" and has another chance down the hectic social runway. Renew or die!

I count the days to the closing sale. I plan assisted suicide. I indulge in the reverie of a gay bathhouse in the heavens above where all are disrobed and visceral and basic, a queer heavens where bones and humours have no pity or indignity and will be ablaze forever. Beatification they call it. It happens to all queers eventually, like gentrification. In this one pill morning, before I put one foot on the grave sidewalk, I forgive myself and others for the way we treat ourselves, nasty, self-indulgent, indulged little sexual minorities, and our fastidious liberations and marriages, fetishes, and sexualities, accoutrements, purchased children, the accessorizing of the middle class. I forgive us for forgetting the heritage of AIDS and thinking of it as a resolved issue, a medical victory, for the years or neglect, for the subterranean stigma and shame—dear family of choice I sometimes can hardly tolerate—for filling our pockets with the currency of Presbyterian self-entitlement. I forgive but do not forget. Would you? On the corner of my eye I see a ray of something filtering slowly into the kitchen, it might be the day that has broken.

"I propose a kind of universal queerness
where we, as strangers, momentarily find
each other in the middle of a simple and
unsophisticated exchange of air: mine for
yours, and yours for mine."

DISTANT TOUCH

Bogdan Cheta

TUESDAY, JANUARY 16, 2013, 11PM, CALGARY

The train ride to the studio feels long. Last night I met a man who offered me meth. He lives in that brick apartment building in Bridgeland that looks like a Frank Lloyd Wright knock-off. His condo fees must be expensive. He was handsome. I wanted to forget my arrest, meth made sense. What saved me is the Greek-Orthodox church next to his building. It reminded me of the church I snuck into as a boy in Bucharest. He wanted to have sex because his lover left him. His apartment was furnished with pieces inherited from his parents. He refinished them with a cappuccino stain. And I thought it was interesting—for someone to preserve his youth through these objects that used to live with his parents. I wonder why people hold on to the past. He proceeded to initiate me to meth or Tina, as he called it. I couldn't think of an argument to leave. I sat down on the couch with him. Numb to reality. Even with porn playing in the background, I kept staring at the Greek church that I could still see outside the window. After two hours of smoking, I told him I had to leave and that I wasn't interested in sex. So I left. I went outside and sat down beside the church, to talk to myself. It felt like I was in the company of a friend—which represented an alternative. Then I went back to the studio.

NIGHT WORK

As any handbook of psychology or self-help book will attest, often the only way to achieve the central object of one's desire requires deviation or working around it. Like a naive ikebana arrangement, the mythology of desire wants to naturally arrange itself and to be by itself without markers borrowed from reliable patterns of performance. Growing up, I practiced some weird rituals, though they were not without meaning. If I left the house and went on different roads, I would always retrace my steps coming back home; I did this so as not to describe a circle with my path in which houses and trees would remain enclosed. In this regard, my walk resembled a thread, and if, once unwound, it had not been rewound along the same road, the objects collected in the knots of the walk would have forever remained irremediably and profoundly bound to me. On these walks, I also had a box of matches in my pocket. Whenever I was very sad I would light a match and pass my hand through the flame, first one, then the other.

BUCHAREST, 1997

In Bucharest, I grew up in a house that was next to an old cemetery. Since we didn't have a backyard, the cemetery became my playground. There, among many other activities, I attended an exhumation and a reinhumation of a corpse (a regular event in eastern-orthodox cemeteries). The deceased was a boy who had been buried in an oversized suit. Years later, like the echo of a strong cologne lingering in the air long after it's been absorbed by a man's skin, the memory of this boy still haunts me: I continue to encounter the elegance of his dead body in the shadows cast by the men I follow, and meet with, in the night. His suit had a gold laménthread embroidered through it, and once in contact with light, these metallic laméedots gleamed like faraway stars, while the suit's blackness gave a background to this temporary constellation, which continues to implode and to spread itself inside the foreverness of his coffin and in my mind. At the time of our encounter, his face appeared intact, however, and almost all of the features had been preserved. The livid colour of the face made the head appear to have been modelled from pasteboard soaked in water.

When the coffin was taken out and opened, someone passed his hand over the face of the dead boy. It was then that all of us who were watching received a terrible shock: what we had believed was a well-preserved face was only a thick layer of mold, about two fingers deep. The mold had completely replaced the face of flesh, down to the bone, preserving its form. There was only a bare skeleton underneath.

That is how I see my head, today, if I stare long enough in the mirror—a skull, temporarily occupied by something that parallels my present. Then, there is the air—the air from the inside of our heads, whose stillness we all share in a Venn diagram kind of way. This head-air is different than the air around us in that it gently witnesses the proximity of our thoughts. When the mold was brushed off, out of some unexplained reflex I leaned over the coffin and began inhaling the air released from the inside of his head—the same way strangers exchange breaths as they walk through the street, likely unaware of the intensity of their shared queer intimacy. His air entered my stomach. Years later, and through this early encounter, I can imagine the identity of the penetrated male body to resemble a performative situation. In my writing, for example, this performative situation becomes the documentation of encounters with characters that through unforeseen circumstances are confronted, at one point or another, with the possibility of inhabiting an architecture meant to lubricate the exchange of air between thoughts—much like the way that some urban post-industrial sites, through their relative openness for being repurposed by/for emerging needs and desires, negotiate and re-negotiate their complicity to the fleeting sexual encounters that develop the concept of the behind as site of both fascination and fear.

THE ADDRESS BOOK

Remember those times when you were young, and you snuck out of your parents' house to go to the movies and see, you thought at the time, the most amazing films, mostly because these movies represented a secret opportunity to stare at beautiful men from somewhere in the dark? Like a scientist, you could ignore the big screen and, instead, consume a slow and calculated study of the men around you, and their bodies. You could spend hours just to stare at the shape of their eyes— or at the way their lips moved in the dark, as they quietly, and also in secret, kissed their girlfriends or boyfriends.

Written sometime in the 1980s, *The Address Book*, chronicles Sophie Calle's gradual, but distant immersion in the life of a filmmaker, whose address book she accidentally finds abandoned on a street in Paris. I find the gestures that Calle invents as she insinuates inside this man's life, to translate the way I imagine homosexuality: as a chance to relate to someone whose body is like yours. For Calle, this filmmaker's mind becomes like a body that, to her surprise, resembled her own. Perhaps Calle and her filmmaker shared the same head—the way that I shared my head with the boy that is buried in an oversized suit in Bucharest.

While in her 20s, and after years of drifting through Europe, and working as a stripper, Calle once said that she had to follow strangers because she was lost. I also follow men—because I am lost. When I am really lost, I turn to Calle's books, which have become maps that find my way out of the wilderness. Guiding my way out of the night, I've come to understand Calle's encounters with people she hasn't met as an imaginary lighthouse, beaming its jolts of light into the night as it directs us—walkers that continue to seek opportunities for getting lost—perhaps in the same way that my grandmother secretly keeps bottles of oil from Jerusalem in her purse, when walking in Bucharest during the night. Calle's object of protection is the stranger. Her books are either pink or red—pocket sized.

As site for double events, the most meaningful encounters with queer sociability find me when I trace, or re-trace, the architecture built from how people in my life—like my grandmother or my father for example—arrange their relationships with the geography of their adult lives. While always doubtful of the ways that mainstream queer literature regulates its distrust of heterosexual norms, I choose to look at the way my father loves my mother, for example, as an alternative that I can trace in my relationships with other men. Doubt is important in a young man's life. As is allowing strangers to choose the course of his future desires. In his memoir *Salvation Army*, Abdellah Taïa suggests that trusting strangers is a queer gesture in the same way that trusting our father's advice is radical. And as Sophie Calle dissolves herself in strangers only to reinvent herself, I propose a kind of universal queerness where we, as strangers, momentarily find each other in the middle of a simple and unsophisticated exchange of air: mine for yours, and yours for mine.

CALGARY, 2013

The following recollection documents a personal encounter. Structurally, the narrative presents the encounter as site for a double event that could be read like a marker which guides the reader through a personal space, but when observed in parallel, through a performative reading, this encounter also positions the penetrated male body and its performative potential in relation to an architectural complicity. As you proceed reading, imagine that you are a hiker who must interpret painted markers on trees, to find your way out of the wilderness. Like in an exchange, I am offering my encounter as your marker.

SUNDAY, SEPTEMBER 22ND, 2013, 11PM, CALGARY

Somewhere on a bike path.

This is a safe space in Calgary where I can follow men whom I don't know—by walking behind them, step for step, until they return to their houses where I usually stand in front of closed doors—sometimes devastated, but mostly desperate.

This evening, (after the usual targeted 10:30 pm police raid where men that find themselves walking without a visible purpose in the dark are sanctioned with $300 tickets) I accompanied a man up to his doorstep. I made sure that I camouflaged myself enough to disappear in the background.

With a sudden urge, unsuspected in me, I opened the gate and followed the man stealthily into the yard. Meanwhile he entered the house without observing me, and I remained alone in the middle of the path leading up to the house. A strange idea passed through my head.

There was a flowerbed in the middle of the garden. In an instant, I was in the centre of it and kneeling with my hand to my heart, head uncovered, and assuming a position of prayer. Here's what I wanted: to remain standing like this for as long as possible, immobile, petrified in the middle of the flowerbed. For a long time, I had been tormented by this longing to commit an absurd act in a completely foreign place, and now it had come to me spontaneously, without effort, almost like a joy. The warm evening hummed around me, and in the first moment I felt an enormous gratitude to myself for the courage of having made this decision.

I told myself to remain completely motionless even if no one chased me away and I had to stay like that until the next morning. Gradually my legs and hands stiffened and my position acquired an interior shell of infinite calm and immobility.

How long did I stay like that? All of a sudden, I heard vociferations inside the house and the outdoor light went off.

In the dark I was better able to feel the night breeze and the isolation in which I found myself, in the garden of a stranger's home.

A few minutes later the light came back on and then went off again. Someone in the house was turning the light on and off to see what effect this would have on me.

I continued to remain motionless, resolved to face more serious trials than the game with the lights. I kept my hand over my heart and my knee planted in the ground.

The door opened and someone came out into the little garden while a deep voice shouted from the house: "Leave him alone, let him be, he'll go away by himself." The man that I followed earlier, in the dark, came over to me. He was wearing an old Disney shirt and his briefs. He looked into my eyes and didn't say anything for a few seconds. We both remained silent. Finally, he put his hand on my shoulder and said gently, "Come...it's over now," as if he wanted me to understand that he had understood my gesture and had remained silent for some time in order to allow it to play itself out in its own way.

This spontaneous understanding disarmed me. I got up and wiped the dirt from my pants. "Your legs aren't hurting you?" he asked, "I wouldn't have been able to stay motionless for so long...."

I wanted to say something but couldn't manage anything other than to murmur, "Good evening," and left hurriedly.

"Unfortunately, for some people
who have never met me, my lesbian
identity is all they can see."

CROSSING THE LINE

Chantal Vallis

8

Stepping into the conference room, I scan the crowd and breathe easy. I can pass as just another young female teacher without putting in too much effort. I take off my jacket and quietly ease into my seat because the superintendent of the school board has already taken the stage. He's graciously welcoming his staff and makes an effortless transition to paying incredible lip service to the importance of equitable practices in supporting students. In my opinion the day is off to a rather generic start. He hasn't even introduced the first speaker and I already feel fatigued.

Equality in the school board has become a rather sexy topic in the last few years with a magnifying look on bullying and mental health awareness. Entire professional development days are dedicated to equality training, deconstructing power and privilege, and encouraging teachers to self-reflect. But as teachers reflect, children and youth struggle and community development workers, myself included, are stretching our arms farther and wider. I can't sit here comfortably knowing that today will be more talk and less action. It makes me wonder how the students I work with are doing today.

A representative from the local poverty roundtable is introduced. She is as somber as her PowerPoint and presents provincial data on her topic. She is not even halfway through her presentation when she loses most of her audience. People begin whispering, busying themselves with coffee or heading to the washroom. Many more are thumbing through their phones. "Pay attention!" I want to shout. If this were a classroom, these very same teachers would demand better behavior, so why not demand that of themselves?

A round of applause breaks my train of thought. I reel my criticisms deep within and mechanically clap along. The next speaker, from the University of Toronto, takes the stage and has us on our feet immediately for an activity called Across the Line.

The premise is simple: the group gathers on a single, straight line, marked out by masking tape, facing the facilitator. Silently, we wait for the facilitator to read a series of statements. If you want to acknowledge that a statement is true for you, you take a step. You step forward for statements that indicate privilege, whereas you step backwards for those that indicate disadvantage.

I feel the heat drain from my body and my head begin to thump as the facilitator explains these instructions. The activity fills me with anxiety. It stirs up unpleasant emotions and experiences I am still coming to terms with. Although I know I don't have to participate in this activity, I feel guilty if I don't. If I stand and watch everyone else, what does that say about me, my values, and the work I do in the community? I'm struggling between balancing my personal and professional identities when silence falls on the room and the facilitator begins.

"Step forward if you were given a good job opportunity based on someone you knew." I walk forward with half the crowd, noticing the line behind me, and the separation that has already begun.

"Step forward if you had a nanny growing up." I stand still and watch others affirm this statement.

"Step backwards if you are part of the LGBTQ community." My heart sinks. "It's only the third question!" I silently object. I take my step and my throat contracts. I feel terribly exposed. I am the only person in a crowd of 150 educators who has moved. I may still pass as a teacher, but I won't pass as straight now.

Unfortunately, for some people who have never met me, my lesbian identity is all they can see.

The crowd ebbs and flows with a steady rhythm of statements. Our differences and shared experiences are becoming more apparent as we drift in opposing directions across the line. Step forward if:

- You are White.
- You come from an affluent family.
- You went to a camp growing up.
- English was your first language.

Step backwards if:

- You were raised in a single-parent home.
- One or both of your parents was an immigrant.
- Your parents had to work more than one job.
- You question holding your partner's hand in public.

It feels like for every step forward, I take two backwards. Unsettled and irritated, I tap my foot impatiently and crack my double-jointed fingers, concentrating on those sensations rather than the ballooning emotion in my eyes and the back of my throat. As hard as it is for me, I know it's just as hard for others who are stepping backwards admitting that they were unfairly treated because of their ethnicity or that they have a family member with a mental illness.

I'm far away from the line now. I'm at least six steps back, despite all the steps I have taken forward. Consequently, I'm no longer registering what the facilitator is saying because all my senses are clogged. I'm doing my best to concentrate on my toes and fingers, working faster and faster to block unwanted sensations. For me, it's best to feel on the outside rather than the inside in these situations.

I look down to watch my toes tap, tap, tap and stomp out the words, but instead I see a tear shatter onto the carpet and another one shortly follows. Not even my tears are allowed peaceful solitude. I lift my head and try to choke back the others, but my tears won't hold. They stain my cheeks, revealing my turmoil to others.

A new line is crossed. Despite my best efforts to keep my emotions locked down, the personal has saturated the professional. I've quickly escalated from a few reserved tears to choking back sobs and wiping away unwanted fluids with the sleeve of my sodden sweater, as unwelcome eyes peek and pry. Uncomfortable with my starring role in these teachers' lesson plans on power and privilege, I look up, ready to confront their curiosity. Some heads abruptly turn to face the instructor. Others just avert their eyes. Passivity leaves the deepest scars on the soul.

Festering in abandonment, I catch the eyes of one curious onlooker. She is staring at me, tilting her head gently to the side with raised brows. She is the sort of person whose every gesture has a thousand captions. In this particular moment I read: "Are you alright? Is there anything I can do?" and "Would you like a tissue?" Her genuine concern softens me. I acknowledge her with a small, tight-lipped smile. A meek offering, but one that she takes as an invitation. Against the continuous ebb and flow of the crowd she stands still and extends her hand. She waves at me to take it, but I hesitate; isn't this breaking the rules? She smiles at me again and steps backwards, towards me, as if to say, "I'll meet you half way." I walk forward and meet her at the masking tape line and grab hold of her hand. We stand in solidarity as the activity wraps up. I can feel her energy and strength binding me to her. I desperately want to express my gratitude, my admiration, and so much more, but I don't say anything at all because sometimes our actions really do speak louder than our words. Hers, mine, all of ours.

> "I suffer because of what I am, and what
> I am saved me from that which I suffer."

LEARNING MY PLACE

Tucker Bottomley

When I was ten years old my family moved across town. New school, new people. The problem wasn't that they were new to me but that I was new to them. Pre-pubescent, chubby, short cropped hair and only boy's clothes led the entirety of my peers to believe that I was of the male gender. Even despite the fact that my name was Anna. The girls were flirtatious, the guys accepting and friendly. I was over the moon with the way I was being perceived and terrified of what would happen when they found out the "truth." I was lucky because it wasn't one big incident when everyone found out; I think it was more gradual. In fact, I find it hard to recall the details, mostly just people asking me to confirm, "You're a girl?" It was easy to tell they were confused by me, and felt uncomfortable with the way they had previously treated me.

They then proceeded to try (to my great annoyance) to force me into female gender role situations, and then poke fun at me for being so much like a boy. It was a strange and difficult experience.

Their confusion and awkward reactions toward me sparked my own insecurities when it came to my gender, and then the most popular girl in the class enthusiastically chose me to be her partner when the teacher said we had to choose someone we hadn't worked with yet.

It was hard going back and forth from feeling like people were disgusted by me and then feeling like they really enjoyed my company. Of course everything got more difficult when puberty set in. No longer able to get away with being "mistaken" for a boy, I couldn't hide from my body anymore. Having no information, everything got perpetually worse in every aspect. North American societal gender norms were very strict on the subject in my mind and in the minds of my peers. I didn't know anyone else who defied gender norms quite like myself, or ever expressed wishing they could be the opposite sex to the degree I did.

I often had the thought, "Who could love me?" I wasn't interested in boys and assumed any girl who was straight wouldn't be interested in me, nor any lesbian because I wasn't like a real girl at all. Many of those questions were answered just a few years later when I met my first girl friend. It is because of her that I believe now you can love someone based purely on who they are, not what they are. She proved to me that despite the fact she'd never been interested in girls, she loved me because of who I was. She also reminded me of a few life lessons a lot of us are taught as children, like "treat others the way you want to be treated." That's probably the one that sticks out the most because it seems like we loose the capacity to do that as we get older. To a ridiculous degree.

A few years later and all of a sudden I had found my place among a myriad of peers, including LGBTQ people, who had extensive knowledge and interests like arts, music, spirituality, politics, science, and math, everything! It was during my first and only tour (I played with my best friend in an accordion and guitar duet, folk-punk style) that I decided to pick a new name and change my pronouns from female to male. It was almost an accident really. It didn't feel like "coming out," I'd already come out as a lesbian years prior, but somehow the switch from female to male was a lot easier and felt a lot more natural. My friends had never really stuck a gender on me, being the open-minded people they are. So it was more just like I was finally making the decision to pick a new name and start presenting myself as male in a more public way.

Finally, feeling somewhat better about myself, I had no clue what was really in store for me during those few weeks of travelling.

I was finally able to live as a boy when, funnily enough, at the same time I started to accept the concept that part of me (mentally not physically) was female. "You just have to remind yourself, Tucker, that inside that brain is a mature sophisticated woman."

It wasn't an insult. It was a compliment, and I felt it right away. A quick lighting flash inside my head of a dawning realization— she was completely right. I had lived twenty years as a woman and suffered some of the same challenges women have overcome for thousands and thousands of years. Then I realized I was proud to have experienced woman-hood. To think about the many heroines of history, who (unlike men) I have a definite passion for, makes me feel a little closer to greatness because I was a woman too. It makes me feel like I've already accomplished a life goal.

I have experienced life as both genders. I've read that many Native Americans believed LGBT people (especially transgender people) to have two spirits. They were known and functioning people in those communities.

My brother also once told me of a Greek myth about a man named Tiresias who was punished for killing two snakes by being turned into a woman. There are many different versions of the story, but in every one of them, after she became a woman, she was blessed with the gift of prophecy and considered to possess magical powers. So why have we been hiding for all these years? Why do we have to suffer at the hands of those who do not understand us?

In a lot of cases people tend to fear what they do not understand. I know it's tiresome and often uncomfortable to answer the same questions, but maybe the more questions you answer, the more understanding will happen. We just need to meet them on even ground and allow them to question us relentlessly, so they may see that we are not monsters. We can be intelligent and beautiful people. We just need to help them see it.

Lately I've found myself looking at strangers and picturing them as the opposite sex. I've found that with the majority of people, it's not hard to picture at all. Even for every woman with especially "feminine" features, or men with a massive jaw and bushy eye brows, I know that somewhere there is a man just as delicate and graceful as that woman, and there is a woman just as big-boned and heavy-browed as that man. What I'm trying to say is that I believe every single person has physical or mental "feminine" and "masculine" attributes. My question is why aren't we all celebrating the femininity and masculinity within us? Both femininity and masculinity have pros and cons, but for some reason a lot of people tend to think we need to be just one of those categories.

I have learned how to get along within society and feign confidence in myself and the few endeavours I undertake, but pretending to be okay with the way some people will think of me just because of what I am hurts me deeply. Not because I care about what they think of my life choices, but because I think that if they go through life judging someone (or something) by its nature then they may miss out on a lot of beauty. I'm not insinuating that someone may be "missing out" by not becoming my friend, I'm asking why would anyone want to turn down the feeling of being accepted and appreciated for who they are by another human being? Don't we strive for understanding and meaning in life? Isn't love the ultimate idea of happiness and meaning for most people? Or am I just crazy? Despite feeling this way about some people, the people I do know and who know me I deeply appreciate and feel deeply appreciated by.

Since I was a child I felt like I had some special privileges. I remember in the playground at an early age (before gender norms really kicked in) when it came to boys vs girls I was asked to be on both teams. It was like I was a special member of the boys' club and the girls' club. People who are open minded enough seem to be very comfortable with me whatever gender or sexuality they may be. That is my gift, and without that I would not be as special as I am. Even though in person I come off as confident, funny, and possibly mildly intelligent, on the inside I'm bloody terrified.

Society has had the same effect on me as most other people. Feeling inadequate in so many ways, I worry constantly about how I appear to other people, even my friends and family. I suffer because of what I am, and what I am saved me from that which I suffer.

I'm not trying to say I'm holier than thou. In fact, I've done as many stupid and wrong things as the next person. But I know for a fact that if I weren't transgender I would not be as open-minded and (in my opinion) would not be able to understand both genders as I do. In fact when I really think about it, I think I probably wouldn't have been as good of a person as I am if I was born with male genitalia. I do want to change the way people think and help them become more openminded. Not just because I suffer on account of the ignorance that plagues our society, but also because I know everyone else is suffering too. I've considered the fact that I'm incredibly lucky to have been born in the 1990s, because a hundred years ago I would have been forced to live a life I couldn't be happy in, or even longer before that I would have burned for being a sexual deviant which was associated with witchcraft.

So what I'm really saying is I'm like a super hero. I didn't want this gift, and I'm often misjudged or looked down upon by people who don't understand me. I fight battles internally and externally. My super power is my ability to empathize with people to gain their respect and love. I, like so many people (who don't even know it), have the power to make a change. Being who I am helped me to realize my dream. I want to entertain people, teach them, and help them if I can. I still don't know how I am going to accomplish these feats I have fantasized in my head, but maybe this essay is a first step towards that dream.

"I long to feel comfortable in my own skin. I yearn for the confidence to express my sexuality and identity in public. I wish for my community and the world at large to be the just and equal place it has the potential to be."

CAUGHT IN BETWEEN

Krista McCracken

No true statement of acceptance has ever included the words "but," "if," or "maybe." I didn't so much come out of the closet as stumble headlong onto the floor while exiting the closet. My family learned of my relationship with a woman without me telling them. To say they were shocked would be an understatement. Baffled might come close to describing their reaction. It was the first of many auspicious beginnings. My mother's response stuck with me most. She was ambivalent at best, soul crushing at worst. Our conversation started with, "We will always support you, but I don't think you're strong enough to be in a gay relationship" and went downhill from there. Her words were filled with good intentions. But those intentions were wrapped in barbs of doubt and wishful thinking.

That conversation happened close to ten years ago. My immediate family and I have never openly spoken about my sexuality since that first discussion. The profound silence doesn't surprise me. Feelings were never spoken about openly in that house. Feelings were something you stuffed down deep inside you and hid from the world. But, even if my family didn't want to acknowledge my feelings or my identity, they still existed. And those words my mother spoke so long ago often permeate my self-conscious and reverberate through my psyche. What if she was right? What if I'm not strong enough to express my sexuality? What if I am better off hiding my true self from the world?

Since my first adventure out of the closet, I've come out a hand-ful of times. I've stood in the mirror practicing what I'm going to say to a new friend. I've built new communities of strength for myself, overcome mental health challenges, and embraced my identity as a bisexual person. This embrace has been a delicate one, and the path has been full of trials and errors.

Like many bisexual people, I've been accused of taking the easy way out and of merely going through a phase. These accusations have come from inside and outside the LGBT community. These statements have made me feel stuck between the straight world and gay world, without a home to call my own. I try to tune out the words of dismissal, but they haunt me as a struggle to define myself.

Yes, my partner is a man. To outsiders it often appears as though I am straight. I can pass for straight if I so desire. But my identity as a bisexual woman is integral to my sense of self. It's not a phase I went through, and I didn't magically become straight when I started dating a man. I have struggled to realize my relationship does not make me less of a bisexual.

I still find it challenging to be open about my true identity. Moving to a small conservative community of under 1,000 people hasn't helped. I have imagined my neighbours finding out that I'm a bisexual with polygamous leanings. In my head, this results in a

witch hunt with an angry mob chasing me out of town. Intellectu-
ally I know that nothing so dramatic is likely to happen. A few
people might shrug their shoulders, others might gossip, and I
might lose a few acquaintances. It's highly unlikely that I would be
burnt at the stake. But the possibility of losing face locally pushes
me back into the closet. Maybe my mother was right. I'm not strong
enough.

But maybe I could be. I yearn for a support network, for others
to talk to who are experiencing the same thing. My partner, close
friends, and others know I'm bisexual. But I've never been willing
to share my identity with the whole world or even my small local
community. I'm not ashamed of who I am. But I am afraid.

I long to feel comfortable in my own skin. I yearn for the
confidence to express my sexuality and identity in public. I wish for
my community and the world at large to be the just and equal place
it has the potential to be. It is getting better. But there are thousands
of people like me struggling to find their voice, to find their place
in the world. This struggle can be heartbreaking, gut wrenching,
and awful. I choke up when someone says something derogatory
to my face. I need to speak up. We all do. The world can be a better
place, but not without effort.

> "So for a long time,
> I felt I was only watching a life,
> rather than living one."

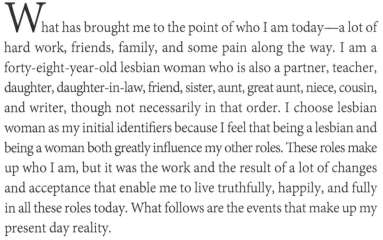

MY STORY OF PRIDE:
A LIFE IN PROGRESS

Lisa Walters

What has brought me to the point of who I am today—a lot of hard work, friends, family, and some pain along the way. I am a forty-eight-year-old lesbian woman who is also a partner, teacher, daughter, daughter-in-law, friend, sister, aunt, great aunt, niece, cousin, and writer, though not necessarily in that order. I choose lesbian woman as my initial identifiers because I feel that being a lesbian and being a woman both greatly influence my other roles. These roles make up who I am, but it was the work and the result of a lot of changes and acceptance that enable me to live truthfully, happily, and fully in all these roles today. What follows are the events that make up my present day reality.

"It's a girl," exclaimed the doctor, and thank goodness I turned out to be a girl. My mother promised to send me back if I was another boy since she already had two. But not only was I a girl, I was also a very unexpected surprise. At forty-four, my mother didn't expect to be able to get pregnant since she had already started menopause. My mom's doctor originally thought I was a tumour of some sort and x-rayed me. I later considered using the effects of radiation as my defence against family disapproval for why I turned out to be a lesbian. However, perhaps I was destined to be gay because I spent a few extra days in the womb doing somersaults that caused me to be born with one limp wrist, resulting in my spending the first six weeks of life in a cast to *straighten* it out. In the long run, it was only my wrist that ended up *straight*.

I grew up in a lower middle-class home with parents from Newfoundland who had moved to Nova Scotia in the 1940s with only enough money to admit them to Canada (since Newfoundland had not yet joined Confederation). They both worked hard: Mom cleaned rich families' homes and Dad worked on the boats. They struggled for every dollar and believed in saving money for a rainy day, values passed on to me. These and other values my parents and other family members possessed were very traditional and common at the time. When I grew up, topics such as inter-racial marriage and homosexuality were usually not talked about, or if they were, the conversations made me feel very uncomfortable to express my thoughts. Not quite understanding or agreeing with others' opinions, I just knew there were some friends from school I shouldn't bring home. I remember wondering what the problem was with being or doing something different. However, I was not courageous enough to speak my mind until much later, particularly when the topic of homosexuality came up because, even as a pre-teen and teenager, I felt this label applied to me.

Mom first married in her late teens to a man who was killed in World War II a month before his second son was born. Left with two young sons, she sought a means of support, mostly financial, and married my father because it was hard for a single mother to make it in the 1940s before social programs were available. Living in a mostly loveless and lonely marriage led both my parents to find means of escape. I don't remember much of my childhood, I think mostly because the good times and pleasant memories were overshadowed by arguments between my parents and other family. However, I do have some happy memories of time spent with my dad in his workshop and helping him around the house as my tomboy ways began to shine. I also remember a few good friends and the fantasies of running away and living in some enchanted land that helped me escape. I liked to hide in my room, often in my closet (which would have much more meaning in the future) where it was harder to hear the arguments below.

I lived in my childhood home until my mid-twenties. I grew up the "perfect" daughter because that's what my mother expected as she tried to live the life she had wanted through me, and I also didn't want to do anything to rock the already shaky boat called my family. I always did exactly what I was supposed to do and not necessarily what I wanted to do, so I never felt as if I was really being me. So for a long time, I felt I was only watching a life, rather than living one. This began to slowly change when I went to university, made more friends, and "came out" of my shyness. After university, I spent the next few years in the "perfect" job, making more money in my starting salary than my father ever did during his life, and in the "perfect" relationship with a man my family and friends loved. But then everything changed.

In 1990, my father died. It was one of the most sorrowful days of my life, but a day that changed the direction of the rest of my life. As death often does, it caused me to reflect on my life like I had never done before. After working through the grief, I took a look at where I was and where I wanted and needed to be, and I began to make changes. Though they often say not to make major life decisions during a highly emotional time, the decisions I made helped bring me to where and who I am today.

I had known after the first few weeks of working in the "perfect" job that I had chosen the wrong career, but I felt trapped after spending four years in university. I had also known for most of my life that I was attracted to women, but at the time I kept thinking that if I tried hard enough, I could be with a man and be happy. The job felt like the easier change, since I knew I wanted to be a teacher, but the idea of admitting I was a lesbian frightened me so much that all my past attempts at coming out were unsuccessful. I was so afraid of being alone. I was afraid of losing my family and friends because I had heard only negativity around the topic of homosexuality.

I started my career change by enrolling in some courses to work towards being a teacher. This gave me a distraction from work and my relationship. But when those courses ended, decision time came, and within a month, I quit my job just a few months before a big promotion, ended my relationship, and opened the door of my closet by deciding to come out to my best and oldest friend. My best friend, who is heterosexual, helped me in my search for self and took me to the only gay bar in our city on women's night. That night I walked cautiously across the street watching to see if anyone was around to notice me going in. As we walked through the door, I thought everyone would be able to see my heart pounding through my shirt. My friend, asking if I was nervous, received only a nod in reply because my voice wouldn't come, but as we walked through the crowds, my mind kept screaming, *Lesbians: real live lesbians! I'm here, and I'm in heaven.*

Unfortunately, this heaven turned into a bit of a hell as I met a woman that night with whom I spent the next year. The only explanation I have for this relationship is I needed to be with someone. However, despite the dysfunction, it was my first lesbian relationship, and nothing will ever change the feelings that came with that experience. This relationship forced me into therapy where I finally began to take a deeper look at my life and the influences on who I was. Thanks to a very caring and capable counsellor, I am still alive today and in a healthy, loving relationship with a woman with whom I just celebrated my ten-year wedding anniversary.

My process to get to where I am today was often incredibly difficult and would cover more than this essay would allow, but I truly feel it has happened how it was supposed to. It has allowed me to grow as a woman and a lesbian and allowed me to better and more truthfully fulfil all of those other roles. The process has created many new friendships, helped me start a lesbian group in the early 1990s when many women needed support and a place to be themselves, and, on a dare, took me to the 1993 Gay and Lesbian March on Washington where I yelled, cheered, and marched with pride.

Life is good now. I am working at a teaching job I enjoy, and I am sharing my life with a wonderful woman and our fur baby. I am open about my life with my family and friends and at work. Though not all of my family and friends have been accepting, I have been surprised by the support I have received. I had always hoped life would be this way, but I never really thought I would have the opportunity to get married and be open everywhere because that's not how the world looked in 1990. Coming out and being who I am reflects my pride and my courage with a few acts of social justice thrown in through the years.

"If you're a child of the rainbow, you're pretty much assured life won't be easy."

LIVING OUT EVERY DAY: AN EFFORT TO FIGHT HEGEMONY IN ITS MANY INCARNATIONS

Amy Soule

Heterosexism refers to the idea that all of humankind is assumed to be straight, making it relevant to sexual orientation alone. However, my life experience has shown me that it's possible to (only half-jokingly) talk about other kinds of hegemony or oppression due to assumptions people make about other elements of my life, including diet, faith, and education. No matter the kind(s) of cultural domination I encounter any given day, I strive toward making people aware it's alright to be different.

It's a rare day, especially between September and June, when I'm on the job as an educational assistant, that I'm not confronted with a challenge to out myself as gay due to the effect of heterosexism (or its more sinister cousin, homophobia). Despite any anxiety it may provoke in people who care about me, I refuse to let heterosexism, let alone homophobia, rule the roost in any class I find myself working in. Dealing with students' heterosexism is generally easy, though I'm sure I confuse some of them when I confide, "No, I don't have a spouse, though I'm grateful I have the right to marry if I want." As for dealing with homophobic abuse of the word gay? Oftentimes, it's as easy, and boring, let alone repetitive—sometimes I seriously feel like a wind-up music box!—as telling students, "Excuse me, I'm pretty sure [insert object] is unable to be happy or attracted to [insert object] of the same sex. Due to that, I'd appreciate it if you used 'gay' according to its proper meaning if at all. Thank you for respecting this." If they push harder, saying they're not offending anyone, I don't have a problem responding that they're actually offending me due to the fact that I'm gay. If that leads to me having to run a thirty-minute Q and A session to educate them more or answer any questions they have, I'm cool with it, as awkward as it can have potential to feel, since I've been asked some pretty intimate questions during these times. As for adult-to-adult interaction, it would be nice if my pride jewellery was adequate to out myself, but all too often I'm read as a straight ally when people notice it due to my appearance; their heterosexism and stereotypes about gay peoples' appearance conspire to prevent them from understanding that, yes, a boring-looking person like me can actually be gay. According to this, I've come to realize most people aren't meaning to be insensitive when they ask me if I have a boyfriend; they are simply the results of a heterosexist culture and want adequate proof that I'm a sentient human, able to fully experience love. Of course that means I'm great at feeling guilty when I shatter their stereotypes via "setting the record straight" and gently telling them, "No, I'm actually gay." Letting people down is hardly something I enjoy, but sometimes it happens and I have to live with the consequences, no matter their effect. Then again, maybe I could, according to one definition, claim to have a boyfriend. After all, I have a friend who's a boy. Does that make him my boyfriend, according to a mathematical understanding of the word? Hard to be sure a hundred percent though, as a literal creature living with the effect of a learning difference, I can hardly help but wonder.

Dietary hegemony is a second influence that has a large effect on my social life since society seems to believe we are all supposed to consume everything on earth, and people think you're odd, unhealthy, etc., if you deliberately choose to avoid eating or drinking something. In an effort to exert some control in my life ten years ago, since I was trapped in a cult (for the life of me, I cannot call the place a school), enduring physical, psychological, and social abuse, I went vegetarian. After learning about everything that happens to virtually all animals that contribute toward making food and drink for people, I stopped being able to rationalize consuming dairy and egg, turning vegan eight years ago. Odd as it may seem (since vegans are often portrayed as militant people, hail stereotypes), I'm fully supportive of anybody consuming animal-derived food or drink if they have to, despite being unable to rationalize such behaviour for myself. I also despise having conversations about nutrition with strangers, something I'm all too aware has a high likelihood of happening if I outright call my diet vegan in public. Due to this awareness, I've learned to tailor my responses according to the exact questions I'm asked, since experience has taught me a generic "no thank you," especially when it comes to being asked about sweets, earns me undeserved and offensive accolades for having such a strong will, something I don't believe myself to have, on top of the evident fat phobia inherent in comments of that kind. If I'm offered something containing egg, my general rebuff will feature an allusion to allergy. Any time I'm offered food containing dairy, my usual retort includes a reference to lactose intolerance (and frankly, I'd be shocked if I wasn't after so many years of being a vegan!). Obviously if somebody offers me meat I don't have any problem voicing a certain longer word starting with V, since vegetarianism is much more understood in our current society and it's not half as likely to generate queries about health, etc., as mentioning veganism. At maximum, you can expect to be asked about protein as a vegetarian; as a vegan you're asked about way more than that.

Trust me when I tell you it gets boring and exasperating refuting everything.

Though it's more prominent at certain times of the year than others, religious hegemony also exerts a strong effect on me. Society at large seems alright with its implicit assumption that all of humankind is—or at minimum should be—Christian, and that non-Christian holidays can be analogized to Christian celebrations. As an observant Jew, I'm simultaneously driven nuts by this phenomenon and left feeling as if I could blow a gasket due to laughing so hard. Advertisements on television that only involve Christian symbolism and then have enough chutzpah to tell people "Happy Holidays," to give one example, are great for mixing and matching my emotions to this effect, especially due to their inaccurate math. After all, Christmas is a single holiday, making pluralisation of the word grammatically improper due to the context advertisements of this nature put it in. It stands to reason, though, that there are definitely times where I'm simply driven psycho due to the results of religious hegemony being outright offensive. I've had one too many encounters with it on the job that make me want to scream, whether it was a song pretty much insisting December should be students' favourite month of the year because Santa will come, bearing goodies, to their homes (hail socio-economic assumptions also, note the sarcasm); students having to write a letter to Santa asking for something; students being asked to count down the days until Christmas; or students being told they have to write "Happy Easter" above a generic spring picture. All of these instances could have been substituted with something more inclusive, but their teacher couldn't—or didn't want to—think like that. Sometimes, though, I almost have to smile at incidents involving religious heterosexism due to their fighting against traditional heterosexism. To give one example, somebody on the job once gave a crossword puzzle to her class that asked about Santa's spouse, something that left me smiling since it half-implied Santa had potential to be gay; on that theme I've come to almost love a certain Christmas carol due to its positive usage of the word gay, helping educate students that it can mean happy, cheery, or festive. People's emphasis on Chanukah, to throw out one evident contrasting example, almost makes me feel guilty about reminding them that, "No, it's not the 'Jewish Christmas' you want to make it out to be in spite of its appearance completely in December most years." Sometimes humour helps, since it's easy to give a 'punny' response to people's questions about Chanukah via retorting, "Nope. Chanukah is light," although that's reliant on them grasping the fact I'm using *light* to mean multiple opposites simultaneously. Something else I will never understand at all is why people seem to believe I'm supposed to feel deprived due to my Judaism. One student I was helping a number of months ago, out of nowhere, announced to the class, "Jews don't celebrate Christmas." My prompt response to that was, "No but we have many other significant holidays that we celebrate." He seemed shocked, whether due to the fact we Jews have significant holidays or because of my proud affirmation of my Judaism, I'm not completely sure; either way, it was an interesting and educational encounter for both him and me.

Educational hegemony, in my mind, is the widely held belief that university is superior to college. This is an additional force that has wreaked its fair share of havoc in my life. Most people have it drilled into their heads that if they go to college they'll be a failure, never amount to anything, or be unable to demonstrate their true potential. Despite having a learning difference, I wasn't exempt from this, even if no one had any real idea where to put me in terms of educational stereotypes. Prior to kindergarten, some educational psychologists told my mom a miracle would be necessary if I was to ever graduate from high school; come grade seven, I started, late as it may have been according to the social clock, to be put under pressure to pursue and complete university studies. Neither of these extreme ideas has proven true. Finishing high school (thank God I was able to escape the cult!) was actually relatively easy after

I was able to devote my energy to classes that catered to my intelligence strengths (musical and verbal-linguistic), though university was an epic disaster—as I had known it was going to be, despite feeling I had to appease certain people in my life. Anyway, leaving that toxic environment and attending college was a real relief. I was able to breathe and enable my true potential to manifest itself (and yes, I shocked myself with this, since I had never obtained a hundred percent through an entire class). It may even stand to reason that I was tempted to claim I felt proud of myself, despite having so many issues with the word due, appropriately enough, to my learning difference making me extremely literal when it comes to understanding anything linguistic. If anybody's desperate to perceive me as a failure for being an EA rather than a teacher and for leaving an environment I never should have been in, they totally can. I've always known my strengths and needs and, despite anything others may tell me, I refuse to judge myself for that. College is great for so many people and I'm a proud member of that group, thank you.

If you're a child of the rainbow, you're pretty much assured life won't be easy. As somebody queer on multiple levels and thus subject to many versions of heterosexism and hegemony, I'm constantly pushed to out myself and affirm everything that combines to make me different due to people's supposedly innocent actions, comments, or questions, no matter whether they relate to sexual orientation, diet, religion, or education. Though it's daunting at times, I enjoy believing that I have enough pride (confession: I think self-acceptance is more accurate since, to me, pride has connotations of success and I'm all too aware that being any difference I am isn't an accomplishment of any kind) to offer appropriate, sensitive responses to anything people throw at me as I'm simply striving to live my life as I'm supposed to. *L'Chayim* (to life)!

"In a world of labels and labellers, for me
it's the most liberating thing to be unlabelable,
to defy easy categorization, to be both
something and not something at the same time,
the Schrödinger's cat of queer males."

A MANUSCRIPT
THAT'S NEVER FINISHED

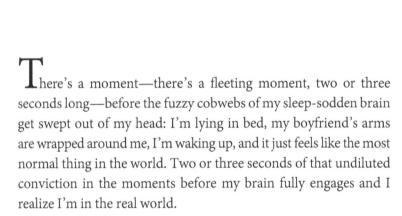

Nathan Downey

There's a moment—there's a fleeting moment, two or three seconds long—before the fuzzy cobwebs of my sleep-sodden brain get swept out of my head: I'm lying in bed, my boyfriend's arms are wrapped around me, I'm waking up, and it just feels like the most normal thing in the world. Two or three seconds of that undiluted conviction in the moments before my brain fully engages and I realize I'm in the real world.

Long ago, right around the time I decided I'd come out to the world, I decided I wouldn't let the world's taken-as-gospel rules dictate my life to me. An early confidante told me the best part about being queer was that you could make your own rules, and I've lived by those words ever since. This was before I went to university and learned that there was an entire branch of humanist studies devoted to this: critical theory. Here at last, one could earn grades for holding a magnifying glass up to the general rules society has handed down to us; one could look closely, past the lines scratched on the stone tablets, carved on statues, enshrined in ruling documents—the rules ordering a paradigm of one man/one woman, because that's the way it's always been—and see that behind these rules that by and large society insists are the only ones, there's a blank slate. There's a fresh piece of loose leaf and a brand new fountain pen, and there's the chance to live entirely on one's own terms.

More on this later.

I think sooner or later, every queer person holds a mirror up to him- or herself and asks, "Would I be happier if I were straight?" I have looked long into the mirror, and I have no answer other than, "I can't imagine being any way other than I am right now." If I were straight, if I were part of the majority, I would be presented with the paradigmatic life trajectory that's handed to every straight person: you grow up, you meet a member of the opposite sex, you marry that person, you have children with that person, you raise those children to follow the same arc through life, you die, and your line continues. For straight people, straying from this trajectory is not accepted with indifference. If you're unmarried later in life and you're not a member of some sort of religious order, people treat you as an object of suspicion. If you're in a marriage with a member of the opposite sex and you have no children, people assume there's some sort of biological impediment, and they adjust the way they treat you as though you had some other medical condition to be pitied. If you raise children and don't heed the meaningless but somehow carefully protected societal constructs—blue for boys, pink for girls, just for example—people assume you're doing some sort of lasting harm to your kids. There's no real escape from the natural order of things—the starling with painted feathers is set upon by the other starlings and pecked to death—and this is what it means to be a member of the majority: To be placed on a path and given a map with strict instructions not to deviate from the gently wending black line lest you should stray into the brambles and be eaten by lions. (I use rhetorical overstatement, of course. I know straight people who don't follow the prescribed societal expectations, and so far as I know, they bear no beak wounds. But I think I'm not wrong in that the fellow members of their tribe invariably view them as odd, strange, eccentric, weird, or whatever other adjectives people use to describe a wholesale breach of convention.)

As with many things that are unchangeable, it is difficult to say whether my relief at not being held to these standards comes about because I'm queer, or whether I'm just naturally an outsider and an iconoclast and so it's just a happy coincidence that I'm queer and therefore not held to these standards.

Whichever it is, I am continually thankful that, as I was once told, I am able to live life however I best see fit. I am automatically excluded from the expectations of heteronormativity. My boyfriend and I have been together seven years, which is nearly the entire duration of my being out to the world. During this time, I have never once consulted a rulebook written by anyone else, queer or straight: my boyfriend and I have been the sole authors. Seven years together in a variation of monogamy that suits our mutual needs (that is to say, flexibly applied, when necessary). What a sublime relief it is not to have to follow someone else's rules. I've learned a lot in seven years. One thing I never would've thought of beforehand is that the day he and I moved in together (prematurely, ten months or so in, but that's the subject of another essay altogether) my wardrobe increased by several orders of magnitude. My boyfriend and I—roughly the same height and the same build, with roughly the same size feet—have shared one colossal omnibus assortment of clothing ever since (and that, it must be said, has been much more to my benefit, as a sartorial amateur, than to my boyfriend's). We divide the domestic duties according to who is feeling more energetic at that particular moment. He does most of the driving, except when I, as a reformed alcoholic, can serve as a designated driver. I'm currently earning the bigger living and supporting both us, but I fully expect that once he's finished training as an accountant, he'll out-earn me for the rest of our lives, and I'm fine with that. (Unless twenty years down the road the English language has degraded so much that they pay writers the same wages they pay doctors. Maybe?) Neither of us feels particularly compelled to exercise our relatively recent rights to marry or have children. For that matter, neither of us particularly cares for the conversationally ambiguous label "partner," though that seems to be the standard these days—"boyfriend" suffices nicely for our purposes. Spending our earnings on ourselves *ad infinitum* sounds perfectly fine, thank you very much. We have been discussing dogs for the last couple years and gradually, glacially reaching a consensus on which type we want. This is life, on our own terms.

I mentioned critical theory earlier because once exposed to it, once trained to dissect everything with critical thought, there's no turning back. There's no smiling and unquestionably accepting the natural order of things, no matter how pervasive. I see these societal constructs as the bars of a cage that engirds large swaths of humanity. I mention this again because the fact is, I've found there are societal expectations placed on queer people too, and I'm equally uncomfortable accepting those.

When I meet straight people and they find out I'm dating a guy, I usually perceive that they're expecting me to measure up to a certain definition that they've learnt. (Here's the point where I say I am eternally grateful for all the activists who have made life as an out queer person in the western world so bearable. I wouldn't be typing these keystrokes if not for you.) The normalizing of queerhood has certainly changed the stereotypes. Instead of gay men being viewed as deviant sodomites, or libertine hedonists, they are now viewed as fashion savvy and gym obsessed, dance-pop loving and effeminate, catty and shallow. These, I realize, are just the stereo-types—the easy definition the media has accepted. And these are changing quickly too, right before all our very eyes in fact. Now gays want nuclear families. They want to marry their partners and have kids. All of this is incredible forward progress, and I don't for a second think it's in any way negative. But having said that, I feel equally uncomfortable being defined by these narrow parameters as I would if I were born a straight person.

I'm speaking purely for myself here now. One thing that has always fascinated me is masculinity. Our definitions of it— what it means to be male. Maleness. On one hand, I reject the traditional definitions of masculinity outright. Feminism, queer theory, poststructuralism have stamped that way of thinking out of me, if I ever did entertain such thoughts. On the other hand, the idea that straight people (or even gays) expect me to be some sort of feminized version of male, some diluted strength of masculinity, makes me all the more intent on being masculine, and yes, the brand of masculine society prizes. This has been autonomic, for the most part. I know within the gay male subculture there's a subset of guys who venerate masculinity. This isn't my reason. Nor is my reason that I myself don't like feminine males—on the contrary, my boyfriend's demeanour skews to the feminine and I love that about him. I have just been intent at every turn to challenge people's ideas of what a gay man should be. I wish not to fulfill some sort of expectation, or to fill in the lines of a stereotype, but rather, to define my queerness in my own way. And so, with this mandate humming ever in the background noise, I live, satisfying no one's criteria but my own. I'm happier listening to Sunn O))), Big Black, and The Replacements than I ever could be with Lady Gaga or The Scissor Sisters, but I'm also happy listening to Owen Pallett, Roxy Music, Robyn, and Matmos. I get my hair cut at the punk-rockest barbershop I can find, and spend my time in the chair talking to the barber about Jawbreaker and Obits. My favourite thing to do is to strap crampons onto my boots, wrap my gloved hands around the hilts of ice axes, and chase death up the sides of mountains—but I also enjoy my daily workout in the gym. I've spent a couple of summers building a house with my father in his ancestral homeland, and I love hunting and fishing (but then again, I also love cooking).

If I've learned one thing, one complete and absolute truth in this lifetime, it's that people, gay or straight, love labels. They live for them. People feel a burning need to sort every person and thing, every concept, every thought, every idea, every event, every action, into tidy boxes, into discrete spheres with legible distinguishing text taxonomizing every single one. I'm probably the same way, truth be told. "These books are Victorian. She's my Sudanese friend. That's a fallacy. Gang of Four is post-punk. She's a doctor. He's straight. She's a lesbian." In a world of labels and labellers, for me it's the most liberating thing to be unlabelable, to defy easy categorization, to be both something and not something at the same time, the Schrödinger's cat of queer males. Whether or not it's been a conscious decision at all times, this is for better or worse how I've chosen to live my life. And that's queerness to me. Normalcy doesn't mean anything. Someone else's definition is not my definition. When I wake up and realize I'm not part of the majority, I don't care. I embrace it. Those are my rules, written in sweeping, amendable phrases in the idiolect of how I define myself.

CONSTRUCTING COMMUNITIES

"Change is not impossible; it's inevitable.
The real question is
what kind of change will come."

MAKING HISTORY, MAKING COMMUNITY: ONE CANADIAN LESBIAN STORY

Melissa Sky

The feisty feminist writer Rebecca West once said, "It is sometimes very hard to tell the difference between history and the smell of skunk." As far as cynical quotes about history go, this is one of my favorites, not only because it reminds me of my feminist unlearning of history as "His Story," the deceptive fables of the powerful, but also because a dead skunk features centrally in my own personal history as a Canadian, lesbian activist. It showed up on my doorstep in 2003, after my partner and I were featured on the front page of the local paper under the weighty title, "Local Couple Makes History." Same-sex marriage was brand new in Ontario, hard-won and controversial, and we were its face locally as the first same-sex couple in our county to get a marriage license. The journalists were eager and objective, but also dangerously naïve. They foolishly printed our home address and the location of our wedding, which necessitated the creation of safety plans. Luckily, the worst thing that happened was the dead skunk, which appeared on our front stoop one morning shortly after the article ran. It was laid out on a 2 x 4 of wood, like some bizarre ritual offering.

I've always wondered about it. Who left it? Were they saying lesbianism stinks? Was it a threat? And how did it get there? I amused myself imagining possibilities. Maybe some random homophobe happened to have this dead skunk lying around in his yard. He can't stop thinking about this article and how it just ain't right, so he calls up his buddies. They down a few beers then decide to drive the skunk over to our house in the middle of the night. They drop it off on our front step then run away laughing and jostling like bored teenagers pulling a stupid prank. Or maybe it was some pearl-sporting, middle-class churchgoer who read the article and just cracked, grabbed a BB gun and went out and killed the skunk on purpose to send an angry message on behalf of her version of God. Whatever the weird backstory of the skunk's appearance, it has become a curious symbol of my experience of homophobia in Canada, a homophobia that is often silent but reeks. You smell it in the air, but everyone politely pretends it's not there. We're *Canadian* after all.

Of course, homophobia can be more than symbolically violent. It can be as putrid and ugly as that decaying skunk. It's just that as a white, feminine, educated woman, I don't often face homophobia at its ugliest. I pass as a good, everyday, middle-class, straight woman, unless I *choose* not to pass. My partners and friends often can't rely on this privilege. But no LGBTQ person lives an unscathed life, even in this most liberal of countries. I've never been beaten up for wearing a tie like my friend. I've never been harassed out of a washroom like my partner. I wasn't disowned by my parents like my ex-wife (oh, yes, I was on the trendy first wave of queer divorce too, lucky me). But I did give up and remove the rainbow sticker from my car after it was vandalized for the second time. And I did have to file a complaint with the Ontario College of Midwives after my first midwife point-blank refused to serve me, stating outright that, as a Christian, she did not believe lesbians should have children and couldn't support a child being raised in that environment. It's a testament to Ontario that I won and that she was forced to take "sensitivity training."

However, it's a testament to the persistence of homophobia that that was not the last time I had to make a complaint to a governing board and force such training on others. It happened again in 2012, at a well-known university where I trained to be a teacher. The Catholic teacher candidates were often blatant in their homophobia. During an activity on "controversial issues in education" they divided the class into stakeholders on the issue of "homosexualism," [sic] and put me, the only out student, in the stakeholder group representing religious parents. I was supposed to read this outrageously misinformed and discriminatory article about the threatening "gay agenda," then role-play as a parent concerned about it. Instead I had a panic attack and ran out of the classroom to cry in the bathroom. The student leading the activity actually put her hand on my shoulder and whispered that she had put me in that group on purpose because she felt it would be good for me: "Try to open your mind to another perspective." Later, when I was more composed and tried to explain to them how this exercise was wildly insensitive, like asking a Black kid to try to understand a racist's point of view, I was, predictably, labeled as dramatic and overly sensitive. But the administration was shit scared of trouble and promised to bring in LGBTQ trainers as I requested. This experience reminded me of both how much things have changed and how much they haven't changed at all. Those students are no less homophobic than before, despite the training, but now they are scared to voice it.

Still, overall, I've seen incredible changes in how Canada treats LGBTQ people since I first came out in the nineties. History never used to interest me, but now I find it rather fascinating. I suppose that history is often boring to the young because it doesn't have relevance. It doesn't have meaning in the same way it does for those of us who've lived long enough to witness the present somehow inevitably roll into the past. All those things that were once a normal, everyday part of your life—crimped hair, turquoise eyeliner, leather skinny ties, knotted pearl necklaces, leg warmers, etc.—are now dated, recognizable emblems of a time that is no more. And yet when they were, they just *were*, as much as everything now just *is*. Ageing is a startling, unimaginable process. Suddenly, the past bears meaning. Nostalgia flourishes and with it the desire to record. To preserve. To remember. Spaces that were once critical to my development as a queer woman are now demolished. Friends and lovers who were once so dear to me are now gone.

Becoming a mother, and growing older myself, inspired a curiosity about history that lead me to start working with the Grand River Rainbow Historical Society to create a feature-length documentary, *Rainbow Reflections*, to capture local queer history. I began videotaping oral history interviews of everyday people in the region, asking them what it had been like to be LGBTQ in Kitchener-Waterloo, Cambridge, or Guelph in the 1960s and beyond. I was floored by their stories. I lost my composure behind the camera more than once, trying to hold onto all these gorgeous, painful, funny, and courageous stories.

I listened as people who protested against the Bathhouse raids in 1981, Canada's Stonewall, recalled that turning point in Canadian queer history, and the growing sense of solidarity amongst the LGBTQ community.

I bore witness as old men broke down, speaking of the legion of friends and lovers lost in the 1980s to the tragedy of AIDS.

I cringed as assaults were remembered in halting, haunted voices.

I was taken aback as a charming senior citizen marvelled, "I haven't been called a faggot for over a year now!"

I stifled laughter as epically tacky 1970s community dances were recalled.

I beamed as a trans woman spoke of finally finding love and acceptance for who she really knew herself to be.

Overall, I was left utterly stunned at the incredible resilience of the LGBTQ community. At the ways we found meaning, created connection, rose up together to fight, and gathered together to laugh away the wounds of quotidian bigotry with an outrageous drag show. The LGBTQ community is my family. My tribe. My people. I have found comfort, joy, support, and strength in this community. The neo-pagan writer Starhawk once wrote something that I believe truly captures the essence of community. She wrote:

> We are all longing to go home to some place we have never been—a place half-remembered and half-envisioned we can only catch glimpses of from time to time. Community. Somewhere, there are people to whom we can speak with passion without having the words catch in our throats. Somewhere a circle of hands will open to receive us, eyes will light up as we enter, voices will celebrate with us whenever we come into our own power. Community means strength that joins our strength to do the work that needs to be done. Arms to hold us when we falter. A circle of healing. A circle of friends. Someplace where we can be free. (*Building Community*)

We all "make history," like I did. Every day, our choices help to determine the kind of community we live in, whether those choices make the front page of the newspaper or not. We make our own story as well as moments in the stories of those around us. We open spaces for possibility and growth or we shut people down and close opportunities off. We embrace others and all their messy, weird, and wonderful differences, expanding this feeling of community that Starhawk so aptly describes, or we fear others and further all the myriad ways in which xenophobia, the root of discrimination, plays out in the world. While I despise the current conservative administration of this country, I love this land, its people, its imperfections and striving. I am very conscious of the privileges I enjoy as a lesbian who happened to be born in Canada. So while there's so much more we can be doing for all kinds of disempowered people here, truly, I have faith in this country, in its promise and possibility. I work every day to make this the kind of country I want to live in: a compassionate, generous, celebratory, equitable country.

I work right now as the GSA Coordinator for OK2BME, a set of support services for LGBTQ youth. I go into classrooms and work with youth on understanding human rights and celebrating diversity. I get paid to do this. That alone is incredible progress. It gives me hope that when my son gets up in class to share his "Special Me" bag, and shows a picture of his blended family, which includes "not one, not two, not even three, but *four mommies*!" as he likes to say with great dramatic flourish, then I trust that people will smile, will get it, and will support him. And whether he discovers he's gay, bi, straight, pan, or whatever, whether he continues to identify as a boy or not, he will be embraced for himself. Because we all deserve that.

In my lifetime, I've been blessed to have witnessed and been a part of a huge cultural shift in how sexual and gender minorities are treated in this country. This is our rainbow civil rights movement and much of the progress on LGBTQ rights has happened in just a few short decades. I am awed and proud to be doing my small but vital part, alongside many wonderfully inspiring people. Sometimes activists are dismissed as dreamy idealists, set on some lofty mission impossible to "change the world." But change is not impossible; it's inevitable. The real question is what kind of change will come. History shows many examples of successful activism for positive social justice. As Mahatma Gandhi once said, "A small body of determined spirits fired by an unquenchable faith in their mission can alter the course of history." This is my story, a queer Canuck activist story that continues to be written by me and by all of you. A classic, scrappy underdog tale. Now what could be more Canadian than that?

"Suddenly I was lost amongst a crowd.
Surrounded by bright colors, clouds of glitter,
and an overwhelming sense of acceptance.
Acceptance."

INATTENTIONAL BLINDNESS

Dorian Cliffe

Like a rambunctious pup, I could hardly contain myself while I sat there surrounded by this rag tag bunch of queers. The room was bustling with friends I wanted to make and I could not wait to tell my roomie Charlene all about it. We were convinced this queer event would end up as another gay monoculture men's group, another space from which she would feel alienated. But no! The abundance of queer women, people of colour, and trans* folk, transformed this rather ordinary room into a truly queer and diverse space. I was so thrilled I didn't see it coming.

It was supposed to be an innocent icebreaker. Members introduce themselves and then gossip a bit about their weekend. Excited at this chance to make a horde of new queer friends, I was anxiously listening so I could have something to gab about when

later I would go up to one of them. I was so absorbed by the intro-
ductions that when it was suddenly my turn, I just blurted out:

"Hi. Heylo. I'm new to the city and new to the school. I guess
my weekend…hmmm. Well I was having a pretty shit Sunday and
couldn't bring myself to head to work. So I ended up munching
on a bunch of shrooms instead. After the visual trip, I was in this
boundless creative head space, and wrote a whole new chapter for
my book."

The silence that followed weighed down on me. This was my
community. These were my comrades. The shame swallowed me
whole.

I remember the buzz of the cheap fluorescent bulbs and the squeal
of the chair's feet against the stained laminate tile flooring in the
high-school counsellor's office. My heart was pounding in my
ears, my hands so clammy that when the counsellor reached out her
delicate hand, ordinate with large opal rings and glistening with a
soft coral nail polish, I froze.

Thirty minutes blurred by as we dropped courses, signed forms,
and shifted my schedule. After the papers settled, she asked me if there
was anything else she could do for me. Digging my nails sharply
into my thigh I croaked, "I'm gay." Effortlessly, she rose out of her
high-back 1990s ergonomic chair, gently swished the door closed,
pulled a seat up next to mine, and just smiled. A smile that was worth
more than any half-hazardous phrase could have been.

Lifting the cool glass pipe to my lips, I flicked the lighter alive and
heard the sizzle and crack of a bowl of fresh greens roasting under
the flame. I filled my lungs with a long smooth pull of smoke that
left me in a gentle daze.

"It'll work out, though. The counsellor hooked me up with a place
to crash at this all-boys' home," I say as I pass the pipe over to my besty

and the only other queer at the high school. We were in the lower level pits of the underground parking at the downtown Covent Market in London, Ontario. This place was kept heated throughout the winter, and tonight we found a mini-bulldozer we turned into our fort.

"It's suhweet. I get my own lil basement unit. Some shit about em being worried about me and the other guys. Puh-*leaze*. Like I couldn't take care of myself."

We were only fifteen and thought we were so cool. Shoved into adulthood way too early, we often retreated into a pot-hazed night when we just couldn't keep those masks on any longer. We had to be brave. Without it we would crumble, and we just didn't have the place to fall apart. Or anyone to tell us it will all work out. No matter, it wasn't going to all work out anyway.

"Shit," I muster under my breath as the bus driver starts his way to the back of the bus.

"Hey! Kid! What do ya think you're doin? You've been on her for nearly three laps now. This isn't a fucking carousel. Ya gotta get off."

"Fuck you!" I spit back at him. "I paid my dues. I'm a customer and ya got no rights kickin me out." That's what I want to say. What I wish I said. Instead, I toss my duffle bag over my shoulder and scurry off.

Making my way to the downtown Galleria, I head over to the south entrance. It's past p.m. and the place will be locked up, except for the third double door on the left. My heart always races when I approach the door. It looks locked. It always looks locked. I absentmindedly bite my inside cheek as I grasp the handle and—swoosh—the door pushes open.

The downtown mall was once a thriving shopping district in the late 1980s, but since then has gone the way of miner towns and is little more than a relic of better economic times. I bound up the lifeless escalators towards the second-floor food court. Usually, I avoid this area during the day with its luring scents that tempt the betrayal of my fortitude against the hunger. I head there now because there exists a hidden side enclave that houses a few tables and booths. The security guards rarely poke their heads in. I grab my favourite spot, a place where I can see around the corner and out the windows looking over the entire city aglow. A glimpse of beauty is easy to find if you have the courage to look past the obvious and into the surreal.

There we all were crammed in a rattling Jetta making our way to Toronto Pride. My first Pride. As we descend into the city, I crank the window down to steal a better view of the towering buildings. I couldn't believe it. If I tried hard enough, I swear I could hear Billy Joel's "New York State of Mind" playing in the background. But then again, who doesn't wish their life had a running soundtrack?

Suddenly I was lost amongst a crowd. Surrounded by bright colors, clouds of glitter, and an overwhelming sense of acceptance. Acceptance. It's often a buzzword thrown around and co-opted of its affective reality. But after years of inner solitude. After years of ridicule. After years of quiet desperation. I stood lost among them all. And I wept.

Ten years have crept by, and I'm standing lost in the crowd again. Charlene and I just moved to Toronto and it's our first Pride here. I purposely lose her so I could stand alone at the four corners of Church and Wellesley.

The world starts spinning. My vision blurs. Tears fall down my cheeks. I'm bumped and jostled by the crowd. Images start flashing through my mind.

Sitting on the edge of the elementary school playground, cow fields behind me and swaths of strangers in front of me, I dream for more.

Sitting in the corner of my room at 3 a.m., pulling at my hair while spiralling into a nightmarish crack withdrawal.

Sitting in my first university classroom, feeling like the biggest imposter amongst a crowd of Guccis and American Eagles.

Sitting on the Greyhound, all my worldly possessions on my lap and the CN Tower slowly rising into view.

My knees buckle and someone in the crowd grabs my shoulders to holster me up. He could have been anyone. He could have been Sandra, who was the first to pull me off the streets and offer me a couch to crash on. He could have been Mr. Alexander, without whom I would have never even thought I could dream of something more than a GED. He could have been any number of my queer friends, who them, and them alone, know how to sit with me and my pain. It was because of strangers like him, like them, that I can even stand here. We supposedly live in a world of meritocracy, but there is no way I could be able to sit here, pen in hand, and write this down if not for the community that surrounds me here and has always offered me an outstretched hand.

> "Etymologically, the word ally
> means bind to, and intriguingly the
> word religion also means to bind fast."

SIX MOMENTS

Kerri Mesner AND Carl Leggo

1

Kerri: I remember a turning point in fifth grade when everything changed, a pivotal before-and-after moment in my own life. Before, I was a social leader, articulate and popular, part of a group of friends, and rarely questioning my place in the mysterious hierarchies of elementary school. After, inexplicably, it seemed like my peers had some kind of inside knowledge that I'd somehow missed. Suddenly, I was on the outside looking in, and everyone around me was speaking a language and playing by rules of a new game that I'd never been taught. Even worse, though (and eventually more dangerously for me), it was gradually becoming clear, to all of us, that something about me was different than everyone else. I couldn't pinpoint what it was, and I'm not sure they could either, but they didn't like it. I know now, in retrospect, that these were the earliest days of my sexual and gender differences beginning to emerge, though I wouldn't have the language or the frames of reference for those identities until my mid-twenties. When the bullying started, I was taught, as was common wisdom in those days, to "rise above it," to ignore the bullying until the perpetrators got bored and stopped. Anti-bullying research and praxis now contradicts this "sticks and stones" wisdom, but back then, all I knew was that no matter how energetically and intensely I ignored it, the bullying escalated. Childhood became about trying (quite unsuccessfully) to blend in…and even more basically, about survival.

Carl: I grew up in the 1950s and 1960s in Corner Brook, Newfoundland, a town that once boasted the biggest pulp and paper mill in the world. I grew up in a distinctly working-class neighbourhood in a town constructed around class and economic status. I grew up in a culture of fear where authority was hierarchically sustained by people who wore white shirts. As my father, an electrician in the mill, often reminded me, "Don't fraternize with the bosses!" And I grew up in a culture of silence where sex and sexuality and sexual orientations and sexual possibilities were simply not discussed. So, my sexual desires and sexual identity emerged in a complicated story of ignorance, frustration, and fear, and that tangled story continues to haunt me.

2

Kerri: I recall another turning point, in high school, where I quite deliberately cultivated my rebel's voice. Perhaps I realized that if I couldn't blend in and disappear, I would take the opposite tack and stand out as much as I possibly could. For my teenage self, it was my explicit f-- you statement to the educational and social system within which I simply couldn't fit. I dyed my hair a vivid burgundy, dressed in as many clashing colours as I could wear in one ensemble, wore fluorescent pink scarves and neon green berets.

I installed myself as the campaign manager for a satirical student council presidential race where we lampooned what we saw as a hypocritical political system, and I stirred up trouble with the school paper in my attempts to expose those political undercurrents. I delighted in being named in my school's annual as the strangest dresser of our graduating class. More importantly, I began to find my people.. fellow theatre geeks, poets, musicians, and imaginative explorers. I know now that this rebel's voice saved my life.

Carl: During high school in the late 1960s, I recall occasionally hearing classmates make disparaging comments that I now readily understand were homophobic, but at the time, the comments were just another expression of self-centered meanness, a kind of ignorant back-biting dismissiveness that was always rampant in the high-school culture I knew. The students had so long been trained to be competitive that they didn't know any way to be with one another except mean-spirited. And exacerbating the culture of meanness was a school system based on governance by several Christian churches. Schools were operated and administered by Roman Catholic educators or Protestant educators. When Roman Catholic and Protestant Christians from the United Kingdom settled Newfoundland in the second half of the second millennium, they exported the rivalries that have historically divided the United Kingdom. I grew up in a culture of fear, silence, and hatred. Of course, that is not the whole story, but it is an integral part of the story that I need to articulate, especially because out of that maelstrom of fear, silence, and hatred, I emerged with a steadfast commitment to living in the world with imagination, creativity, and love.

3

Kerri: Like many LGBTTIQQ2SA folks, I internalized a great deal of the sociocultural homophobia, heterosexism, and transphobia that was embedded in the communities around me. Even before I'd consciously come out to myself, I knew there was something integrally different about me, and I intuited that this mysterious "something" was also inherently wrong. When I did eventually come out to myself and the world at the age of twenty-six, I knew that, as a lesbian, I'd be going to hell. I couldn't tell you (as a mostly un-churched young person) where I'd picked up this certain "knowledge," but I knew it as fact.

Carl: I will celebrate a sixtieth birthday soon. I have been in school since I was four years old. All my life I have been a student and teacher. In the beginning of my teaching career in Robert's Arm, Newfoundland, I initially thought I could frighten my students into obedience and diligent devotion. I carried a big stick for the first month of September. I shouted often, and I threatened a long litany of earthly and eternal punishments. One day near the end of September, I smacked the big stick on my hardwood, fortress-like teacher's desk, and it shattered, and I finally recognized that my classroom management skills were violent and vile. I apologized to my students and recommended that, hereafter, we would have one rule in the classroom. When a person was speaking, everybody else would listen. That was the beginning of a pedagogy of love, and ever since that day, I have deliberately sought to support and promote a culture of love.

4

Kerri: Perhaps it's not surprising, in retrospect, that coming out into my queer identity was, from the first, as much a spiritual process as a sexual one. Eventually, these two strands of my life emerged as deeply interwoven threads; as I moved into queer activism, art, and expression, I was simultaneously moving into queer Christianity and formation as a lesbian/genderqueer Christian minister. I understood the call to Christian ministry as a call to the prophetic, radically inclusive, deeply embodied praxis exemplified by Jesus. For me, it was no longer a question of whether I could be lesbian and Christian. The two were absolutely integral to one another.

Carl: When I met Kerri, I was impressed by her many gifts for creative scholarly research, but I was especially moved by her commitment to Christian living and ministry. From the beginning, I realized I could speak with Kerri as a Christian believer without equivocation or censorship. I could speak truthfully. I have taught many students who are aligned with the LGBTTIQQ2SA community, and I have learned much wisdom from their stories and their willingness to teach me. Years ago, a student sought me out to supervise her in a study of Canadian lesbian fiction. After a lifetime of study, I have a wide-ranging acquaintance with Canadian literature, but I knew little about Canadian lesbian fiction. So, with the invitation to supervise a study of lesbian literature, I engaged in a journey of learning together with the student. Like an overstuffed photo album, I can share many stories of walking with LGBTTIQQ2SA students in unique places of teaching and learning, our guiding one another in challenging and questioning the cultural experiences of fear and silence that many of us know daily and intimately. But none of these stories are as enlivening as my journey with Kerri. I have been a Christian believer since I was twenty-one years old. I have studied in a Christian seminary, and I once planned to be a Christian pastor. I have fellowshipped in United Church, Baptist, Pentecostal, and Brethren communities in five provinces of Canada. And in all this long Christian experience, I have never been able to understand the opposition of so many Christians to a sexual orientation that is still labelled simplistically and anachronistically homosexuality. I have never understood why so many adherents in the various traditions of Protestant, Roman Catholic, and Greek Orthodox Christianity claim to hold fast to the church's historic view of sexuality when that historic view has been challenged again and again with thoughtful and scholarly interpretations of biblical and theological texts.

5

Kerri: While I know I'm far from the first LGBTTIQQ2SA student Carl has mentored, there are some unique threads to our scholarly and interpersonal journeys that make for intriguing conversations. It's fascinating to me, for instance, that early on in our work (perhaps our very first meeting), I remember Carl saying that he was engaged in ongoing learning around LGBTTIQQ2SA issues, and yet, in the years that followed, I found myself best able to do my queerest work within this particular supervisory context.

I suspect that a part of this, for me, was around having to really get clear about how I articulated the queer aspects of my scholarship. At the risk of mixing my metaphors here, I wasn't just "preaching to the (queer) choir" in ways that I might be, say, within more explicitly queer theoretical or queer theological contexts. Moreover, however, I wonder if there is something particularly "queerable" within arts-based educational research methodologies; they already depart pretty radically from academic orthopraxy, and maybe that makes our shared arts-based inquiry approach particularly amenable to queer perspectives.

Carl: I teach in my local Christian community about once every three or four years. The last time I was invited to speak, several years ago, I was asked to focus my sermon on a significant person in the Bible. I chose Mary Magdalene, and I pointed out how the story of Mary Magdalene has been traditionally misinterpreted. Instead of being a repentant prostitute, Mary Magdalene was a businesswoman who supported the public ministry of Jesus as a significant leader in the emergent Christian movement. Many members of my local Christian community were surprised by how a fiction had been composed and promoted in order to suppress the role of women in the initiation of Christianity. And they were surprised by how a close textual reading of the Bible and theological scholarship can open up new possibilities for understanding. (Still, in spite of the surprise, I have not been invited to speak again.)

6

Carl: Kerri is an ordained Christian pastor, theologian, actor, and writer. As we walk together, learning to trust one another, we open up new possibilities and perspectives for promoting a culture of love. Etymologically, the word ally means bind to, and intriguingly the word religion also means to bind fast. As a privileged white man who has been married to one woman for almost forty years and who has been committed to the Christian church for almost that long, too, I am an ally in the LGBTTIQQ2SA community, and I am grateful to be included in this growing community that requires an expansive acronym because it promotes openness and inclusion.

Kerri: In reflecting on Carl's and my journey together, I'm particularly struck by how many of our conversations have moved beyond "queer 101" issues, oftentimes out of necessity. As I've navigated multiple, intersecting, and deeply challenging issues as a queer, genderqueer, and Christian scholar in a secular and arguably oftentimes gender normative/heteronormative institution, there have been many times when I've experienced Carl not just as supervisor, but also as ally, in those situations, and in terms of his ability to understand the depth and complexity of the issues at hand. At a workshop I recently attended entitled "Creating Genuinely Safe Space for Queer and Trans Folk," the presenter, Anna White, Director of UBC's Camp Out!, noted that the identity of "ally" is not one that can be self-claimed—but that it needs to be given by the community to the individual seeking to serve as ally, and that the difficult, bumpy, and transformative work of allyship is spiritual work. It occurs to me that in engaging those kinds of conversations, we are, indeed, engaging in spiritual, scholarly, and artful work in the academy.

> "What surrounds the human
> we love is just packaging."

FINDING MY
INSPIRATIONAL STORY

Jennifer A. Barnett

Being bisexual and living in a Northern Ontario community, it was always very easy to hide. The hiding was not intentional; it was a natural situation. I like men and women, and when others saw me with a man, a heteronormative understanding naturally came into effect. Further, living in the rural north makes it very difficult to meet women, so being seen in this type of relationship is not common. I was able to go through my life blending with mainstream society without having to out myself in any way. Thus, I found it extremely challenging to think of a topic to write about or a story to share.

Of course, even if I lived in a larger, more diverse urban centre, this would not guarantee me a litany of inspirational anecdotes upon which to draw. Being bisexual, I know I am not fully accepted by either the gay or straight communities. In my experience, lesbians tend to view me as someone who has not yet fully stepped out of the closet. One has only to venture on to a woman-to-woman dating site and note the vast number of profiles which specify that bisexual women and questioning women need not respond to realize how many individuals think bisexuality means undecided. I know bisexuals who are in the closet in the LGBT community and publically identify as lesbian in order to avoid criticism and/or increase their chances of getting a date. I have to admit that I have done this myself on two occasions. All human beings crave acceptance.

On the opposite side of the spectrum, straight men tend to view me as a loose woman who can enact all of their porno fantasies. I have come to realize that these men think bisexuality means sexually starved or sexually audacious. I have had the most ridiculous invitations from straight men that assume bisexuality means sexually adventurous. In truth, I am pretty "vanilla." While it is true that I do not care whose arms are around me as long as they are around me with love, I differentiate between love and sex and see the former as much more desirable (not that I have anything against the later).

There are very few people whom I have met who understand that, for me, being bisexual means I am attracted to the person and the rest is just packaging. After all, once the years pass, what attracted us physically is gone to gravity and what we are left with is the human being. What surrounds the human we love is just packaging. While my friends who are straight and gay see the logic in this once I explain it, they still have a difficult time coming to terms with attraction existing towards both sexes. I have had gay friends tell me that I will never be able to commit to one person because, being bi, a relation-ship would mean I can never get what I need. I have had straight friends tell me that I am really straight but just need to find a man who is open-minded and possibly eager to watch and/or participate some-time. This attraction to both sexes is very difficult to accept for those who see the world in binary terms. In truth, the world is not binary and even how I am bisexual differs from others who identify as bisexual. Bisexuals are as different as members of any group. I know bisexuals who are primarily attracted to the opposite sex, the same sex, believe in polygamy, or believe in monogamy, and don't believe in relationships at all. I know bisexual women who identified as straight until they met one specific woman. I know bisexual women who believed they were lesbians until they met one specific man. Our LGBT community is as diverse as the individuals who make it up, and even amongst ourselves we have closets. Writing a short narrative that is inspirational for our community is extremely challenging.

When thinking of this challenge, I found myself reflecting on a workshop I gave the summer of 2013 on Understanding Bisexuality at the National Affirm United/S'affirmer Ensemble Conference for the United Church of Canada. Though baptized and confirmed Roman Catholic, I am now a member of the United Church. Given the history of the treatment of LGBT individuals by various churches, finding the United Church was a pleasant surprise. I was welcomed immediately and found the people so friendly. Age, race, ethnicity, ability, and sexual orientation were irrelevant as members valued the individual and welcomed all. After a few months, I became involved in the Affirming Committee of the Church and this conference was a celebration for us as at the time we had just joined other United Church Affirming congregations in publically announcing our acceptance of LGBT individuals. Being surrounded by diverse people who believed in inclusion and practiced acceptance was amazing. For a bisexual woman living in the rural north, this conference's environment felt liberating. I felt I could breathe.

After my presentation, three men came up to talk to me. All identified as bisexual. One in his mid-twenties from Western Canada spent his free time with a group of men and women who all enjoyed each other's company. Another in his late sixties from Southern Ontario was happily married to his spouse of the opposite sex for over thirty years. They had an open relationship. The third in his mid-thirties self-identified as heteroflexible as he had a preference for the opposite sex but also enjoyed same-sex relationships. These three men and I talked and laughed. There was no judgment about sexual preference as it was not considered a preference but accepted as just the way we are. In fact, bisexuals have more in common generally speaking then gay men or lesbian women. While the later share a preference for the same sex—the women are attracted to women and the men to men—bisexuals are all, to one extent or the other, attracted to both sexes. What was interesting to note during our conversation was that biology seemed to hold less importance when dealing with people who were not perceived as potential partners. During our conversation, there were no gender/sex roles in play— we all talked and we all listened. There was no hierarchy based on cultural heteronormative concepts of men's roles and women's roles. We all seemed to be on an even playing field.

At the conclusion of the weekend I had made many good friends. I said to another member of the church that I didn't want these people to go. Being in a space surrounded by no judgment, no assessments, no political manoeuvring, and no sex-role expectations, was freeing to the point of tears. After the conference was over, I sat down and wrote the following:

Have you ever watched a flower in full bloom? Connected to earth, it seeks the sun. It turns its face in companionship and acceptance. The flower cares little if the sun is approaching from the east or journeying to the west. It is the essence of the sun itself the flower loves. It will always orient itself towards the essence of the sun. The sun, regardless of its orientation in the sky, provides sustenance.

The flower is unaware of its name or label. It just is what it was born to be and responds to the world as God intended. The flower does not seek a male or female counterpart in order to feel complete. It continues because of the way God made it. It is content when it finds the sun.

The flower is a plant. Our world accepts plants. Plants can reproduce sexually or asexually. No one defines the plant by how it reproduces. A plant is allowed to just be a plant. The world accepts it for how it is, not what it does.

230

I am a flowering plant. I exist the way God intended. One day the world will see me as it sees plants. Until that day, I simply remain beautiful. And I will seek the sun.

Like the flower, I spent much of my life not associating myself with a label. I knew I was different, but growing up in a traditional, conservative family in the wilds of Northern Ontario, I did not see any others like me and assumed my difference was just an aspect of who I was. After all, no two people look the same, act the same, or achieve the same. When I first encountered the term bisexual, I did not associate it with myself at all. In fact, as a young adult I wondered if I was a lesbian who was in denial to herself, but then I would meet and be attracted to a man and would forget all about my self-questioning.

When I finally came out to myself and accepted that the term bisexual applied to me, it still took me a long while to come out to others. I began with my friends who were gay men. They seemed the most accepting though there was some static from one as to why I kept it hidden for so long. I guess I needed to feel it was the *Right* term for me.

I had a difficult time as a child understanding the concept of *Right*. My parents would tell me what was *Right* and my church would tell me what was *Right*; my community would tell me what was *Right* and the television would tell me what was *Right*. Music would relate stories of what *Right* looked like and movies would illustrate *Right* larger than life before my eyes. My teachers always knew what was *Right*. What I had difficulty with was how the concept of *Right* seemed to vary depending on the messenger. On occasion the messages even contradicted each other. Of course, I also had to deal with situations where the message of *Right* and the messenger's actions of *Right* did not align.

As a result I spent a long time trying to figure out what was *Right*. In extension, I also had to come to terms with the fact that if my *Right* was viewed by another as *Wrong*, this did not mean I was any less of a person or that my worth to society was diminished. Eventually I came to my own understanding of *Right*—if at the end of the day I reflect and I can look myself in the mirror, what I did and who I am is *Right*.

Philippians 3:17-4:1 defines the *Right* way to exist as coexistence with other members of the community. Instead of focusing on worldly possessions, self-gratification, or increasing your own reputation, this reading reminds us to be aware of others. It does not suggest that you shouldn't take joy and pride in your successes—to do so would be to ignore the results of some wonderful blessings bestowed upon you. It suggests you should be open and aware of others in a positive fashion. It asks that we simply see. At the end of this passage, it is pointed out that God loves us and is proud of us. Following God's example, it is thus *Right* to love others and ourselves. As it is pointed out to us in Corinthians 13:4, "Love is patient, love is kind. It does not envy, it does not boast...It does not dishonour others." This sounds pretty *Right* to me!

If I was going to honour myself I had to be kind to myself, patient with myself, and honour myself. Once this was realised, I was able to enjoy my bisexuality and find humour in myself. I remember watching a very badly produced movie with even worse acting. There was a scene in the movie where a man and a woman decided to have sex in an airplane bathroom. As the clothes started to come off, I discovered I was giving myself a bit of whiplash. I couldn't decide who to ogle more. My head was swivelling left, right, left, up, down. I burst out laughing at how funny my behaviour was. Accepting my bisexuality has become a source of laughter and joy for me, laughter expressed during the joy of discovering myself.

I am a bisexual woman. I am a member of a diverse community of bisexuals who are as different from one another as snowflakes. We are members of the LGBTTIQQ2S community. All those letters indicate differences that combine together to make our community. While some consider us on the margins of society, in truth we are part of society. We have always been part of society. This is my inspirational story.

> "I wonder when people will
> no longer be oppressed and demeaned
> for falling in love, when we can
> truly come into this world as we are."

COURAGE, MY LOVE

Nicole Doucette

I was once told that courage is deciding between paralysis and action in the face of fear. If so, the queer folks I have met are some of the bravest people I know. They constantly have to choose between action or inaction—deciding to come out, to speak up for their rights, to simply choose every day to be themselves. You would think it's a basic human right to be who you are; being queer has never harmed anyone else. Unfortunately, in this backwards world of ours, we aren't always encouraged to be true to our nature.

The queer community in Canada, although widely accepted and loved, still faces hardship, injustice, and bigotry. Some members of the community hear homophobic comments from strangers daily or have been kicked out of their homes because of their sexuality. Others have been subject to horrific acts of violence:

murders, beatings, rapes. Life for a queer individual can be hard and unfair. Of course, we've all heard that you'll be stronger when you make it through. But not everybody does.

Every day I feel incredibly lucky to have the life that I do, and that I am still here. There were times in my youth where all I wanted was to fall into the comforting warmth of death, days that I could barely get out of bed because I didn't want to be gay. Society taught me to hate myself. It has been a long journey to love and self-acceptance, but an ultimately rewarding one. And now that I love myself, I have been able to find it elsewhere too. And so my story is quite an ordinary one. All that happened to me was I fell in love. But I did what you're not supposed to do, although it happens to most of us. Did you guess it? I fell in love with my best friend.

I still remember the first time I met her, and that should've been a sign if any. It's rare that I can recall the exact moment I met someone. Though the whole world was spinning on its axis, at that moment, it must have stopped.

Perhaps our hearts know before our brains which moments in our lives will be the pivotal ones. It took me a very long time to admit to myself that I loved her, although not as long as it took for me to realize I was gay. It seems that my brain is very far behind the rest of my soul.

When I met her, it was my very first day at university. I was moving into residence, dragging several heavy suitcases and followed by my tired and anxious family who were dragging several more. I was feeling awkward and sad about leaving my comfortable suburban high-school life behind. And as any new university student, I was also nervous about fitting in and finding new friends. I remember peeking into the room next to mine and seeing the silhouette of a tall girl unzipping her suitcase. The way she was standing, the sun was coming in from the window behind her and lit the room with fire. A most appropriate backdrop as she had flaming red hair, and as I would come to learn, a personality to match. We introduced ourselves, and that was that.

This seems to be a rite of passage for most queer individuals because logically why wouldn't you want to be with your best friend? They're someone who knows you as well, or perhaps better, than you know yourself. Someone you can share everything with: crushes, hopes, fears. They know all of you, and they love you anyway.

But being in love with your best friend is never easy. What if they don't feel the same way? Or what if it ruins your friendship? And as a queer individual, the issues become even more complex. What if they're straight? Religious? Homophobic? Afraid to come out?

Luckily I dodged most of these issues as my friend came out as bisexual soon after I came out as a lesbian. I thought—or I should rather say, hoped—she liked me, but I was too afraid to say anything. We had our evenings of drunken fun where we would hold hands and sometimes kiss, and nights that turned into mornings while we shared whispered secrets lying on the grass. However, throughout that whole time we remained best friends, and at one time became roommates, but never anything more. We were walking a shaky tightrope between friendship and love.

This summer, I decided to drunkenly tell her how I felt. From what I can remember of that conversation, she said she had feelings for me as well, and had for a long time. The stars were all aligned, everything was in my favour. Except for one thing. She had a boyfriend, one who she's still dating now.

I decided to leave it alone. I had kept it inside for so many years; another few wouldn't hurt, right? But it was so much worse because I actually knew I wasn't crazy, that all those times in the past I thought maybe she liked me, she actually did. I decided to avoid her and hoped the feelings would go away, as any mature adult would do. I was telling another friend about this dilemma, and she said something to me I will never forget. I told her, "My story's typical. Everyone falls in love with their best friend. It's no big deal."

She said, "Yes. But it's not very often that they love you back."

Up until that point I was paralyzed: no action. Fear. I cared too much to lose her but I was terribly afraid of getting close again. Now, all I wanted to know was why I wasn't enough for her. I wanted to push hard against the walls that had closed me out, so maybe I could find a way back in. I wanted to explore her body and soul with my weathered palms, to have a place to keep my heart safe.

But inevitably, as they always do, doubts found their way into my mind. What if she didn't love me as much as I loved her? What if her feelings had already gone away? What if they never were true to begin with? And my greatest fear. What could I offer her compared to a man?

I could offer her catcalls and jeers when we're holding hands, unwanted pictures if we kiss in public, threesome requests from ignorant men if we go to a bar. I could offer her uncomfortable stares, unwarranted comments, and questions about what sex toys we use in bed. The remarks of men who think they can "turn us straight," or that we "haven't met the right guy yet." Or even that we're not gay, just stupid.

I could offer her the criticisms of the queer community as well, some of whom don't believe in bisexuality. So many times I have heard queer people say, "You can't be bisexual. You *have* to have a preference." We are fighting amongst ourselves when we're all on the same side.

I once met a FTM transgendered individual, and he told me how hard it was because he was once a part of this community, but as soon as he transitioned, he was an outcast. He was rejected from the community he loved and had once belonged to. I saw the smiles of the women there turn to disgusted looks when he explained that he was transgendered and not a gay male. Some women were worried he would try to hit on them, and why was he at a lesbian event in the first place if he wasn't one? I've had other experiences like this as well. Last year, I was with a group of lesbians, and when I invited my male friends to come hang out, they said "Sorry, we don't like straight males." And they left. When did we become exclusive? The community is supposed to be inclusive.

I wonder where the courage of our community has gone. We form a strong front, but inside we are still broken. Yes, we stand up for the community as a whole, but not for the individuals within it. We need courage within the community, courage to love everyone for who they are; love should never be conditional.

I mourn the loss of my best friend more so than the love lost. It has been many months, and it hasn't gone back to the way it used to be. There are days where it feels like my chest is going to cave in with the heaviness, and everything I see reminds me of her. We do still speak, but without really saying anything. Someone who knew the entirety of my naked soul is now a stranger.

I begin to wonder if accepting that everything will be different from now on will help ease the transition. But then I wonder if the feelings of love will ever really go away. I know now that time does not heal everything. I am old enough not to be deluded about that anymore. It does not heal pain, it only lessens it. And a friendship built on the ashes of an old love is not really a friendship at all. Perhaps the braver choice is to leave this behind; friendship will never be enough when I know I want to be with her forever.

I realize now that courage is not just deciding between action and inaction. A story of bravery is always interwoven with love. We push ourselves to do courageous acts because of love, whether for our friends and family, a complete stranger, or simply ourselves. You cannot have one without the other.

I wonder if my old eyes will look at a grey world because I let something that mattered slip through my fingers. I wonder if I will tell younger generations about "the one that got away" or if I will laugh with a future partner about how young and silly I was. I wonder if I will share memories with my friend in the years to come, and if we will humor ourselves with recollections of our awkward adolescent romance.

I wonder too about the future of our community. I wonder when people will no longer be oppressed and demeaned for falling in love, when we can truly come into this world as we are. I wonder when we will find the strength to make the queer community whole from within.

Every person is capable of courage because we are all born with the ability to love. And although being brave is sometimes the hardest decision you can make, it will be the most gratifying. In the end, the only thing that will really matter to you is what you choose to fight for.

> "I felt in my heart that God
> made me different from others
> and being gay was part
> of His plan for me."

A SPIRITUAL JOURNEY

Anthony Mohamed

I decided to put my trust in Jesus during my early teens at a youth retreat. It was at this time that all self-hatred and confusion about my sexuality began to dissipate. I felt in my heart that God made me different from others and being gay was part of His plan for me.

The early 1980s was a time when media, religion, government, and other sectors were not so LGBT aware or friendly. There were no formal protections in the Ontario Human Rights Code or the Canadian Charter of Rights and Freedoms, and the only role model I can remember was the character of Jack Tripper pretending to be gay in the sitcom *Three's Company*.

Religion can be a taboo subject within the LGBT communities. Various religious institutions have hurt many community members who had difficulty reconciling their gender identity or sexual orientation with their faith. This often resulted in an outright rejection of their spiritual lives. In addition, many organized religions have looked the other way while those claiming to be followers promoted all kinds of discrimination or committed atrocities. Some may even question why an LGBT person would want to be part of these belief systems, given the social divisions created in the past.

The reality is that many LGBT people have reconciled their spiritual life with their true gender or sexuality, and this has become an important part of their identities. Paying attention to my spiritual as well as other aspects of health has contributed to an increase in self-confidence and given me a sense of direction and hope. In addition, as LGBT people become more visible and faith groups grow in their understanding of diversity, we are seeing more LGBT-affirming spiritual spaces. It's important to note that not all faith groups are homophobic or transphobic and many have always welcomed LGBT members.

Growing up in Toronto, I was heavily involved in my church's operations and attended up to five days per week. I volunteered to run the sound system, teach Sunday school, and peer-manage the youth group.

During this time, I was slowly coming out and some of the leaders in the church had difficulty accepting me. I was eventually asked to stop attending, which I remember being very painful as I had been so involved from a very young age. I called the relatively new Metropolitan Community Church of Toronto (MCCT) that was reaching out to members of the LGBT communities. I wanted to make friends my own age who were also gay. They recommended Lesbian and Gay Youth of Toronto (LGYT) which held regular meetings at The 519 Community Centre. These meetings were the first time I was surrounded by peers with similar feelings, and we could talk about them openly. Unfortunately, LGYT was not very diverse, and I found the family context of other members to be very different from my home or culture. Luckily there were other LGBT groups that helped meet those needs. I joined Zami, a social group for Blacks and

West Indians and Khush, another directed at South Asians. I felt part of a welcoming community, a fledgling rights struggle, and a supportive environment to help others. I joined the steering committees of these and others groups, including the Lesbian and Gay Youth Line, a peer counselling service. This also gave me the courage to come out to my parents and family. Although they did not understand how I could be gay, the unconditional love I experienced could not have come from anywhere but their strong faith.

There is a real difference in the way society handles discrimination. When I was told, "Paki go home," in public school, my teachers, other students, and my parents made it clear this was unacceptable behaviour. Also confusing to me was that these statements referred to Pakistan, a country very far from Trinidad and Tobago. Of course, adults explained how indentured labourers were brought from India during British colonialism to work on the sugar-cane plantations. A few of them were part of my family's heritage. As a result, I understood our cultural connections to South Asia. However, when racist terms became homophobic ones in high school, my options for seeking support were severely limited. It was hard to approach my parents on this subject, so I went to see the guidance counsellor in my school. He said that he would get in trouble if he talked about "those issues." Around the same time in health class, there was a discussion about the love between a father and son, and not unexpectedly, a lot of guys made homophobic jokes. Instead of challenging them, the teacher said, "Love had nothing to do with homosexuality. It's only lust." I really felt alone, but later I discovered this teacher was very wrong as a few years later I experienced being in love for the first time.

It was a cold winter's day in 1990, and my boyfriend and I returned to a tiny apartment from our daily walk along the *rue Saint Jean* in Québec City. I remember seeing our neighbours on top of a very high roof using sledgehammers to bang down the built up ice before it literally caved in from the weight. Although I loved our walks exploring this beautiful old city, it was good to be back in the warmth of the home.

After a light lunch of pasta and canned sauce (the gourmet choices of youth on a budget), we found ourselves reading the paper and struggling hard to improve our French. We were listening to *Rock Détente*, a local radio station, tapping our feet, and snapping fingers to the likes of Philippe Lafontaine, Vanessa Paradis, and Michel Rivard. It was a lazy Sunday afternoon, and you could feel our connection in the artificially warmed up air.

We hugged in a gentle embrace while we took turns praying, giving thanks for the continued blessings on us and our families. It was in the middle of this, our hands held on a little tighter. I have heard some folks say that you fall in love only once in your life and the rest is just a memory. I'm not sure if that is true, but I wonder if this was that time for me. Celine Dion was singing, "Trop jeune pour aimer, qu'est-ce que ça veut dire," on the radio now. During that prayer, I felt like we were in a dream state as we simultaneously explored our spiritual, physical, mental, and emotional beings. That experience reflected an unspoken love created and blessed by God. I could feel his heart pounding against mine, and it felt like they were beating at the same time. Our romantic relationship ended shortly after returning to Toronto, and he passed away in 2009. Regardless of the ups and downs of our friendship, I continue to miss him dearly.

A few years before that relationship, AIDS was starting to have a devastating impact on significant parts of the community. I remember a time when I was attending at least one funeral every month. Everyone who was involved in the LGBT rights movement immediately started doing safer sex education, forming political lobbying coalitions such as Queer Nation and AIDS Action Now! and caring for those living (or in those days dying) of HIV/AIDS. People formed round-the-clock care teams for the many men who were dying from something not at all understood. The AIDS

Committee of Toronto was established in 1983 to help coordinate some of these activities. Science had little to no understanding of HIV, and mainstream health institutions were often places of discrimination that did not respect our relationships or desires. We didn't even know for sure how to prevent transmission. HIV fear and stigma grew within the gay male community, and guys were often trying to identify who had it and who didn't, resulting in severe rejection and isolation of those perceived to be HIV positive. Governments were not talking about this health crisis, and there were public messages of AIDS being a deserved punishment from God. How do you respond when most of the major social, religious, and political leaders, and even other LGBT community members, were blaming gay men for bringing a plague? In the politically active LGBT community, we did what we could.

I'm grateful that our community has come so far in addressing specific health needs, but clearly there are struggles that remain. Addictions, body image issues, and breast, colorectal, and other cancers tend to affect LGBT people at a very high rate. As the population gets older, LGBT seniors need safe and welcoming environments to continue to live valuable, healthy, and happy lives. Clearly, getting HIV medications to everyone everywhere that needs them remains a priority. Although HIV has been terrible for Canadian LGBT communities, it also served as a galvanizing force that contributed to the many rights we have today. At the start of the pandemic, it was the first time I could turn on the eleven o'clock news and see a person who had similar desires as me, helping me and others to feel not so alone.

A few months after I left my former Church, I returned for a visit. I was amazed when some of the congregants told me things had begun to change but that it would be a long road. Their love for God and for me allowed some reconsideration of the painful actions that had been directed at LGBT people. My faith in Jesus continued to grow, and I sought spiritually welcoming spaces within the LGBT community. More than thirty years later, I remain active in a Baptist Church near my home. My specific congregation has been a warm, inclusive, and welcoming environment for me to worship, fellowship, and learn. I wish all churches could be growing like my church, and that youth never have to feel like they have no one to talk to.

"After years of being silenced and terrified
of showing the world who I was, I found the
voice that had always been inside of me."

A RED CORVETTE
WITH A RAINBOW STICKER

Jessica Del Rosso

I remember the screech of the tires on the wet winter road to this day. I remember the feeling of my stomach plummeting as if I was on the largest roller coaster heading downward. I had been spotted. I had been caught. I was exposed. I remember letting go of her hand as fast as I could. Although deep inside I knew it was too late. I knew I should have been more careful based on the traditional values passed onto me as a child. I had been holding her hand, trying to keep it warm. We only had a little way to walk before we got to her house anyways. Little did I know that holding her hand would drastically change the direction of my life. Although I had experienced feelings of fear and uncertainty before in my life, the level at which I was feeling these emotions was indescribable.

She and I ran as fast as we could towards the safety of her house. My heart was pounding with the fear of what would happen now that I had been found out before we arrived to safety. Once there, we locked all the doors and windows. She called her mother who appeared shortly after, worried. I remember being told, "You just experienced your first act of homophobia." I went from having almost everything to having nothing. I did not know how to stop the landslide which was unfolding underneath my feet.

According to my court papers, this happened on December 27, 2006. I have a tattoo on my arm of this date. I mention my court papers because, ten days after this occurrence, I found myself in foster care. I did not really understand what had happened. I did not understand what it meant to be gay—to be a girl who liked other girls. My world became an abyss of confusion. My life went from being one way one day to being completely different the next. I felt like I had hit the ultimate low in my life, and I had no strength in me to go anywhere but down. I went into survival mode. I stopped caring about school and, therefore, my grades began plummeting lower than ever before. I got fired from my part-time job because I couldn't keep up with the requirements and expectations. I began struggling with anxiety and symptoms of PTSD and depression. Pot, unhealthy relationships, trauma, self-harm, and a newly discovered, confusing sexual orientation were all that defined me.

One day, reality hit. To this day, I cannot pin point what day it was or what was different about that day, but I finally realized that the first part of my life had been full of negative experiences and that unless I wanted the rest of my life to continue as my past, I needed to take control. I had experienced abuse, rejection, and loss. I had never learned how to make friendships or learned about social cues. I never learned stability or what it meant to have a healthy relationship and be loved for who I truly was. But I needed to move on from the past and make my future what I wanted it to be. Although I did not know exactly what that looked like, I knew it did not look like where my life was headed at that time.

I needed to begin with reevaluating the people with whom I associated and eliminate negative and unhealthy relationships from my life. I began going to school regularly and building relationships with my teachers and counsellors who became significant supports for me in both good and bad times. I set the goal for myself to graduate high-school on the honor roll and attend the University of Waterloo, both of which I achieved. I also began volunteering at my local Family and Children Services. Through this volunteering, I learned and discovered my passion for public speaking and advocacy.

I began sharing my story louder and louder. I wanted to raise awareness about LGTBQ topics, especially homophobia experienced by youth from their parents and gay youth in foster care. I became a peer mentor for younger youth in foster care, especially youth who identified as LGTBQ. I was offered the opportunity to be a part of the *Youth Leaving Care* video, which was a video that addressed the difficulties experienced by older youth in foster care. This video led to my working at a provincial level government position on a working board. The working board's mandate was to develop a document to present to the Minister of Child and Youth Services on the changes in policy that needed to be implemented in child welfare agencies for youth in care in Ontario. I then started appearing on local news channels, radio stations, websites, and in newsletters. People began recognizing me in public and individuals from my past were now hearing my story.

As I began taking control over my life, supports were being built. My life filled with people who loved me for who I was, not who I pretended to be. I met my partner who I have now been with for five and a half years. She has taught me how to love myself more than anyone ever has. Despite whether or not we remain together in the future, she will always have had a central part in my life and my healing. I also found my extended family through the use of Facebook. They have redefined my idea of what true family is. I have built a relationship with one particular aunt and uncle that is stronger than any I ever had with my biological family.

Through the tears I cried for both the good and bad that has happened in my life, and by utilizing the support I have received, I realized something. I realized that, after years of being silenced and terrified of showing the world who I was, I found the voice that had always been inside of me, waiting to make a difference in the world. I started using it to help others who could not find theirs just yet. And the most amazing part of all this was that people were listening.

I have set new goals for myself. One of these goals is that I will continue to grow as an individual and continue to have only positive, accepting, and healthy relationships in my life. I have begun to look at life in a new way. To look at the things I do have rather than the things I do not. I have learned to listen to my body and my heart in regards to what their needs are. I have learned that tears and emotions are not a sign of weakness, but a representation of roads once travelled. Happiness and peace are now two focuses in all that I do. I strive to learn new ways of coping with my past trauma and anxiety in a healthy and constructive way. Lastly, I have learned, and still aim every day, to love myself for who I am.

I now incorporate yoga and physical fitness into my regular routine, and I try my best to nourish my body with healthy foods. I have begun journaling again, something which I had not done in years. I am also back in therapy, where I learn more about myself every session. When life becomes overwhelming, I try to take things one day at a time, and I remember that some things are not worth becoming stressed about. I review my priorities, to ensure they are only things that will bring me happiness. Things in my life that bring me unhappiness, I try to distance myself from.

While growing up, my father always told me that when I graduated from law school, he would buy me a red corvette. I always loved to debate and argue. I also loved red corvettes. It was a win-win in my mind as a young girl. I do not know if I still want a red corvette after I've graduated with my social work degree, but if I do, I will buy it myself. And, I'll place a rainbow flag sticker right on the back of it with pride. Because one thing I have learned throughout my life, which continues to be written, is that you need to stand tall and be who you are. Everything in life happens for a reason. Obstacles are given to those able to overcome them and at the end of the day, your life is what you make it. I am happy with who I am today, and of who I was back then. I will always continue to use my voice to encourage others to also be happy with whom they are no matter how hard it may be at times. We all deserve to be happy, and to be proud.

"I spent a few sleepless nights considering the words and attitudes of my coworkers, wondering if I would ever be able to come out to them and what would happen if I did."

BIG TALK: THE FAILURE TO BUILD LGBTQ* POSITIVE SPACE FOR YOUTH AND YOUTH WORKERS

Kate Miller

I became a queer Child & Youth Worker (CYW) with very limited experience with what it meant to be a queer youth. I had spent my teenage years ignoring my queerness and distracted by other challenges in my life. In my mid-twenties, I went back to school to complete a CYW diploma as a relatively out bisexual woman. At the time, I had identified strongly as a survivor of sexual violence, as a feminist, and as someone who believed that children and youth are disempowered and ignored; These were things that I was determined to have shape my work. Living in Canada's largest urban centre, home to North America's largest Pride celebration, I had assumed that my education and workplace experiences in the social-service field would be relatively queer-positive.

What I have learned in the two years since I made the decision to change careers is that many of the environments where CYWs work are oppressive to both LGBTQ* staff and the children, youth, and families seeking support. While there is a great deal of recognition systemically of the rights of LGBTQ* staff and youth to be treated fairly and have their identities affirmed, this isn't reflected on the front lines in a consistent way. In my experience, the education that CYWs receive does not prepare them to confront homophobia and support queer and trans youth, and CYWs who are already working in the field, or have been for a long time, are not given training opportunities to build these skills. In residences, schools, and mental health treatment centres, I have seen that children and youth are not protected from oppressive attitudes and prejudicial treatment and are exposed to violence and coercion. While I was aware that the environments I would be entering would not be ideal, I had not expected how this would affect me specifically as a queer person.

I spent my first weeks in college trying to discern if any of my thirty or forty classmates also identified as queer. We were all given rainbow bookmarks, and the campus, located a few blocks from the Gay Village, was littered with similarly-decorated posters advertising the Diversity, Equity, and Human Rights office. But by the end of my first term, it became clear that none of my classmates were openly queer, nor were any of my teachers. References to the inclusion of queer and trans youth in CYW programs were tokenistic—usually cropping up once per semester per class. There was little acknowledgement that as CYWs it would be our responsibility to respond to the needs of queer and trans youth beyond a list of things not to do or say. Worse still, the representation of LGBTQ* clients in our case studies often fell into one flat stereotype: bisexual girls who were missing the attention of their parents. My classmates would bring up the possibility of "sexual trauma" or "a need for attention," and often conflated the terms "bisexual" and "promiscuous" in our discussions. I often found my stomach clenching and my cheeks flushing as I attempted to block out this ignorance. My teachers did not validate or confirm my classmates' uninformed speculations, but the statements were not challenged for what they were: homophobic attitudes and hurtful stereotypes about bisexual women.

This knowledge gap extended beyond the classroom to the formal networks for Child & Youth Work that I was exposed to in school. In our curricular online resource, I found only six articles in the database discussing LGBTQ* youth, compared with hundreds of articles on residential care, and seventy on family dynamics.

The most intensely negative experience that I had in my post-secondary education was the required sexuality class I took as part of this Child & Youth Worker diploma. Delivering comprehensive information about sex, and being able to listen and talk with teens in a non-judgmental way about their sex lives, is a cornerstone of youth work. In this fourteen-week course, we spent only one class talking about queer and trans* sexuality, sex, and gender identity. In this one class, the three topics were awkwardly blended and treated as extra, non-essential learning.

The content of the class included watching a sensationalist UK television broadcast on gender independent children and youth in which the journalist constantly misgendered the people he was reporting about. At the end of the class, students were encouraged to share their opinions on the how gender independent and trans children and youth should be treated, and our teacher reinforced the idea that we had the right to our opinions and that these are "complicated issues." I did my best to express that the transphobic and cissexist attitudes being shared in the classroom and communicated in the film were out of date and inconsistent with the policies and values of the organizations we would be working for and, most importantly, are damaging to the children and youth we were supposed to serve. However, this idea was not supported by the instructor, who appeared stunned that I was taking such a decided stance on the treatment of queer and trans children and youth. I then followed up with an email to my class and instructor with resources such as "Let People Be Who They Are: Best Practices When Working With Gender Independent Children and Their Families in Ottawa," and links to Rainbow Health Ontario and others. I also took any opportunity I had to do a presentation, to choose a subject related to queer and trans youth. I was enrolled in school to learn how to do Child and Youth work. I found myself the only openly queer person in my class, working to supplement the curriculum for myself and my classmates in any way I could.

My first field placement for school was at an open custody mental health treatment centre for young men charged under the Youth Criminal Justice Act. On my second day there, a co-worker printed a photo off the Internet which she thought looked like one of the youth in the house, but was an image of someone cross-dressing, and passed it around to staff and residents to laugh at. It was clear to me that this would be a very unsafe place for queer and trans youth to live.

The only person who knew I was queer was the house director, whom I spoke to one day on the way to a Pride celebration, an event the rest of the staff had also been invited to but chose not to attend. I let her know about my experiences of homophobia in the house and my witnessing staff condoning sexism and transphobia and trans-misogyny. She was sympathetic and made attempts to change the atmosphere of the residence, but change was unwelcome, and she eventually left the job.

My second placement was at an elementary school in my neighbourhood. I was ecstatic to get the chance to work with younger children and be connected to the community where I lived. I again experienced the rhetoric vs. practice gap when I expressed an interest in running lunchtime activities for the Day of Pink, a day to celebrate diversity and fight homophobia and transphobia in the school system. My supervisor thought this was a great idea and pointed me to some resources, and we also ordered t-shirts from the school board specifically made for the Child & Youth Workers to wear on the Day of Pink.

A few months into my internship, I had already noticed some of the same disturbing attitudes and values I had experienced in my first placement. One was the lack of visibility of queer people on staff. There was one teacher who was open about her same-sex relationship to staff, but she was subject to regular "playful" teasing. Unfortunately, this experience, combined with the fact that I was presumed straight by most staff members, kept me from talking about my sexuality. I had to leave a big part of myself at the door.

Another trend was the poor treatment of children whose expressions fell outside of accepted gender norms. Staff members regularly speculated about their sexuality and policed behaviour seen as inappropriate gender expression in the name of protecting them from being bullied. I will never forget seeing a boy told by a teacher not to sway his hips when walking down a hallway where there hung a poster, produced by the board of education, that said, "There Are No Rules for Being a Boy or Girl." I did my best to reinforce the amazing resilience of these children, who were able to maintain and express these parts of themselves in an atmosphere that rejected them daily. I also tried to communicate and reframe discussions about these children when talking with teachers or fellow Child & Youth Workers, but as a placement student, my words weren't given much weight.

After finishing school, I was hired at the residence for young men where I had done my first placement. I was sure I would be able to start advocating for more change within the house, and eventually the system. During this time, I took two of the residents for a walk through the neighbourhood, a densely populated, mixed-income area that was experiencing gentrification. The young men living in the house had to be chaperoned wherever they went, so it was an incredibly constraining and controlling atmosphere for them.

We stopped in at Popeye's chicken, and as we waited for our

order, we saw a conflict brewing. One man sat at a large table reading a newspaper. Several other small tables sat empty. A group of four or five men, mostly queer, two of them holding hands, asked the single man to move to another table. He looked them over and refused.

The boys giggled as they looked on, and I sanctimoniously asked them not to stare and reminded them of the possible consequences of getting into an argument while on an outing. This didn't feel good; it felt awful and feeble, and power-wielding. I knew the system of limiting youth's access to community space was a broken system. They resented my intervention, and when their food came up, they yelled "Faggots!" at the group of men, several times, as we left the restaurant.

On the way back to the house, I talked to them about hate speech and homophobia. Their response was that it was just wrong and they didn't know anyone who was gay.

Once back at the house, I engaged the group of six or eight young men in a discussion of homophobia. I did this alone while my co-workers sat in the office laughing at my attempt to bring this "hopeless" issue up in the group. My own sexuality came under attack pretty quickly, with the guys assuming that I must be gay or I wouldn't care about this. I told them that I was not going to respond to these questions, confirming or denying.

The next day when I came to work, I was told that it had been "dealt with," and the young men had been told that they were allowed to think whatever they wanted about gay people, including that they should be killed, as long as they did not say it out loud, especially outside of the house. The assumption was that there wasn't anyone who was gay within the house. I spent a few sleepless nights considering the words and attitudes of my coworkers, wondering if I would ever be able to come out to them and what would happen if I did.

It was clear to me that I needed to move on. I made a binder of activities and resources about homophobia, programs for queer youth, and popular education ideas that I left at the house, and did my best to find other work. I still have no idea whether any changes were made.

One month after deciding to leave the residential position, I was incredibly lucky to be hired by a program that celebrated and prioritized the needs of queer and trans youth. I was so excited to be able to work in an art-based program where I knew my identity wouldn't be under attack, but after experiencing homophobia in my previous work, I had many reservations. I was worried about being tokenized or being expected to have all of the answers and speak to the experiences of all queer and trans people.

I quickly learned that neither of these things was true. One of the greatest things about working in an environment that took supporting queer and trans youth seriously was that the atmosphere for staff was also completely different. I became part of a team that included experienced queer and trans youth workers who I could look up to and learn from. This was such an important part of my ability to focus on being the most supportive and skilled youth worker I could be. I didn't have to worry about being the only one advocating for change while absorbing a lot of hate and ignorance. I had a team to set the tone of acceptance, inclusion, and challenging ourselves.

After working in this program for eight months, I've realized that being able to work free from the stresses of a homophobic staff gives me a lot more energy to put into my work, and additionally challenges me to work on my own knowledge gaps when it comes to inclusion and equitable treatment of youth. This results in better services being delivered to young people, from a person who is more engaged and available on a daily basis, and for queer youth, it means being exposed to an adult who they might be able to identify with and look up to, the way that I look up to my queer coworkers.

While I have found a safe and nurturing place in my career after choosing to become a Child & Youth Worker, this isn't a reality for many queer and trans people working in this field. There are some incredible programs that exist for LGBTQ* youth, and the staff in these programs are often working hard to share their knowledge and advocate for changes in other environments, but there is still so much that needs to change in order to fulfill our obligation to children and youth.

The knowledge and skill gap in the field of Child & Youth Work is failing both employees and youth. Policies that are supposed to protect young people from prejudice based on their gender and sexuality are not backed up by action. Ambivalence on behalf of managers and frontline workers when it comes to addressing homophobic actions of staff and youth put LGBTQ* people in harm's way. Change needs to happen on multiple levels, and this requires the effort and commitment of all people in the field. It is my hope that as Child and Youth Workers we will make good on our common goal to support all youth, regardless of our identities, by working to create safer and more affirming environments for LGBTQ* children and youth, and our colleagues.

"Things are above ground
and changing rapidly."

AFTER THE DANCING

Valerie Windsor

Here I am, fifty-two years old, single, and trying to navigate a new lesbian scene, make new friends, and hopefully find a love that lasts.

After coming out a long time ago and being away for twenty-eight years, I found my way back home to St. John's. Two children, two marriages, and two divorces later, I am not the same person as when I left at twenty-three years old.

I grew up in a small fishing village on the south coast of Newfoundland. I can safely say I knew nothing about being gay until I was in my mid-twenties. I thought lesbians were characters in romantic fiction with platonic relationships.

I came out in Ottawa at twenty-eight and was welcomed with open arms. Women connected emotionally and politically. We connected as mothers, as activists, as lovers and survivors. We marched to Parliament Hill and the Supreme Court of Canada in large numbers, brothers and sisters in the fight for LGBTQII rights as human rights.

It was difficult at times to ignore the small contingent of people condemning us, fuelled by hate and ignorance, from the sidewalk while we marched by in the thousands. Thankfully, we had the comfort of each other, the support of a small number of spiritual and community leaders, family (sometimes), and friends.

The lesbian community was still very much underground in the 1980s and 1990s—literally and figuratively. We even had an underground dance club in the parking lot of the Rideau Centre, downtown Ottawa. Someone had to bring you there the first time to show you the inconspicuous yellow door that led downstairs. I was told, "If you have the courage to walk from the door, cross the large room to the bar, then you must be dyke." Thankfully, I passed that test. The Coral Reef was sometimes jokingly referred to as the Oral Grief. Those were the days of Doc Martins and plaid shirts—except for the women that crossed the bridge from Hull and Gatineau. They were more stylish than us Anglophones. Occasionally, jealousies would arise and one time a fight broke out with five or six women practically brawling on the floor. But mostly we danced.

Twenty years ago, we hid the places where we danced for fear of violence. There was a time in Ottawa when 200 very peaceful women danced in a community hall until police arrived to clear the building because of a bomb threat.

In the late 1980s, AIDS was like a plague in our community affecting mostly men. Women were affected in far lesser numbers, but the consequences of AIDS spread beyond the victim and survivors to their family and friends. There were regular deaths in our community. A lesbian friend of mine took her life one night, unable to shake depression after her ex-husband died of AIDS. Two small children were left with that terrible legacy—no mom or dad.

My daughter went with me to my first Pride march in Ottawa.

She was eight and I was twenty-nine. The family picnic at the end of the march was a wonderful positive place full of happy gay people and children. Unfortunately, we had to leave early because a group of young men threw eggs at us from the sidewalk. Police were present to keep things safe. Disappointed, we left immediately and talked about oppression all the way home. That experience formed a base understanding of social injustice and laid the foundation for our beliefs and understanding of homophobia.

My children and I lived a very open and positive life. We had to deal with homophobia from time to time in their schools, our neighbourhood, and with friends and family as it came up. The kids would ask why we didn't live in a gay friendly neighbourhood rather than the suburbia we lived in then. My son, at ten, asked me one day why did he always have to check the "other" box to define our family when filling in a school form. Yet another lesson in the invisibility of lesbians and the slow progress of our educational system.

My first lesbian relationship was with an aboriginal woman and lasted five years. She is a beautiful, artistic, gentle soul who was haunted by the years of separation from her parents and family as a child growing up in a residential school.

My daughter came out at seventeen, and initially I was stunned and then realized my own internalized homophobia—I actually said, "I think it's a stage." I found it more difficult to tell my family that my daughter was a lesbian than myself. My family lived in another province and didn't give me a hard time when I came out, so it seemed unreasonable for me to think that way.

The organization Gays of Ottawa was so important to us at that time. They offered safe space for people to meet, to come out, and to dance even more. The old GO Centre was above a laundry mat. It was like you had to have a map of hidden safe havens. Thankfully, things have changed—for the better. Now LGBTQII communities all across Canada and the US are vibrant, diversified, busy, wonderful places to be. Things are above ground and changing rapidly.

In some big cities, there are resource centres, churches, sports teams, seniors' homes, theatre and arts. I have visited gay villages in Vancouver, Montreal, Toronto, and Dallas. There, I felt part of the majority and safe, walking with my partner hand in hand.

But you can still walk into a bar in a small city, cross the threshold, and think you took a step back in time. At times I feel there is a psychological barrier to our growth and visibility. It seems some people like it on the edge of a forbidden sexual world. We have pushed the limits and broken taboos. How we coped to survive worked for a long time, but today is different and a lot of queer folks just want to love, have a family, and live a normal life—whatever that is. I believe there is still room for the queer community to rise above the subversive world of an underground culture to celebrate ourselves, our diversity, and our contribution to the world we now live in.

My partner and I moved to Halifax in 2002. Nova Scotia was one of the first provinces to have a domestic partner registry. They seemed ahead in many ways when it came to human rights for the queer community. My partner and I spoke publically about our right to marry and participated in as many events as we could to help further the rights of the rainbow community.

We could have been charged with fraud if we didn't file income tax returns as couples, but we couldn't get legally married. It was frustrating times but worth it when all the hard work of Egale and other LGBTQII organizations in Canada came to fruition and we were allowed to legally marry. We were one of the first same-sex couples in Nova Scotia to marry and divorce. We were married for four of our thirteen years together. I had settled into a lifetime together. Somewhere in the final year, she changed, and I didn't. That was another starting over point for me.

My daughter and her wife also married in Nova Scotia, overlooking the Atlantic Ocean in Peggy's Cove. They are still madly in love after ten years.

The ocean and family brought me back to the east coast, first Nova Scotia and then Newfoundland. I am starting over in a new city, and for the first time in a long time, I have to build friendships in a lesbian community. There aren't many events or activities for lesbians, and women seem to be integrated into mainstream society with large families to keep them busy. I have heard women here say they prefer to be with family and straight friends than to be with other lesbians in group activities. When I asked why, the answer was that as couples it could threaten their relationship hanging out with other lesbians. There doesn't appear to be a lot of women interested in activism, or at least, I haven't met the right women yet.

Many gay people flock to big cities and anonymity to avoid small town judgement and being ostracized. There are some inherent dangers in living your life underground, in the closet, with no family support. Young men and women start going to the clubs and enter into a drug culture. I call it the dark side. There are a lot of street kids, homeless kids, and couch surfing among gay youth. It is dangerous. Along with addictions, some of the kids I met also had mental health issues that contributed to being on the streets with no safety net of a loving family to fall back on.

While volunteering for one youth organization, I met children as young as twelve coming out. They use different language and don't always like labels. Parents would sometimes drop them off and pick them up after a few hours. The best parents were the ones who came in to say hi and see what the organization was about. There were programs and information for parents and schools, gay/straight alliances, information on healthy relationships, anonymous testing for STIs and sex education. Kids also came from the streets, homeless and hungry. It is vital for youth to have a safe space to live, to gather and have fun. They are just like all other kids, needing acceptance and support.

The Metropolitan Church of Ottawa and Metropolitan Safe Harbour of Halifax were two religious organizations that worked hard for the queer community. Safe Harbour held a wonderful celebration every Christmas with young and old coming out for the delicious free turkey dinner in the warmth of the St. John's United Church hall. There was music, decorations, and china teacups. They raised money through raffles for Manna for Health, which fed and ministered to isolated members of our community. It was mentioned to me that many older transgendered people often were alone and isolated. The dinner offered a rare opportunity for a lot of older folks to catch up with old friends.

Also while living in Halifax, I volunteered to proofread and edit for an Atlantic Canadian magazine aimed at the LGBTQII community. I quickly moved on to writing a few articles and loved it. It was fun, challenging, and an incredible learning experience. As with a lot of volunteer organizations, in-fighting caused dissention in the ranks. We haven't learned how to always play nice, and we don't always agree. I made a couple of friends at the magazine. Not too long after I left, one of them was brutally murdered on the street by a raving homophobic lunatic.

In spite of that, I believe the world is safer now for our LGBTQII community, but it is not perfect, and we have to learn how to fit into the larger community with a sense of pride and belonging.

Over the course of the last twenty-five years, I have met wonderful, amazing queer folks who brought us to this point where many of us can live openly and safely. I am grateful for the women of the Tatamagouche area who gave us a warm place to dance in January. I am grateful to the queer communities of Ottawa and Halifax and, in particular, all my lovely, caring friends who still stay in touch. These women are part of my soul, and I love them very much. I am also a very proud mother of a lesbian daughter and a straight son.

I am making friends in St. John's and discovering the hidden gems of the queer community here and how much the women love dancing, given the opportunity.

UN-LEARNING LEARNING

> "It's hard for me to believe that only a year ago I was making plans for a future that included a wife."

LEARNING TO BE ME

Jamie B. Laurie

Some days, I still have to pinch myself to make sure I'm not dreaming. It's hard for me to believe that only a year ago I was making plans for a future that included a wife. One year...and my whole life has changed. It took 365 days for me to settle into this role I was born for. Being gay feels as natural as breathing, as truthful as the passing of a day, and as right as living the way I'm meant to.

That being said, the road to accepting myself has been long and twisting. The words "I'm gay" still taste strange on my lips when I say them out loud, and I'm reluctant to offer this bit of myself up as an introduction. Maybe that will get easier with time...maybe the road has not yet come to an end.

I don't think my homosexuality came as a major surprise to most of the people in my life. My mom often says that she always knew the truth. Maybe my running like a butterfly across the soccer field as a child tipped her off. I'd like to steer clear of the clichéd expression, "I always knew I was gay." I think it's safe to say that as a little boy who used to perform the entirety of *Mamma Mia!* for my family (complete with feather boas and choreographed dance routines), I wasn't aware I would one day feel compelled to have sex with other men. At the time, I only knew that I was different.

In my elementary school, a Canadian boy was expected to eat, sleep, and breathe hockey—if you didn't play the game, you at least had to be up to date on your NHL statistics. That was a problem for me because I was much more interested in devouring books and auditioning for after-school theatre productions. But I was happy, content with my group of almost-exclusively female friends. The other kids in my grade, on the other hand, weren't so understanding.

I remember a particular incident from the first grade vividly. For well over a week, I spent my lunch hours in the schoolyard evading a group of several kids. What had started as a simple game— they would chase me, and I would try to run faster—eventually became something far less innocent. I would beg them to stop, my heart a jackhammer in my chest and my lungs burning by the time I returned to class. None of the supervising teachers did anything to help me, so one day I took matters into my own hands. As a little boy who felt like an outcast, I didn't know who to turn to for help, so I took a pair of scissors with me into the schoolyard one lunch in case I needed to defend myself. I didn't use them of course, and the bullies tattled on me right away. The administration didn't punish the bullies or put measures into place to ensure I would be left alone. Instead, I was sentenced to a week without recess and had my scissor privileges revoked.

Things really changed when I started high school. The turning point of my sexual confusion came at puberty. My elementary years were riddled with crushes on one girl or the next because I was more of a personality-over-looks kind of guy at the time. When my pituitary gland finally fired up and pumped me full of new hormones, I started to really *notice* what people looked like—specifically, what *guys* looked like!

It became harder and harder to hide my true self. As my friends discussed which guys they thought were attractive, my lips were sealed. I occasionally contributed to the conversations by offering up the names of actresses I thought were pretty.

I was a "sensitive" guy, which led to one of my best friends developing a crush on me. I felt horrible for rejecting her, and the pressure of my deepest, darkest secret weighed heavily on my heart and mind. I wondered at the time if I should have started dating a girl because that would have trained me for my inevitable future as a straight man—there was no question in my mind that I would not or could not live a happy and "normal" life with another man.

The first person I came out to was my mother, though not by choice. My mom sat me down because she was concerned about the change in my mood: "You just haven't been yourself," she explained to me. And she was right. I told her that I had a lot on my mind. That I thought I needed some help. That I was confused. And then I said, "Remember that time you told me you'd always thought I was gay? Well, I think I might be." A long, tear-soaked hug sealed the deal. I had inched my way towards those closet doors. Coming out to my mom put a crack in the metaphorical dam of my resolve; the water pressure was there, my secret wanting more than ever to escape.

Still, I wasn't quite ready. The next year saw me seeking professional help. A program had been set up at the hospital to help people through the struggles of sexual identity. I met with a therapist several times, learning about potential strategies for coming out.

Fast-forward to Christmas of 2012, and I found myself chatting online with one of my closest friends. She was talking about a boy band that I secretly adored and I had the image of a cute guy I'd seen at the grocery store in the back of my mind. I thought how much easier it would be to just...*talk*. No more secrets, no more hiding. Just being. So I told her I was gay. And it really made no difference to her in terms of our friendship. In fact, we likely grew closer with the truth out.

After that first friend, I had the confidence I needed, and I told several more friends over the following days. I had a small group of confidants, guardians of my most private skeleton in the closet. They swore their lips were sealed, and I began to feel a sense of lightness where before I had felt such a crushing pressure.

I started attending meetings at a local LGBTQ youth center with my close friend, a boy I'd met earlier that year. It was an enriching experience socially, as I started to learn how to come out of my shell. I made so many new friends who existed in a world outside of the walls of my somewhat sheltered private school. I learned that some people don't identify with a gender, and so they prefer gender-neutral pronouns like "they." I learned the difference between HIV and AIDS. More than anything, I was simply learning to be myself.

At that point, I still hadn't come out to my father—not out of fear, but just because I think these kinds of things are said more easily to a mother. I knew it had been a long time coming, and I was finally ready. Battling an army of butterflies in my stomach, I said those two words out loud: "I'm gay." My dad told me he was so very proud of me, and wrapped me in a hug. Soon after that, my grandparents were in on the not-so-secret secret.

I asked my friends to slowly spread the word; I didn't want to make a big show of coming out. I wanted things to flow organically. I never thought that coming out had to be a grand affair that demanded all kinds of attention because I had reached a point where I realized that being gay wasn't *all* that important. In my opinion, a human being is made up of so many more factors than his or her (or their) sexuality. I changed my Facebook profile to say, "Interested in men."

As the news got around, I received occasional messages from classmates I'd never really talked to. One girl told me how brave she thought I was for coming out in high school. I thanked her and simply said that I was looking forward to a day when people wouldn't have to come out. A boy I'd always considered a typical "jock" stood up for me on social media when someone was making fun of me, which ended up teaching me about how I was sometimes judgmental in my own way.

I continue to be grateful for the outpouring of support I received from my classmates and friends. My family continued to love me as the same person I'd always been. Possibly more importantly, I learned to love myself. As I write this, happily settled into life as an openly gay teenager, I have to acknowledge the fact that not everybody has it as easy as I did. I have to hope that we are moving in the right direction and that people's opinions will continue to evolve. I feel for the young people like me who are shunned by their friends and rejected by their families. But I am optimistic for a future where sexuality is no more important than the colour of one's eyes.

Sometimes, I still have to pinch myself to make sure I'm not dreaming. Then I remember the friends I made at my youth group. I realize that not all "jocks" are bullies like you see in the movies. I still feel the nervousness of my first kiss with another boy. I look back on the boy who never felt like he fit in and find myself in the shoes of a young man who knows where he's going. I can picture a future with a husband by my side and a baby in my arms. Being gay is not a curse, because love is never wrong.

In the words of Aliya-Jasmine Sovani, a woman who inspired me greatly: "…no matter what you are in terms of race, gender, religion, ethnicity, or sexual preference…the truth of humanity is that love is love, is love…"

"That's when I realized that
the drive to be with a man was not
something external, was not something
bad, was not my cross to bear."

HOME ALONE
WHEN *LIFE* INTRUDES

Tom Churchill

The glossy photo shows the blacked-out silhouette of two men, standing side by side on a hill, facing the camera, legs spread apart, holding hands. The backdrop is evening in San Francisco.

On the same day I see it, I also see an article whose heading—in large block letters, grainy grey against a black background—reads: "Homosexuality in America." It is *Life Magazine*, June 26, the summer of 1964.

Ancient history. Living history.

Picture a small New England town, and on a slight rise a white, wood-shingled colonial with a red door and black shutters, shrubs of mature mountain laurel beneath the first-floor windows, a green lawn, the hill down to the sidewalk covered in lush pachysandra. Now picture a fourteen-year-old boy at home alone on a June day when the mail arrives. Peace, prosperity, and puberty in the protective arms of America.

I was that boy. Something went *kerchunk* in my gut when I saw that picture—a tightening, an excitement, much like the reaction I would experience countless times when a man locked eyes with mine. It was a kind of recognition, but it was all in my gut, not in my head.

In the *Life* issue there were two articles on homosexuality, "The 'Gay' World Takes to the City Streets" and "Scientists search for the answer to a touchy and puzzling question: Why?" The first is, ostensibly, an attempt to provide an accurate view of the nature and extent of homosexuality in America, although in referring to a photo of leathermen it says, "They are part of the 'gay world,' which is actually a sad and often sordid world." (Throughout the article the word *gay* appears always within quotation marks.) The second article is a compendium of then-current scientific thinking about homosexuality.

The two-paragraph lead-in to the feature ends with this sentence: "The myth and misconception with which homosexuality has so long been clothed must be cleared away, not to condone it but to cope with it." The introduction, however, actually mimics myth and misconception. Homosexuality is a "social disorder." Homosexuality is "deviation." The feature includes quotes such as, "The pervert is no longer as secretive as he was," and, "Anybody does any recruiting [in my bar], I say shoot him. Who cares?"

Very scary stuff.

By the time I'd read the articles, and notwithstanding that wrenching in my gut, I knew in my head that I couldn't be homosexual. I was a good kid. I was Catholic. I lived in a good home with two parents, four brothers and a sister, two dogs. I had good friends, both boys and girls. I was in with the in-crowd. I wasn't an outcast. I wasn't a sicko. I wasn't a deviate. I couldn't possibly be a pervert.

And so life went on, despite *Life*. I liked hanging out with the boys and girls in my crowd. I always had a girlfriend, and she was always pretty, smart, and fun to be with. When it got down to the heavy petting, my body always reacted to her touch. Pleasant as it was, though, I always wondered why this was something the other guys were so obsessed with.

And so life went on. Moving to Canada. Going to university. Going into business. Getting married. Having kids. And all the while, men on the side. It wasn't until I was in my forties that my head caught up with my gut. That's when I realized that the drive to be with a man was not something external, was not something bad, was not "my cross to bear." It's when I finally saw that it was part of me, part of what makes me who I am, that the physical compulsion was a relentless guide, always pointing me to myself, to acceptance of specific affectional needs, to the realization that I have much more to offer a man than my body, that I want much more than his.

That's when I could finally say to myself, with some peace and some pride, "I'm gay."

Not that it's been an easy path since then. But it has been a rich one. It's funny how whatever path you choose is the right one because every path does its best to lead you to where you ought to be. It would be hard to count the many blessings my wandering has bestowed upon me—impossible perhaps. Impossible to describe how profound the grounding, how enduring the hope.

Ancient history. Living history. Still looking for the man I can stand with on that hill. Ever grateful to the ones who have travelled with me toward the top.

It's Complicated
by Tom Churchill

We were hungry when we met
went from hello to deep kisses
with hardly a word
into what bliss our bodies could offer—
muscle on muscle
the pure beauty of man on man.

You came so quickly;
It's your deep throat, you said.
And when I asked, Meet again?
your answer was clear: It's complicated.

Years later, though, at Bruce's birthday,
there you were—
a handsome man across a crowded room.
We spoke then, mostly of books
of bad backs and Pilates
pornography and current affairs,
careful to skirt our brief history
though there may have been references
too obscure to be sure of.
Or maybe you really have forgotten.

At any rate, you were right.
It is complicated.
My wife   your partner   our separate lives
issues of honour and trust
the thrust of passion—
a full ration of conflict
in a full portion of care.

Listen, I wanted to say,
I long to hold you near.

> "'Go die.'
> When a young guy in my class looked
>   at me and said this to me one afternoon,
> I looked him directly in the eyes
>   and said to him, 'I'm trying.'"

COMING OUT
IN RURAL LABRADOR

Katy Craggs

My coming-out story is a little different considering I was in elementary school, and about ten years old, when I did so. This being a small town in Labrador, and having never even known what the word lesbian meant, I never knew what coming out as one would entail. I never really "came out," as such, after years of telling my parents, "If I marry a guy, he's shaving his legs and changing his last name." I just started saying, "I like girls instead." It was as straightforward as that.

It wasn't long before the news that I was a lesbian spread like wild fire. In grade five, I was having the word "dyke" yelled at me every time I was seen in the halls. It wasn't long before I got fed up and decided to speak out about it when my classroom had a speak off. It wasn't a day later that my rough draft was sent home explaining I couldn't use the word "dyke" in my speech. It wasn't appropriate for me to say in a speech how being called that made me feel, but teachers would stand idly by as it was yelled at me in the halls? Feeling hopeless and defeated, I wrote about some topic that meant nothing to me. The day of the speeches, however, another little girl in my class wrote a speech about how important her religion was to her. I'll never forget being shocked and appalled as she quoted Corinthians 9 and 10 in front of the whole class, telling us homosexuals are going to hell. Apparently that was deemed completely appropriate.

I moved to St. John's in 2003 when I was twelve years old without saying goodbye to anyone, vowing I'd keep my sexuality a secret and with the mindset that lesbians must only be in San Francisco, and I'll move there when I'm older. I didn't feel that way for long, however, because shortly after I moved, I met my first love. Then, even after my past experiences and warnings from my concerned parents, when asked if I had a boyfriend, I finally told one girl, "Actually, I have a girlfriend."

So I "came out" yet again. I was tired of having to hide who I loved and didn't feel that I should have to. Being proud, however, didn't help how cruel kids are. I deliberately missed the school bus every day, afraid of the torture I'd face on board. When I'd get on the bus in the morning, every student sitting alone would slide to the end of their seats, so I'd have nowhere to sit. Then the driver would drive away as I shakily tried desperately to find a seat or had to eventually just shove another kid in so I could sit down. More times than not, I'd sit there trying to ignore the taunting voices of the guys in the back yelling sexual questions at me. I got in trouble for missing the bus so much though (my parents having to drive and pick me up every day). Forced to ride the bus, one afternoon after school as I got off the bus to walk home, a group of kids on board threw dozens of beer bottles at me as I did so. When my parents and I went to the principal, it was my word against theirs until one kind guy came forward against his friends and said it had happened. Even so, we were told it'd be easier if I'd stopped getting the bus as opposed to kicking half the students off as that's as many that had been involved in the assault.

I fell into a deep depression that year; I was twelve years old and wanted to die. I couldn't see anything getting better, and I was so tired of being degraded for my sexual orientation. Nearly daily self-injury and several suicide attempts followed. I felt completely alone. Even with the support from my first girlfriend and ever accepting parents, I still never wanted to leave my bedroom. I even quit the competitive swim team, a sport I'd enjoyed since I was seven years old, when my cutting got so bad I couldn't hide it anymore. It was a common occurrence at school for other students to look at me and say, "Go die." When a young guy in my class looked at me and said this to me one afternoon, I looked him directly in the eyes and said to him, "I'm trying." And I meant it.

Through the worse days of my depression, I wrote many speeches for my junior high speak offs, in both French and English. It wasn't until I'd gotten my first girlfriend and even thought of marriage that I was bewildered to learn, as the gay marriage debate was just emerging, that even if I'd wanted to, I couldn't get married. I wrote about how marriage is a basic human right, not a privilege for the heterosexual. This time my teachers never tried to silence me, but offered guidance to help improve my writing and better convey my point.

When I started high school, my life did a 360. I met a group of girls who were way more mature than the children I'd known in junior high. I went from being afraid to enter the girls washroom to hanging out in there with friends laughing and doing my makeup before class. I luckily stuck it out as I had started the year trying to change schools. I kept at my speeches, becoming a huge advocate against bullying as I now had the confidence and the experience behind me giving me strength.

When I graduated, I brought my girlfriend at the time with me; not a single word of objection was uttered by anyone. It was the most amazing experience, considering how many times I thought I'd never see my next birthday, let alone graduate high school, and happy at that!

I have since aided the wonderful Egale Canada with their promotional video for the GSAs, spoken on behalf of the LGBT community at an event for the coalition against violence, and been a member of the Board of Directors for St. John's Pride Inc. for the summer of 2012. I am now twenty-two years old, a nurse with the mental health and addictions program in Newfoundland, wishing to someday obtain my master's degree in nursing and practice with a focus on the counselling of those dealing with mental illness.

I believe it to be very important to fight for the rights of our LGBT seniors, youth, and entire population no matter how you identify. Everyone has a right to know they're important. I will always have the scars I gave myself those years ago, but they are a reminder of just how much of a survivor I really am, and how grateful I am now for just that.

"I don't hate the people who bullied me. Instead, I feel sorry for them."

THE PEACEFUL CHILD

Adam Carroll

Looking back on my childhood, my sister was always, and still is to this day, the dramatic one. She tends to be the center of attention in my family. My mom always tells me when I was a child I could sit on the floor for hours entertained by nothing more than a pair of socks. From the moment my sister tried to throw me in a garbage can when I was a baby, I was suddenly pushed into the role of the "Peaceful Child," the child who didn't seek out attention, didn't cause family disputes, and was simply expected to behave twenty-four seven. This being the way my family functioned, when the bullying began at school it was easy to hide it. In fact, no one in my family knew I was bullied in school until June 14, 2010, when I told them I was gay.

Gay.

It was the end of recess and my fourth grade class was lined up to go back inside. Out of nowhere, a boy came up beside me and said

I was "gay." I didn't know what this word meant, and frankly I don't think he did either, but I didn't like it. I thought little about this insult at the time, and I had no idea how it would haunt me through the remainder of my school years.

The bullying seemed to begin around the same time I started taking dance classes. To this day, this is something I can't really wrap my head around. I was being bullied by guys for doing an activity that involved being the only boy in a room full of half-naked girls, when the guys played hockey or basketball so they would be in a changing room full of half-naked, sweaty guys. Clearly if I had my time back, I would have done things differently!

When middle school started I began to close myself off from friends and family. I walked around with a smile on my face and pretended like nothing was wrong when, in reality, I was being eaten up by fear. For years, I wouldn't go out anywhere with my family—to the mall, movies, or even out for a walk—because I was terrified of being bullied in front of them. What would they think of me?

I had people call me names, like faggot and Gaylord, and regularly got shoved in the hallways and even had words engraved into my locker. Because of all of the schoolyard torture, I now suffer from anxiety, depression, and my own little food issue. However, I don't hate the people who bullied me. Instead, I feel sorry for them. When someone bullies, it's usually a reaction to an unfortunate situation that's happening in his or her own life and has little to do with the person they're picking on. When it comes to bullying, we're so eager to point the finger of blame at someone to say, "You're the bully, and you're the victim!" Life is never that black and white. For the most part, people aren't calling others names and beating others up for no reason. As human beings, we're constantly reacting to situations. As children and young adults, that can be very scary. It can make the best of people do the most horrible things. We need to look past this steadfast explanation of the bully and the victim that we settled on years ago and examine each side for real answers.

If I could change that I was bullied when I was younger, I wouldn't! On some level, I'm grateful it happened. Although it left me with scars, it also left me with gifts. It's not something that negatively defines me, but it is an experience that has taught me selflessness, understanding, compassion, and most importantly forgiveness. I understand these in a way that most people don't, and for that I am grateful.

Selflessness.

The idea of putting someone else's needs before my own has always felt like second nature to me. Being bullied as a child and not being able to reach out for help, I learned you should always be willing to reach out and help others even if they don't initially ask for it. If there is something I can do to ease someone's suffering, I believe it's important to do it. I give up my seat on the bus when someone else more deserving needs it, I help out a friend when they're sick, and I'm always there to listen. There's a joy that comes from helping others and making them happy.

Understanding.

There's something to be said about understanding. To understand that people aren't out to be evil or hateful. They truly believe what they're doing is the right thing to do. Of course this doesn't excuse their actions but it is a starting point to finding the common ground that will lead to a conclusion. For a while, I resented my sister for always being the center of attention growing up, but later I realized that's just who she is. For a while, I resented my parents for always giving her the attention, but as I grew older, I realized they did the best they could with what they were given.

Forgiveness.

People say that to be able to move on you need to let go of your baggage. In reality, I don't think that's possible. We all have baggage, whether it's being bullied, your father having cancer, or struggling with a learning disability. It's with us wherever we go because it's a part of us—a part of our history. The best you can do is make peace with it. Make peace with those who wronged you and the things that have hurt you.

I don't know if I'll ever see that boy from my fourth grade school yard again, but if he's reading this, if he remembers me, I hope he knows I forgive him. In fact, I forgave him a long time ago! But now he owes me a double vodka and orange juice!

Be strong, be brave, and always remember to laugh a little.

" As members of humanity, we all possess
within our bodies gifts that have the potential to
save and create lives. However, the
capacity to share these gifts is not equal, for
not all bodies are deemed fit
for such acts of generosity. "

THE PROBLEM WITH 'GAY ORGANS': REFLECTIONS ON A BODY DEEMED UNFIT FOR MEDICINE

Jason Behrmann

A s a bioethicist, analysis of how innovations in medical science benefit humanity is a subject that captures my attention. Of particular interest is the transfer of human materials from one body to another as a means to save and create lives. The transplantation of organs, tissues, and cells is the current state-of-the-art treatment for blindness, cancer, and infertility, to name a few. While impressive in the benefits to population health, implementing bodily materials in medicine also raises concerns. Of importance is that the transfer of tissues between persons carries the risk of also transmitting infectious disease, and it is thus necessary to assess the health of populations that supply human materials in order to minimize this well-known risk. Though essential for the protection of patients, criteria that determine which populations can—or more importantly, *cannot*—provide human materials to benefit the lives of fellow citizens may create ethical shortfalls by socially excluding specific people from acts of great collective import. Indeed, many jurisdictions throughout the world, including Canada, have ubiquitously marked certain people as 'unfit donors,' labelled as too 'risky' for the potential transmission of infectious disease—such as HIV—due to an observed elevated incidence of disease in particular populations.

I am a member of one such population: what health officials term *men-who-have-sex-with-men* (MSM). Restricting tissue donation by all individuals that fall under this broad label provides a blunt tool to lower the probability of procuring human materials that may contain transmissible infections. Though laudable in its intended goals, such precautionary measures have been criticised as being unduly restrictive given the availability of pathogen screening technologies and the fact that experts in infectious disease identify that over 90% of members of the MSM population do *not* have HIV. Many argue that labelling all MSM as 'high-risk'—regardless of practising safer-sex or being in a monogamous relationship and in good clinical health—is unscientific and stigmatising, perpetuating stereotypes that HIV is inextricably linked to homosexuality. And at a time where the supply of human materials in medicine is limited, questions arise as to whether blanket restrictions on MSM as potential donors may exacerbate this scarcity and thus disadvantage the health of all Canadians.

Moving beyond technical arguments, here I provide my personal reflections on being made an unequal citizen because of exclusionary donor-eligibility criteria. I express the injustice I feel from the realisation that the love I share with my fiancé automatically assigns us both a negative label; one that marks us with caution rather than as people whose generosity has the potential to save fellow citizens. Having a body deemed unfit for medicine, I provide a personal account as to why this reality blemishes progress towards a more tolerant society. My thoughts begin with blood.

TAINTED BY MY BLOOD

Commonly referred to as the 'tainted blood scandal of the 1980s,' failures in government oversight resulted in mass contamination of the global blood supply with transmissible infections, namely HIV. With little understanding of the disease at the time, regulators were justified in taking precautionary measures in banning blood donations from populations hit hardest during the early stages of the AIDS epidemic, such as MSM. Though logical at first, this precautionary measure has remained unchanged in many jurisdictions, meaning that the blood of all men that have ever engaged in homosexual sex—even once—is forever banned from transfusion. This now raises contention since revolutions in HIV screening technologies developed in response to the tainted blood tragedy enable detection of transmissible infections in donors within weeks following infection. Forever excluding one's blood—due to a sexual act that occurred years earlier, for instance—is illogical and has led many to argue that such restrictions are outdated.

After over a decade of calls to end the ban, Health Canada did just that in 2013, replacing it with a defined deferral period. Men can now donate blood following five years of abstinence from homosexual activity. Ending the previous blacklisting for all men that have engaged in homosexual intercourse represents progress, yet remains disheartening. By focusing regulatory reform on a deferral period from MSM activity, I feel that amendments to blood policy in Canada missed an opportunity to truly counter discrimination by reforming the MSM criteria itself.

Consider the fact that human sexuality is diverse; while many find love in same-sex relationships exclusively, many others experiment with and experience their sexuality with opposite/same-sex partners without necessarily ascribing to being either gay, straight, or bisexual. Indeed, the MSM category captures this diversity. For this reason, regulators assert that restricting blood donations based on the inclusive category of 'men-*having-sex*-with-men' is not discriminatory because it targets a sexual *behaviour* and not sexual *orientation*. I, however, remain unconvinced. For one, this supposedly non-discriminatory label that fixates upon the criteria of 'being a man whose intimate partner is also male' targets an attribute that is inherent to my identity, as well as that of most gay men. Claims that the MSM category does not overtly target sexual minorities seem dubious, a problem that has only been exacerbated by the five-year donor deferral criteria. Men like me in long-term same-sex relationships have now become especially circumscribed by these restrictions, thus reinforcing our exclusion as blood donors. An arguably better outcome would have been to refocus regulations upon truly risky behaviours, such as unprotected sex with multiple partners. Until such regulatory progress takes place, I will continue to live my life with the sombre knowledge that the blood coursing through my veins is undesired.

This exclusion of my body from medicine extends beyond that of my blood, where blood regulations have set precedence for all my body and its parts, such as the following cases for sperm and organs will demonstrate.

BUREAUCRATS AS GATEKEEPERS TO REPRODUCTION

Assisted reproduction technologies now enable a growing number of Queer people to build families in the absence of heterosexual relationships. However, due to being perceived as unfit parents or too risky as providers of reproductive tissues, regulations in many parts of the world enact barriers against accessing medical reproductive services by Queer populations. Canadian regulations governing sperm donation are an example.

Deemed too risky for the general population of patients in need of donated sperm to conceive a child, I remain banned for life as an anonymous sperm donor. Fortunately, if a friend or relative wants to use my sperm specifically for their family building goals, I can free myself of this ban and become what is known as a 'directed-donor.'

However, to use my sperm for these 'directed' purposes I must first obtain permission from a physician. Enabling a thorough health assessment in this instance makes sense; but I must then obtain permission from a government bureaucrat at the Ministry of Health, which makes no sense whatsoever. First off, when it comes to making medical judgements, such assessments are best left to doctors and not to remote government bodies. That said, once my body is identified as perfectly healthy, I see no discernable safety benefit provided by a bureaucrat rubber-stamping my medical assessment and scrutinising my reasons for wanting to be a directed sperm donor. Instead, this regulatory necessity strikes me as deeply intrusive and hampers my reproductive freedoms.

My unease is made greater by the fact that unlike most other human materials, sperm can be frozen for safekeeping over the long-term—which it is. Regulations mandate that all sperm be frozen and quarantined for six months in order to enable ample time to screen my body for transmissible infections. I am therefore dumbfounded that I am banned—for life—as an anonymous sperm donor, a fact made especially nonsensical by the inconsistency that I can be a directed donor (but only if the government permits it). Such extraordinary restrictions in my ability to help others build families is a matter of concern, where I feel that current regulations carry unsettling eugenic undertones that inadvertently serve to prevent me from anonymously passing on formidable 'gay genes' to unsuspecting parents.

'OUTED' BY MY ORGANS?

Current capacities in transplantation medicine now enable a person, upon death, to save the lives of many. The regrettable reality is that donated organs are rare. Knowledgeable of such scarcity, I imagine few greater honours than to gift my organs to those in need upon my death. However, I feel this honourable act will be marred by the fact that in such an event, patients must be informed that my organs are from a high-risk population, and technically, they therefore are procured from a non-ideal donor. Once my organs are 'outed' as inherently risky, patients must then decide whether or not to accept my 'gay organs' in order to save their lives.

Donor eligibility criteria for organs in Canada and the United States of America are similar to those for blood, with one important distinction. Men who have engaged in MSM activity within the past five years are *technically* ineligible as organ donors; however, due to an exceptional circumstances loophole provision within the regulations, many organs *are* procured from the MSM population. Exceptional circumstances apply to life-or-death situations, where a patient can consent to receiving an organ from an otherwise ineligible population if organs from ideal donor populations remain unavailable. Overall, this loophole provision acknowledges that the life-saving benefits of receiving an organ outweigh the potential risks of obtaining one from a high-risk population. Having a patient consent to receiving such organs further justifies this risk-benefit assessment.

Several aspects of these regulations cause concern. First off, given the scarcity of organs, any organs on offer from the MSM population will likely meet the exceptional circumstances criteria. Moreover, I find it hard to believe that any reasonable patient would turn away an opportunity for a new lease on life, regardless of which body it originates from. MSM donor eligibility criteria, in sum, appear superfluous, but that does not mean current donor eligibility criteria have no influence on the procurement of organs from men like me.

In fact, surveys of transplant surgeons in the United States of America indicate that while many surgeons choose to procure organs from gay men by way of the loophole, some choose not to do so. Additional observations indicate that some surgeons infer that 'exceptional circumstances' signifies that most organs may be transplanted from the MSM population, but kidneys must be discarded since patients can be placed on dialysis (where patients are not destined to die immediately without gay kidney transplantation). The practices of Canadian surgeons remain understudied. However, a recent CBC media report interviewed grieving parents upset that their dying son's organs were rejected for transplant for reasons that they believed were due to him being gay. The observed procurement of some organs and not others, as well as apparent inconsistencies in procurement practices by American surgeons, leads me to wonder what might happen upon my death. Rather than permitting me to save the lives of fellow citizens, will decisions made by a surgeon deem my organs better suited for the dumpster?

CONCLUSION

As members of humanity, we all possess within our bodies gifts that have the potential to save and create lives. However, the capacity to share these gifts is not equal, for not all bodies are deemed fit for such acts of generosity. I, for one, have a body that is gay and thus labelled inherently risky to the health of others regardless of my sexual practices, my health status, or how often my partner and I routinely screen our bodies for infectious disease. Being discriminatory, stigmatising, and unjust, these regulations merit extensive reforms. Until such reforms come, I encourage all those with able bodies to donate as much as they can in order to provide the lifesaving materials that men like me cannot gift. Meanwhile, I will continue to advocate for change so that in the future my blood will no longer be considered inherently tainted, my sperm will be freed from government scrutiny, and my organs will not be judged on their 'gayness', and, above all, gain rights to a body that is lawfully labelled fit for medicine.

"We are not passive observers in the things
that characterize our current historical time
period; we validate and challenge the
reality we live in with the things we say,
the choices we make, and the
way we live our daily lives."

TRANSGENDER TEACHER

Kael Sharman

$\mathbf{M}$y out status at work occurred accidentally but has become an integral part of my contribution as an educator. I am out as a transgender teacher and tell this story in the hope of creating a more flexible public education system, one that reflects gender diversity in practice. It is an ongoing effort but one that gets easier as time goes on and I become—more than the token transgender teacher— an excellent history teacher whose practice has been enriched by my experiences with a part of our social world that too often goes unquestioned: the gender binary.

I am a female-to-male transgender history teacher in a public secondary school in Ontario. I came out ten years into my teaching career. I was terrified of the reaction I might get from my colleagues and students, but as it has turned out, transitioning while teaching—

and the ongoing coming-out that accompanies it—has been a challenging but ultimately wonderful experience.

I am fortunate that my school board's teachers have organized a Teacher Gay-Straight Alliance (GSA). I began my professional coming-out process with them. I was the first teacher in the school board to come out as transgender, and the Teacher GSA was thrilled that I was making this bold move. I told them that I planned to come out to the administration prior to spring staffing for the following school year; I hoped the administration would accommodate my transition by placing me at a new school, hopefully one with gender-neutral washrooms, and by insuring that my name change and switch to male pronouns would be acknowledged and honoured. Teacher GSA members advised me to come out to my union first and the diversity officer with the school board second, which I did. By the end of February, I informed my principal of my intentions: I would be changing my name in the next few months, getting top surgery in July, and returning in the fall as a male teacher. My staffing forms for the following year indicated my new name and my desire to work at a new school. My requests were all accommodated, including gender-neutral washrooms. Human Resources handled all of the details of my name change expertly. The staff at my new school was very compassionate and understanding.

My only frustrating experience was with my professional body. I don't believe they intended to make things difficult for me, but they seemed unaware of their responsibilities. I informed them about my name change and the reasons for it in early April. In May, they let me know there was no problem with changing my name, but both of my names were going to be left on my public online profile. This was their policy in order to make it easier to trace people's careers; they seemed to expect that name changes would occur only for traditional reasons such as marriages. But from my perspective, suppressing my previous name from public view was essential in order to provide me some control over coming out on my own terms to those I encountered in my professional life. I wrote a letter stating I had no problem with keeping my previous name on file privately, but requesting that, for safety reasons, my female name be suppressed from public view. According to the Ontario Human Rights Commission,

> An employer or service provider must have a valid reason for collecting and using personal information, such as from a driver's licence or birth certificate, that either directly or indirectly lists a person's sex as different from his or her lived gender identity. They must also ensure the maximum degree of privacy and confidentiality. This applies in all cases, including employment records and files, insurance company records, medical information, etc. (Human Rights in Ontario: Gender Identity, 2011, Ontario Human Rights Commission, <www.hrlsc.on.ca>)

Thus, I hoped they would quickly comply with my request for privacy, but I was disappointed. An intense period of letter writing and phone calls followed, and it wasn't until October that they finally suppressed my previous first name from public view. Once they finally understood my position, they planned to revise their policies regarding names and online profiles, and they invited my input in the process. While in a perfect world, employers and other agencies would take the initiative to make sure they comply with human rights codes, I also hope that my success will inspire other trans people to be tenacious advocates for their own rights.

While I was waiting for them to comply with my request, though, some students did discover my previous name online, and word spread about my transgender status. I had looked forward to my role at my new school as simply Mr. Sharman, history teacher; it was heart wrenching at first to come to terms with being known as Mr. Sharman, transgender history teacher. As difficult as it was to accept that my new teaching identity would not be simply as a man, but as a trans man, I came to understand that hiding my past meant withholding myself as a genderqueer role model for students at the school. After the initial shock of being outed at work, I realized that accepting my past sat well with me—not just as a history teacher who touts the importance of the past personally, socially, and culturally, but also as a person whom genderqueer—and nongenderqueer! — students can look up to and see themselves in. I remember how difficult puberty was for me, and I imagine what it might have been like to have a transgender teacher: How amazing that would have been, how much easier it might have made looking into the mirror and into my own future.

When I think about what it means to be a trans person in a high-school classroom, I am reminded fondly of an experience from early on in my transition. I had begun taking testosterone in the fall of 2011, and as the changes slowly began to accumulate and second puberty began to take its hold, I had to walk into class everyday as Ms. Sharman. I had tried to slow the visible changes as much as I could, despite my private excitement that they were occurring. But while I was speaking in class, my voice would noticeably crack. I had begun wearing men's shirts to accommodate my growing arms and shoulders. I kept my chin closely shaved to hide the thickening facial hair that grew coarser by the week. But as spring 2012 wore on, it began to get hot in my un-air-conditioned, third-floor classroom. By mid-June I could no longer take the heat, but I refused to shave my newly hairy legs. I decided to wear shorts to work anyway. On the drive in, I thought of turning the car around several times. I could just call in sick and find cooler pants to wear! But I did not. If I could not make this small step, then how could I walk into my new school next September as Mr. Sharman? I had to do this. I walked into my first-period class, head held high, and started the discussion on our topic that day. I gave instructions for the activity and circulated around the room while students worked. I noticed a few eyes glance down at my extremely hairy legs, but for the most part, I don't think my students cared about my leg hair. It wasn't an issue. In fact, I now see that if there was any crowd of people I could blend into, it was a crowd of teenagers with braces, acne, cracking voices, and all-around awkward changing bodies. I was in good company.

Today I have a newfound sense of confidence in my body, in my future, in my identity as a trans man, and in my feminine past. That confidence waxes and wanes with the daily pressures of challenging assumptions and stereotypes about transgender people and gender in general. It is nice to have the choice to be out in contexts where I feel safe. I try to create that space in my classroom, not just for my benefit, but also for the benefit of every student. Teenagers need safe spaces to explore their own growing and changing senses of who they are in time and space. In the same way that all Canadians need to feel connected to our larger national story, we also need to acknowledge that, like our national identity, our personal identities are ongoing constructions. We need to understand history, not just to be good citizens, but also to understand ourselves in social spaces, embodying socially constructed identities, genders, deviances, and normative values. We are not passive observers in the things that characterize our current historical time period; we validate and challenge the reality we live in with the things we say, the choices we make, and the way we live our daily lives. Teenagers love this message and find it empowering at a time in their lives when they are looking for more control over their own circumstances.

It is through this lens that I find comfort and strength in being an out transgender history teacher. I am participating in a social time and space where I can create safety for others and myself, a place where we can sit comfortably in our own skins, even if they don't fit perfectly into the gender binary. That's an exciting thought! I am an active historical subject today, and so are my students. I hope my presence in the school system makes it that much easier for students and educational workers to accept varying concepts of gender that exist in our families, classrooms, schools, and communities.

"Is there an implied duality
between professional and personal
lives keeping my queer existence
separate—*quiet*?"

VICE-PRINCIPAL:
MY IDENTITY...MY EXISTENCE

Hubert Brard

In the professional world, I am an educator, a curriculum leader, a life-long learner, a role model, and an aspiring vice-principal. In my personal world, I am an immigrant, a son, a nephew, an uncle, and a husband... I am also a gay man. Twenty years ago last December, I realized I was gay, this integral and important aspect of my being. For the past eighteen years as an educator, I often question, "Who am I?" Frequently, I question the realization of myself as an aspiring vice-principal, specifically as a self-identified member of the Lesbian, Gay, Bisexual, Trans-sexual and Queer (LGBTQ) Community, navigating my queer existence. How can I realize my duality between professional and personal identities? Is there an implied duality between professional and personal lives keeping my queer existence separate—*quiet*? My narrative, in part, is based on my self-introspection as to how I will navigate my self-identity within a hetero-hegemonic and political administrative world, as a future vice-principal. I must mention that this affects all LGBTQ administrators in identifying their true nature in a public forum—school administration.

In 2012, The Accepting Schools Act passed, and Ontario public education delved deeper in the plight of social-inclusion and social justice for LGBTQ youths and peoples. However, in light of this Act, in an age where Ontario schools continue to strive for social justice, equity, and inclusion, I question whether or not this Act will have an effect on the school administrators' world. In their book, *Brave New Teachers: Doing Social Justice Work in Neoliberal Times* (2011), Solomon, Singer, Campbell and Allen contend that given leaders' pivotal role in either reproducing the status quo or transforming schools for inclusivity and social justice, school administrators are under the microscope especially when openly self-identifying as either LGBTQ. In reality, I see my life as a vice-principal as survival, always on the look-out for those who disagree with my "life-style" and "preferences,"' all the while condemning me and not simply respecting me or just tolerating me. Do I want their tolerance? No. I do not want to merely be tolerated but accepted as a person, a professional, a leader who is gay, but more importantly, as someone who strives for teachers and students to be accepted in school. Consequently, how I will negotiate my social self-identity as a member of the LGBTQ community and as a vice-principal (as a leader) is a new area of both research and self-realization.

Specifically in Ontario, as a teacher, I am deemed a vice-principal when it is earned. Albeit, the promotion to vice-principal from classroom teacher carries a lot of power and clout in educational discourse, yet such power and clout are given by the actions of my direct supervisor, and this clout deemed as fit or faulty by the teachers, students, and community. I will be that proverbial middleman between my principal and my staff/students and the community at large. I ask myself, where does my own social self-identity as a member of the LGBTQ community come in to play as a vice-principal? How will I intertwine my professional self with my personal self all the while being my true self?

I experience marginalization through, and living in, oppression and how my otherness is read via dominant hetero views and how I must recognize the awareness of my identity as integral to my own personal philosophy and approach to leadership. Undeniably, I struggle with my inner-conscience and inner-courage that my non-hetero self-identity stems from the fact that I have experienced, and continue to experience, discrimination and marginalization which propel my identity and, therefore, desire to protect those who are *othered* in society. I do not want my students to experience the hardships of being LGBTQ in school as I had from an early age, starting in elementary grades being bullied for acting too girly. This intensified in secondary school as I was taught that being gay is simply wrong and to avoid it at all costs. We spoke briefly of homosexuality in my grade twelve religion class (ironically called, Marriage and Morality). I was too scared, too timid, and too alone to speak up and question the religious right to silence people just because we were told to tow the religious rope. Ironically, I still find myself silenced again, too scared, too timid, and too alone to speak up. However, I have come to realize that it is within a dominant hetero culture that I *am* an agent of change as a leader in my school district. As a result, my non-hetero social identity is one of empowerment in my leadership journey—I hope.

As a leader, a gay leader, I shall embark on a queer leadership identity. Ideally, the need for the silenced queer culture will be abolished by Ontario's Accepting Schools Act when administrators who identify as LGBTQ can be comfortable (dare I say, "safe") to come out. Unfortunately, society has forced the LGBTQ community to live in the closet for centuries, and even today, the ramifications of outing oneself as an educational administrator is genuinely feared as mentioned in Fraynd and Capper's (2003) article, "Do you have any idea who you just hired?!?" For myself as an LGBTQ future vice-principal, I continue struggle with the self-pressure to maintain my anonymity as it is critical to protect my career and personal well-being—to keep my duality of existence between my professional life and my personal life just that, a duality. Despite my plight as a leader, the heterosexist and homophobic nature of education, in general, makes LGBTQ school administrators virtually invisible for fear of negative rebuttal and illegal consequences. This brings to mind the urge towards assimilation leading to self-invisibility where I must be willing to sacrifice a core portion of my identity—my true identity. To assimilate, I must be constantly on guard that I not give any clues to my personal identity, which, and it bothers me to realize, gives way to hetero privilege where not only is hetero privilege rampant in society, but it is also an extremely large issue in our schools. The reality is there are school administrators who advocate for students whilst remaining securely hidden regarding their authentic queer self. Is that my reality as I face the role of vice-principal? I would prefer to be the administrator committed to being a positive role model for my teachers and students who do not often see themselves represented in positions of responsibility and power. What kind of role model will I be if I were to share my queer affiliations with my students and staff? I would claim, a pretty darn good one!

Although the essence of schooling is to build a better society, I struggle as an aspiring vice-principal. I must navigate my self-identity within a hegemonic and political hetero educational world—sad, but true—where sexual identity might negatively influence my legitimacy as leader in a social climate that assumes public school administrators are heterosexual. On the other hand, disclosing my LGBTQ membership will hopefully serve to protect, help, and/or save those who seek like-minded others to find a place in this hetero-normative society, to connect and to share narratives. As a teacher, I have carefully minded my words to not give away my queer identity. At times, however, to help students struggling with their own homosexuality, I have shared my queer identity knowing that this secret, *my secret*, would be safe as they too were empathetic and aware of our shared socio-locales. As an *out* administrator, to have LGBTQ students realize the potential of professional successes—all the while identifying as queer—would hopefully empower them to continue and be self-proud.

My stories will inform my work and guide my role as an administrator. When one juggles the stresses of the administrative position, while keeping one's personal life separate, it is difficult. I believe that as an administrator, I am charged with the maintenance of the norm, what makes the school run smoothly, so as to ensure the successful futures of my students. The reality is that such duties do not stop there. As an administrator, I need to be empathetic to the struggles of staff, students, and families as it is critical in order to create a safe environment that is all-inclusive. Also, it is imperative to have the ability to understand what it is like to be marginalized as it appears to be a common thread among minority groups, including an invisible queer minority, because we have experience being on the outside looking in. As students, teachers, and community members seek answers, justifications, and reasoning from me as their administrator, I have to admit that my social, queer identity is then intertwined with their realities, their narratives, as I make decisions for the betterment of students.

Moreover, there is a correlation between the responsibilities of my being an educational leader with my social identity. Basically, I am further affected by my personal lived experiences while interpreting the discourses of the educational language. With beginning at the core of my experiences, experiences empower and enrich the ways that I, a queer administrator, interpret school as a whole part of society. Freire (1992) argues that the leader must not be ignorant, underestimate, or reject any of the knowledge of lived experience when it comes to school. To his point, my lived experiences have a direct effect on how the school is run, what decisions I make, and why I make decisions. He also refers to the freedom of the oppressed by freeing the oppressor. I have come to realize that I am self-oppressed. Basically, I am my own oppressor with voluntary self-declination of my enriched queer history, my queer narrative that defines me as an LGBTQ person. I must see myself as an agent of equity through expressions of empathy to my teachers and students. My role, therefore, shall allow students and teachers to advocate for their personal narratives. My work is about developing teachers and students who will contribute to the advancement of the human condition at home, in schools, and in the community; all this through the understanding and reflecting on my personal queer history, which makes up my leadership narrative. I need to delve into my self-experiences and move forward to ensure a school based on socially just actions and equity beyond equality. As a result, the process of self-reflection is a critical aspect of identifying myself in relation to those involved in leading and learning.

My queer identity is my reference to the composed meanings that I attach to my role as a future vice-principal. Understandably, contexts differ with each educator's and leader's role and responsibility in their perspective schools as each and every vice-principal has a different background, travelled a different road, had a different home. I find myself questioning Polonius' advice (as written by Shakespeare)—to thy own self be true. Do I rely on my queer narrative to shape my leadership experiences, or do I assimilate into the hetero-masses? Obviously, with the continual fight against heterosexist discourse (assumed heterosexuality in books, media, language, et al), I feel that I must engage in democratic—almost activist positioned—practices. Although legislative history was made in Ontario with the Accepting Schools Act, allowing the Ontario public education system to delve deeper into the plight of social-inclusion and social justice for Lesbian, Gay, Bisexual, Trans-sexual, and Queer (LGBTQ) youths and peoples. It is my hope that such strides will positively affect and support LGBTQ administrators seeking a place to be supported and safe in their work places, their schools. I can rest assured that as a leader, a leader who identifies as gay, I shall utilize my queer leadership identity to continue to change the hetero status quo.

"A socially just learning environment is
the raison d'être for all of public education
and should figure centrally in the
pedagogical practice of all teachers."

THE HIGH SCHOOL MUSIC ROOM AS A SAFE PLACE AND SPACE

John L. Vitale

*"If we are to achieve a richer culture, rich in contrasting values,
we must recognize the whole gamut of human potentialities,
and so we weave a less arbitrary social fabric, one in which each
diverse human gift will find a fitting place."* –Margaret Mead

Any type of bullying in high school is a serious issue. Bullying based exclusively on sexual identity, however, is particularly cruel and painful. In *The 2005 National School Climate Survey: The Experiences of Lesbian, Gay, Bisexual and Transgender Youth*, Kosciw & Diaz (2005) say that "actual or perceived sexual orientation and gender expression" was the second most common reason for bullying. Moreover, the numerous suicides of gay teens is clear evidence that high schools are obliged to protect and champion the rights of all students, particularly at such a young and vulnerable age.

With well over a decade of teaching experience in the secondary-school music classroom, bullying was simply not tolerated in my classroom. This zero-tolerance approach, however, was not so much a mindset, but rather a philosophy rooted in the very nature of a quality music program. That is, music education is not about music for the sake of the music. Rather, it is about the medium of music as a source of social and communal opportunities, where students build character, overcome adversity, develop integrity, and learn to be respectful, cooperative, and productive citizens. In addition, such opportunities also provide a safe and trustworthy medium for the many students trying to cope with the pressures, tensions, and anxieties of adolescence. Of special significance in my past pedagogical practice, however, were the male students who were struggling with their sexual identity. For these students, the entire music program was a safe place and space (physically, emotionally, and spiritually) to connect, bond, and cultivate friendships. In this essay, I would like to share two important events from my past pedagogical experience that illustrate the "safe place and space" perspective. First is a story called "The Music Room is Always Open," and second is a story called "Building Community through Performance."

> "Every now and then one paints a picture that seems to have opened a door and serves as a stepping stone to other things."
> –Pablo Picasso

THE MUSIC ROOM IS ALWAYS OPEN

As an optional subject, there are many challenges involved with the operation of a high-school music program. It is difficult to tame the demanding nature of orchestral music unless one has healthy student numbers and extra-curricular participation. This demanding reality simply means that music teachers have no choice but to make all music courses fun, engaging, and socially just; otherwise, students simply do not take courses in music. Even with healthy student numbers, high-school music programs are expensive. Buying and maintaining instruments and the sheer cost of sheet music are enough to make any school principal cringe. This is why the music program has to be audible and visible at every possible school and community event as a means to justify the commitment to funding. Hence, the music program is a huge undertaking in terms of providing extracurricular opportunities for students before school, during lunch hour, after school, and even on weeknights and weekends.

I soon discovered, however, that a viable method of providing an engaging and extra-curricular infused program was to implement an open-door policy. Hence, I always maintained and championed an open-door policy for all music students, who were welcome in my classroom at all times throughout the day (before, during, and after school). This open-door policy was feasible as most music classrooms have a number of soundproof practice rooms for students to meet, socialize, practice, and study. Even though my open-door policy raised a few eyebrows by some administrators, I justified it with the argument that music education in high school is not about one course, but rather inclusion in a larger community of music-makers who come together for the betterment of society. The music room, therefore, is the very heart and soul of the community.

Year after year, it didn't take long for new students to realize that the music room was a safe place and space to come together and build relationships with other students. As the years passed, I noticed that a number of distinct student groups, which I always referred to as "little communities," consistently used and benefitted from my open-door policy. I had several groups of Emo students, students more interested in Rap music and urban culture, and students struggling with their sexual identity. It was always the latter group, however, that consistently spent the most time in the music classroom. Although I taught in three different high schools throughout my career, none of these schools had a support network for gay students. Hence, the gay students in my music program simply created their own support groups—true acts of courage, resilience, and valor. These students met on a daily basis and often ate lunch together, shared their love of music by practicing, and even did their schoolwork. More importantly, however, they had an opportunity to convene free of prejudice and prejudgment, conditions which often did not exist in the hallways or cafeteria. Considering that 86% of LGBT had experienced harassment at school (as referenced in *The Struggles of Coming Out in High School* by Goldring & Hopen, 2012), a prejudice-free environment is critically important. Although I cultivated an open-door policy, I truly believe that it was the music program specifically, and the Arts program generally, that fostered a socially just learning environment. In sum, a socially just learning environment is the raison d'être for all of public education and should figure centrally in the pedagogical practice of all teachers.

"An ounce of performance is worth pounds of promises."
–Mae West

BUILDING COMMUNITY THROUGH PERFORMANCE

As previously mentioned, music education is about the medium of music as a source of social and communal opportunities. Musical performance, however, is the vehicle that drives social and communal opportunities. Performance is the culminating event of weeks and even months of practice, and is also an important foray into human interaction and communication.

My students participated in many different types of musical performances ranging from school events to local parades and community happenings, and even national and international music festivals. This diverse pool of performances and venues created a diverse number of opportunities for students to develop and build character not only as musicians and performing artists who shared common goals, but also as students who were searching for a sense of individuality and identity. In many ways, the days leading up to performances (extra rehearsals and last minute preparations), as well as the travel involved, was the very pinnacle of the musical community coming together. Students were working, interacting, and socializing with one another all under the pressure, thrills, and excitement of performance day. It was like a super-charged version my open-door policy. It was during these times that the "little communities" within the larger musical community had an opportunity to convene, connect, and bond. Evidence of this was particularly apparent during international music festivals, which created a myriad of opportunities for student input pre, during, and post festival. Once again, it was the students struggling with their sexual identity who not only supported and comforted one another, but also showed brave leadership and refined organizational skills with regards to the international music festivals, and in many ways, became the principal coordinators of these trips. In fact, year after year, these trips became a significant marketing and advertising tool for my music program that made waves well outside of the high school.

PRE-TRIP

Students who were struggling with their sexual identity were always well represented on my music student council. Hence, they always showed tremendous leadership in the planning and preparation of overnight trips, including the researching of various festivals, planning trip details, and looking for ways to keep costs reasonable for all students. These pre-trip tasks and responsibilities provided numerous opportunities for these students to assemble in the music room and work together, as well as engage in fundraising opportunities during lunch.

DURING THE TRIP

Students who were struggling with their sexual identity were a collective and communal force during the trip. They helped with a wide range of tasks, including the organization of last minute performance details and taking pictures on behalf of music student council and the yearbook committee. More importantly, however, these students also enjoyed the privilege of socializing and appreciating free time outside of the rigid conditions of high school, but within the comfortable and flexible boundaries of the larger musical community. This was particularly noticeable during visits to popular tourist destinations in the various cities that we sojourned in, such as Quincy Market in Boston, MA, as well as Millennium Park in Chicago, IL. At these locations, these students were able to experience new sites, freely mingle, and have fun in a socially just environment.

POST TRIP

Even when the trip was over, these students continued to meet regularly in the music room to promote and politicize the laurels of our international performance experience. They consistently organized photos of the trip for the school yearbook, made DVDs of our performances for all the music students, and announced the success of our trip during morning announcements. They would even start pitching ideas for next year's trip.

> *"Injustice anywhere is a threat to justice everywhere."*
> –Martin Luther King, Jr.

CONCLUSION

In many ways, writing this essay has been an exercise in reflective practice for me as I have earnestly reflected upon my past pedagogical experiences as a high-school music teacher. This reflective process has been very cathartic and therapeutic for me, and has significantly informed my current pedagogical practice as a teacher educator. Moreover, I have come to realize that I had a very symbiotic and reciprocal relationship with many of the gay students I have taught over the years. Through the medium of music education and building community, I was able to provide a safe place and space for students who were struggling with their sexual identity to connect, bond, and cultivate friendships. In turn, my music program received tremendous support, respect, and contributions from these students, which created a viable, successful, and thriving community of music makers. It proved to be an effective, prolific, and socially just relationship that continues to enhance my knowledge base not only as an educator, but also as a human being.

> "So that two boys may feel
> comfortable kissing; so that two girls
> may fall in love without fear."

TO KISS A BOY: WORKING
TO MAKE SCHOOLS SAFE
FOR QUEER TEENS

Julian Kitchen

On my way home from school one spring afternoon in grade ten, I dropped my bag and out tumbled several books. Phil, who was in one of my classes, helped gather my belongings. As we walked together, I felt a spark of energy, a special connection with a beautiful, gentle boy who was like me. In the days that followed, I imagined spending time with Phil, gazing into his blue eyes, and kissing him. But I was scared to let down my guard. I avoided seeing Phil again during my time in high school.

My adolescence in 1970s Toronto is a collection of stories in which little happened, with this being a notable example.

I was a normal enough grade ten student: gawky yet bright, an outsider in a new school. My gay identity was safely locked away, my yearnings held in check, and my mask firmly fixed. I carried on well enough as I progressed through the grades. By grade thirteen,

I had gained confidence, demonstrated academic success, edited the school newspaper, rose in social status, and dated girls.

Yet my brief encounter with Phil haunts me still. Recently, as I read several young adult novels about gay youth, I cried and cried and cried. I cried for lost innocence. I cried for feeling alone and lonely. For learning to be guarded about my feelings. For not having a normal adolescence. For not having kissed a boy. I cried even though I have become a happy and fulfilled person with a great job, close friends, caring family, and the love of my partner, now husband, of thirty years.

I cried because I had made the right choice. If we had entered into an awkward, fumbling teen romance, it would have ended in disaster. I did not have the strength of character to deal with the experience, and the world around us would have reacted cruelly.

I cried because alternative endings remain difficult for most lesbian, gay, bisexual, and transgender teens today. I know, through my work as an educator, that social norms and bullying continue to make it difficult to live and love openly in schools. As a result, queer adolescents are more prone to depression and self-harm. Harassment and bullying led to the suicides of Tyler Clementi, Jamie Hubley, and many others.

As an adult, I struggled for years to love myself and to be authentic in my relationships and work. As a teacher in the 1990s, I was open to my colleagues about my identity and offered support to several gay students. When I began teaching at the university level in 1999, I chose to be *out* to both colleagues and education students. I felt a duty to be a role model to aspiring teachers, queer and straight. When I became a professor of education responsible for teaching about professionalism and law, I drew on my experiences as a gay man when discussing human rights, teachers as role models, and bullying in schools. I also facilitated Positive Space workshops designed to increase awareness and acceptance on campus. I was satisfied that I was making a difference.

Then I met a high-school teacher who ran a gay straight alliance. I was surprised to learn that life for queer teens today is often as hard as it was for my generation. For some, knowing who they are earlier makes it harder to wait until graduation for things to get better. They continue to be exposed to homophobic comments, and bullying seems worse. This straight teacher inspired and challenged me to do more.

Since then, I have become more active in queer issues in education. I now present workshops on sexual diversity issues to all aspiring secondary teachers on campus. Feedback has been very positive, with most education students interested in learning more about lesbian, gay, bisexual, and trans issues, and about the experiences of students in schools. Many expressed commitment to addressing homophobia when they witness it in schools, and some indicated that they were prepared to make equity for gays and lesbians a priority in their work. I have also extended my research interests to include gay straight alliances and am writing about my experiences as a queer educator.

The memory of this incident with Phil serves as a poignant reminder of what it means to be young and queer. It motivates me to help teachers understand the needs of LGBT youth and learn ways in which teachers can make schools safer and more welcoming. So that two boys may feel comfortable kissing; so that two girls may fall in love without fear.

"These programs help us to reach our
goal: to create Generation H."

3-H CLUBS FOR SEXUAL AND
GENDER MINORITY YOUTH:
WORKING AT iSMSS TO
MAKE IT BETTER NOW

André P. Grace

*[We have] two important tasks. One is to join the fight to strip away
the discriminatory and oppressive values attached to masculinity and
femininity. The other is to defend gender freedom—the right of each
individual to express their gender in any way they choose, whether
feminine, androgynous, masculine, or any point on the spectrum
between. And that includes the right to gender ambiguity and
gender contradiction. It's equally important that each person have
the right to define, determine, or change their sex in any way they
choose—whether female, male, or any point on the spectrum between.
And that includes the right to physical ambiguity and contradiction.*
–Leslie Feinberg, 1996

Feinberg's words, in the book *Trans Gender Warriors: Making
History from Joan of Arc to Dennis Rodman*, embody the working
philosophy of the Institute for Sexual Minority Studies and
Services (iSMSS) in the Faculty of Education at the University of

Alberta. Our intervention and outreach work is about opening up spaces where sexuality and gender can exist in all their rich complexities. It is also about helping sexual and gender minority (SGM) youth, including lesbian, gay, bisexual, transgender, Two-Spirit Aboriginal, and intersexual individuals, explore possibilities. Our goal is to affirm the pathways SGM youth choose on the road to being *Happy, Healthy, and Hopeful*. In this regard, iSMSS develops and implements year-round educational and cultural programming that makes the world better *now* for SGM youth and their families. In essence, iSMSS operates 3-H clubs that help SGM youth be happy, healthy, and hopeful. This work is an engagement in critically progressive social education that focuses on (1) youth agency in an emancipatory context and (2) training and development for teachers, healthcare providers, youth workers, and other caring professionals. The iSMSS research highlights the fact that, with mentors, resources, and supports, SGM youth are better able to survive and thrive despite the daily stressors, risks, and barriers they encounter in their schools, families, and communities.

In Canada, SGM youth often experience schooling and healthcare services, as well as government and legal services, as a loose and disconnected menagerie that is insufficient to address the stressors and risks associated with living with adversity and trauma induced by homo/bi/transphobia, which comprise ignorance- and fear-induced responses to sexual and gender differences. For SGM youth, key stressors can include (1) neglect by such significant adults as parents, school administrators, teachers, school counsellors, and family doctors and other healthcare professionals; and (2) abuse and victimization through symbolic violence (such as anti-gay name calling and graffiti) and physical violence (such as bullying that includes assault and battery). Key risks can include truancy, quitting school, and running away; developing alcohol and drug addictions, emotional problems, and mental illness; and suicide ideation, attempts, and completions. These dire realities indicate the urgent need for greater synchronicity in research, policy, and practice arenas so stakeholders in Canadian education and healthcare can collectively help these youth to build capacity (a solutions approach), moving away from unconstructive strategies focused on stigmatizing or fixing these youth as a source of social disorder (a problems approach). At iSMSS, creating this synchronicity to nurture SGM youth is our primary focus. As iSMSS research clearly demonstrates, SGM youth who set realistic goals and engage in problem solving with people who are supportive become self-reliant and more resilient, even in cases of complete family and societal rejection.

iSMSS helps hundreds of SGM youth annually. Our 3-H clubs include Camp fYrefly, which are summer residential, community-based leadership camps for SGM youth, which are held each summer in Alberta and Saskatchewan. 3-H clubs also take form as fYrefly in Schools, a program that is offered throughout the school year to educate students about the pervasiveness and impacts of homo/bi/transphobia. This program is juxtaposed with our Youth Intervention and Outreach Worker program that includes the Family Resilience Project. This project utilizes a holistic model to deliver supports to SGM youth and their families as they construct them by providing social learning opportunities via workshops, group meetings, and networking coupled with offering integrated university, government, and community supports and services. All families can benefit from learning about resilience research as well as specific resources and supports that can improve their SGM child's overall health and wellbeing. In sum, these programs help us to reach our goal: to create Generation H; that is, happy, healthy, and hopeful SGM youth.

> "Schools are predominantly conservative spaces where the status quo is upheld and unquestioned. I challenge my students to be agents of change and to examine the world and their experiences through a variety of lenses."

LESSONS ON AFFIRMING IDENTITIES IN THE CLASSROOM

Christine Cho

It wasn't like I didn't know how conservative teachers could be. I had been an elementary school teacher myself since 1994. Still, one can always be optimistic as I was on a particular evening in 2006. It was the first night of a university course I was teaching to aspiring, future educators on socio-cultural contexts of teaching.

Briefly, the course required students to "consider how inclusive teaching strategies can help us to resist the stereotypes, prejudices, indifference, and power structures that promote inequality and disadvantage students and teachers alike." Many students in the course were obtaining their Bachelor of Education degree part-time in the hopes of becoming an elementary teacher and making a career change while they still maintained their current career in the day and took their classes at night and on the weekends. The students in the course tended to be older than the students enrolled in the full-time program. Typically, they had been out of school for a few years, many had children of their own. In this particular class there were no men enrolled. I knew challenges were afoot on the first night of class as I went through the syllabus and shared the many topics the course would be addressing. When I mentioned homophobia, a student piped up and declared, "What if you don't believe in that?" The words were out of my mouth faster than I could blink when I responded, "Oh, it's not like Santa Claus. It's not a matter of believing or not. You will have students in your class who are gay, and you need to affirm who they are in your classroom." The challenge, for me, became how to make that happen with a group of very resistant and sometimes hostile people. On my course evaluations, some students commented that I was "shoving homosexuality down their throats."

This was the first time I taught this particular course. I constantly work at interrogating my biases and look to people who can help me identify the spaces of inequity in the taken-for-granted. I teach to provoke and to make classrooms better places where everyone's identity is affirmed. In the realm of education, I live in a privileged body. I am reflective of 80% of teachers: white, middle class, female, and born in Canada. English is my first language. I self-identify as an ally. My colleague, a visible and out lesbian, commented on the importance that I do this work in the faculty. She maintained that when she teaches about homophobia it is seen as her "agenda" and often dismissed. I could bring a different perspective.

Over the years, I refined the course and my teaching of the content. I went from teaching one section of thirty students to teaching four sections of the course (or 120 students). The content of my course covered numerous aspects of social location, and sexual orientation was one perspective but still remained the most contentious. I invited a guest speaker from the Rainbow Coalition to do an activity on coming out so future teachers could get a better perspective on the importance of support systems. She ran through the alphabet soup of LGBTTIQQ2SA and engaged in a frank and often humorous question and answer session. We talked about safe spaces and not outing a student. I showed them the films *It's Elementary* and *It Gets Better Canada*. We read books, watched films, and engaged in discussion. However, the work and the conversations still remained in the realm of theory, and the students lamented that they couldn't and probably wouldn't do this kind of work in an elementary classroom.

Finally I embarked on my biggest project to date. I enlisted the help of a local school and arranged to have ninety of my students teach anti-oppression lessons to all the students from Kindergarten to grade six. I was asking my students to create a lesson they would actually teach at an elementary school to address racism, sexism, ableism, genderism, etc. They would work in a group and choose their topic. The topic that was both most feared and most sought out was homophobia. One third of the students in the course were preparing to be Catholic educators. There was the greatest desire amongst these students to have the sexual orientation topic. One student commented that she knew she would not be able to have the same kind of conversation in the Catholic system, so she wanted to take the opportunity to do so in the public system and perhaps develop some skills and strategies that she could transfer into a Catholic school one day.

And so, for three days in January, eager and somewhat scared future educators, taking the opportunity to see if they really could put theory into practice, infiltrated a sleepy little school in a small city two hours outside of Toronto. The students were armed with texts such as "And Tango Makes Three" or "Heather has 2 Mommies." Some showed the *It Gets Better Canada* video. While some classes were having lessons on racism and some on sexism, this story is about the lessons on homophobia. And toward that end, several interesting things happened.

First, the teacher in the grade three to four class was not a full-time contract teacher, but he was there on a long-term occasional contract. In other words, he didn't have the same level of job security as the other teachers in the school. When I stopped by to see how my students were doing, he stepped out into the hallway with me. I was expecting upset, outrage, and possibly anger. Instead, he expressed his gratitude. He indicated that he didn't feel he could personally begin this conversation with his class, but my students opened a door for him, and they began a conversation that he was thrilled and willing to continue after we left.

Next, I went into the grade two classroom. The grade two teacher had joined the students on the carpet, and with tears in her eyes told her class that her brother was gay, and she'd never shared that with her students before. It had never come up in conversation. A little boy in the class announced that his aunt was now his uncle. My students looked at me with stunned silence. They were not expecting this. Normalizing conversations were beginning to happen. The crossing guard reported to the principal the next day that students were walking home and talking about having two moms or two dads like it was okay!

Of course, there was backlash, too. One of the teachers in the school questioned my motives and "agenda." I directed her to the curriculum and the Ontario policy documents on Equity and Diversity and reminded her that we had sent the lesson plans to her a month prior to our arrival. She tried her best to thwart the lesson, proclaiming the equipment the students needed to show their video wasn't working. The principal intervened and got the lesson rolling again.

Before the students went into the school, I obtained ethics approval to collect their written reflections on the experience. I share some of those now (all names are pseudonyms). John wrote, "As educators in this classroom it was not my obligation to preach to these students about accepting people with a homosexual identity, but rather, I spoke with these students about the value of respect and how, even though they may not agree with a homosexual identity, showing respect and stewardship can ultimately make our society a better place regardless of our interests." He also commented, "I feel that our group made tremendous strides in getting students to think about the topic and being aware of the words we use on the playground."

Matilda, who was very resistant at first, commented, "I was uncomfortable with this particular age group, as I did not think it was my job to discuss this matter with them, not at this age." At the end she declared, "These children in their own special way taught me that they were not too young, and that no matter the age, topic areas such as homophobia *should* be discussed in the classroom without discomfort on anyone's part."

The weather was particularly bad on the second day of our lessons. Buses were cancelled and perhaps half of the elementary students didn't make it to school that day. On the third day, all students were back in school. One class, who had had a lesson on homophobia on the snow day were now having a lesson on ableism. My students began their lesson and were interrupted by a student who wanted to know more about what had been discussed the day before. He had lots of questions about sexual orientation that he wanted to ask, and my students, who said they chose ableism because they thought it was the least contentious, discovered something important about being a teacher. As Abbey noted, "Spill over from prior lessons is very likely to occur, and whether you were the one to teach it, or another teacher who has your class for a period, or in the previous year, you have to be prepared to deal with this spill over." They realized that as a teacher you have to develop a repertoire of skills and the capacity to discuss all issues. And on this day, they rose to the challenge.

One of the biggest misconceptions my students had was that children are not aware of their sexual orientation at a young age. Some expressed a perception that young children only know straight people. Working with the elementary school students began to quash some of these perceptions and challenge some unexamined beliefs. Nancy made the following assertion: "I realized it is uncomfortable that elementary teachers do not teach to primary level students sooner on topics like homophobia, since young learners are impressionable and vulnerable to peer pressure."

Talking about oppression and the ramifications of oppressive structures only goes so far. Many teachers, like me, are drawn from the dominant group. They live in privileged bodies. They, without having to think about it, put the photos of their spouses and their children on their desks at school. Our schools are places where great harm has occurred for LGBTTIQQ2S youth and teachers alike. Schools are predominantly conservative spaces where the status quo is upheld and unquestioned. I challenge my students to be agents of change and to examine the world and their experiences through a variety of lenses. Fear immobilizes, but experience might motivate. I have my students work in groups so they can find allies and understand that anti-oppression work cannot be done alone or in isolation. I hope that the work I do with future teachers presses them to examine their taken-for-granted and to recognize the fluidity of identity and the complexity of every life and to open up spaces so they have the courage and the tools to make schools sites of affirmation as opposed to places of conformity.

"Together with our students, we were
able to create *queer* possibilities
for change— in ourselves,
in our students, and in and beyond
our school environment."

QUEERLY HOPEFUL:
MOMENTS OF EDUCATIONAL
ACTIVISM BEYOND THE GSA

Vanessa Russell AND Louise Azzarello

P icture this. The soggy day outside has left its watermark on the students during class. There's barely a beating pulse in the room. They've been discussing sexuality issues for about a week now: violence and healthy relationships, STDs and STIs, queer and gender issues. Their teacher decides a sure-fire way to bring heart paddles to the collective. *Sex Jeopardy!* Students work together in teams and find creative ways to articulate their ideas. Jason and Yukyung start to form teams. Final configurations are uneven with Jason's team one person short. He remembers something really important. Every time a new student calls their school's curriculum leader "*Miss*," she tells them to call her by her first name or Dr. Russell but never

"*Miss.*" When questioned, "Doctor?" she'll yabber on that her dissertation was about "gay stuff." So Jason gets this great idea. "I'm getting the Doctor of Gayness for our team. We'll win for sure in the queer category." Jason runs into the office and grabs Vanessa from behind her desk.

Oasis Alternative Secondary School opened its doors in Toronto in the early 1990s. The school's raison d'être was to re-engage students who are the most poorly served by the education system. These are the students who have felt the deep and enduring impact of multiple forms of oppression—many of whom live in poverty, are street-involved, homeless, and struggle with mental illness and/or addiction. Many people have heard about Oasis solely because it is the parent school of the Triangle Program which is still Canada's only secondary school classroom for queer youth. What most people do not realize is that Oasis has yet another satellite program, the Arts and Social Change (ASC) Program, which delivers an arts-based/equity curriculum and pedagogy. We are writing this chapter as a reflection on a moment in time when we landed in the same school. Being aware of our long histories of teacher activism, we were thrilled for the opportunity to finally work with one another. Together with our students, we were able to create *queer* possibilities for change—in ourselves, in our students, and in and beyond our school environment. As with any individual and systemic change work, there were unique challenges. Deficit notions about the students who end up at the ASC impacted our work every day. Some educators suggest that our students are "too diverse," "too homophobic," "too disengaged," "too *out there*"—with parents who just don't care.

Here are a number of "stories" informed by our own social locations. We are both White, middle-class, fifty-something women. Vanessa is queer, Louise a straight ally (and of course, like everyone else, we are so much more). Our stories are related to pedagogy, curriculum, and school community that move beyond notions of safety for queer youth to one that re-engages students while supporting them to understand their own worth and value, their human rights, and their civic and social justice responsibilities. Within this context, it is not surprising that many of our students chose to come out during their journey with us at the ASC.

OPPRESSION: MORE THAN BULLYING

We developed and team-taught an Equity and Social Change course as a way to engage students to critically analyze and understand more deeply the systems of power and oppression in their daily lives and to consider actions for social change. It was a difficult and sometimes messy process. We developed and adapted powerful strategies to give students the time and space to make connections through curriculum resources, popular culture texts and personal narratives. We began to understand how much we needed to slow down in order to give our students the time to absorb and work through the material.

We worked with the students to understand that homophobia and other forms of discrimination are larger than name-calling. We used the *Power Triangle/Mapping Oppression*[1] activity to help students understand that every form of oppression rests upon oppressive ideas, individual actions, and institutions (each forming an apex of a triangle). We explored the ways in which oppressive ideas reinforce oppressive actions which further reinforce institutional manifestations of oppression. For example, the pervasive belief/stereotype that all gay men are pedophiles reinforces particular actions that marginalize, ridicule, and bully gay men. In schools, these particular actions reinforce the institutional lack of visibility of out gay teachers. Of course, this conceptual framework works in reverse as well. The invisibility of out gay male teachers reinforces negative actions and ideas about queers. Homophobia is easy when people think they've never *met one* before.

[1] The Power Triangle was originally conceived by Barbara Thomas (1987) and later adapted by Tim McCaskell (2005).

We worked with the *Power Triangle* in our course, and students came to understand the processes with which ideas and actions are supported by systems such as education, the law, and religion. Students began to develop a language for their own experiences of oppression and marginalization and to see beyond themselves. Most importantly, the *Power Triangle* opened a window that allowed us to discuss activism and social transformation. The good news that we share with students is that we can pick up tools to challenge each element of oppression: curriculum to challenge oppressive ideas; rules/policy to challenge individual expressions of oppression in the form of bullying and harassment; and community outreach/ political activism to challenge the system.

We used the *Power Triangle* to analyse a number of texts, posters, films, music, and current events. To move from the realm of theory, we grounded our work in the body. The body is an organic way to really link identity categories. We live and breathe more than one social identity at any time. Pedagogically, we refused to teach about race one week, gender another, and social class after that. As well, working with students through their bodies helps them to understand that access to power can be enhanced or limited in the ways we choose to perform and/or represent ourselves. Working with the students to learn a variety of performances gave them options.

In one interactive exercise connected to the *Power Triangle*, we asked our students to create life-sized bodies and to somehow represent the impact of oppression upon that body. We asked students to consider the ways that oppression impacts us physically. Students created a visual representation using the shape of a body as their canvas.

Antoine, a young Black man, represented oppression as bullet holes through his body. Fatima, a young biracial woman imprinted a series of feet, hands, and Xs across various body parts, illustrating pressure, pushing, and repression. Tina, a young East Asian woman created what looked like a huge yellow blob to represent her body.

Within that blob, she drew a cut-out body attached to a pair of scissors. She explained that when people see her, all they see is her Asian-ness. She felt that she needed to do hard work continually with each new relationship in order to cut herself out and beyond the yellow so that people could see all of who she was, not in spite of, but because of her Asian identity. Included in her drawing was a pink cellphone which she believed gave her a connection with her non-Asian friends. Michael, a young White man designated gifted as well as struggling with a learning disability, represented classism as an empty stomach with a "tapeworm of poverty." Beneath the heel of his "boot of machismo," lay the "dog shit of family values"—his push back against homophobia and heterosexism. All of the artwork produced by our students was extremely moving and powerful.

We recognize that in this work we asked our students—some of the most marginalized across our school district—to consider not only their own oppression but also the ways in which we are all complicit in the oppression of others. We carefully used the body in part as a vehicle to move our students beyond their own autobiographies. Like any anti-oppression educators worth their salt, we started with the lives of our students. We managed, fairly successfully, to have them critically analyze the oppressive forces in their own lives. However, when we asked them to look at their own privilege, they freaked out. Supporting our students through this crisis of learning was worth it. It helped them to develop a shared language, cultural currency, and an understanding of how we could push the system together in concrete and *legal* ways to make their lives less of a struggle.

STORY ONE AS TOLD BY LOUISE:
"YA KNOW, THAT ANGRY KID?"

One day after break, Susan, who was in her third semester at Oasis, went to Vanessa and said, "Hey, you know that new kid? Short, diamond earrings, angry looking? Well he keeps using fucked-up language. He says gay this and fag that. I've talked to him but he won't listen. You gotta do something before I do!" Susan had successfully completed our course and had come out as both bisexual and Aboriginal through the work. Vanessa assured Susan that we would talk to this student but that she needed to remember that unlearning homophobia and heterosexism is a process for everyone, herself included.

We talked privately with this new student, Rico. Rico had spent some time in a youth detention centre and shared some of his personal experiences with us in class. He had just begun to articulate his anger at the abuse related to his Latino identity that he had faced from other youth and workers. We were sensitive that he was at a critical and early stage in understanding his own oppression. We did not want to shame him. At the same time, we needed to address his homophobia. We told Rico we had some good and bad news for him. He asked for the good news first—unusual but I think he knew what the bad news was. We told him we really appreciated his improved attendance from his previous records and that we were thrilled he was participating in class. We asked him if he knew what the bad news might be. "Yeah," he responded with his head down and eyes averted. "My language." I asked him to explain. Head still down, he said, "I shouldn't say 'fag.'" I asked why not. He slowly raised his head and looked at us earnestly, "Because you're a bunch of lesbians?" It's important to understand that Rico's response was *not* delivered with any hostility but rather with a sweet sense of resignation—as if to say, I know what I did was not okay. Because of his genuine accountability, we were able to use humour to get to the heart of the issue. Vanessa responded, "Well Louise isn't queer." And there it was, my straightness for the world to see. I laughed out loud and said, "Vanessa, you outted me." By acknowledging my straightness, Vanessa disrupted Rico's notion that anyone challenging homophobia must be queer. This assumption is long-standing with deep roots among students and other educators with whom I have worked. Sexuality matters for both teachers and students in a number of complex ways that intersect with other social locations like race, gender, class, and ability.

Returning to the *Power Triangle*, we began to help Rico understand that it was bigger than us, that his homophobic action was part of a system of oppression that hurt our community—including his peer who came to us and brought the incident to our attention. With time, it was clear that our work together gave him the opportunities and the breathing room to see beyond himself. At the end of the semester, he quietly approached Vanessa and with raw honesty thanked her for all she had done for him both in class and beyond by reaching out and working with his family during some enormously tough times.

STORY TWO AS TOLD BY VANESSA: WITHOUT SAYING A WORD, "OOH THAT'S SO NASTY!"

After working together as a class for several months, students from our equity course began to adopt a shared language about power, privilege, discrimination, and social justice. They not only had the ability to wrap their heads around very complex and paradoxical issues, they began to depend on one another. They depended on one another to wake up and get their butts to school on time and to engage meaningfully with the course content and with the school community. In a parallel and similar experience in English class, students were learning about different social movements in Canada and the United States. They worked their way through civil rights, first- and second-wave feminism, and had landed squarely upon gay liberation. Their English teacher wanted to show her students the Hollywood film *Milk* based on the life of Harvey Milk.[2] We thought this was a great idea and decided to combine classes in order to watch

---

[2] Harvey Milk was the first openly gay city supervisor of San Francisco, making him the first gay man elected to public office in the United States. In 1978, he and San Francisco Mayor George Moscone were assassinated by another city supervisor.

the movie. We had seen the film when it first came out in theatres. We did not remember any graphic sexual scenes and checked the film rating to be sure.

The class was packed with students as we began to watch the film. I had forgotten that there were a number of scenes portraying men kissing men in darkened rooms and a certain amount of sexual innuendo. I looked around our own darkened room and saw students looking down, squirming in their seats, and trying hard to stifle their giggles. I found myself squirming too. I guess being queer myself did not protect me from my own discomfort. I wasn't entirely sure what to do, but I had to turn the spotlight on the elephant in the room. I whispered to my colleague to stop the film. Looking surprised and uncomfortable herself, she asked, "Really?" Slow as molasses, we turned off the projector and turned up the lights. The students began to grumble and asked, "What's going on?"

This was a teachable moment—for myself, for my colleague, and for the students in front of us. I invoked the previous teaching and learning about the power triangle, the concepts of discourse and the body. "Remember that thing we call discourse? Well, your bodies are screaming at me and here's what they're saying." I explained that with every giggle, with every downward looking face, and with every squirm, they were saying, "This is not normal. Men shouldn't be kissing men. Homosexuality is wrong." They didn't deny that's how they felt. I described that these ideas are part of the soup we marinade in all the time and that this is the very process that marginalizes certain groups of people and privileges others. Straight folks get to be normal. My students were screaming at me in and through their bodies—without saying a word, without using a putdown. I asked the students to let their bodies teach them. Their bodies might help them understand just how deeply homophobia and heterosexism run—even when we think we're past it.

Teacher identity is critical to this story. When Louise and I worked together, three of the five ASC teaching staff, including myself, identified as queer. Not only did we happen to be queer, we were out. While the curricular and pedagogical approaches of our work can be taken up in any school, the identities of the ASC staff—public and private—at the moment that we taught together, sets an important framework for our stories. At the end of the film, the students applauded, and one put his hand up declaring, "Gay people are the bomb[3]." At that moment, I knew we had another mountain to climb. Marginalizing the 'Other' includes exoticizing them, exoticizing me. This was a good reminder that equity education, including anti-homophobia education, is an ongoing process which never, ever ends—Argh!

STORY THREE AS TOLD BY LOUISE: IT'S NOT ALL ABOUT ME. STUDENTS MOVE BEYOND SELF

Having the opportunity to combine classes and work as a community was one of the ways we were able to deepen the understanding of particular anti-oppression concepts for all students. The visual arts teacher designed an activity that explored archetypes and stereotypes using photographer Cindy Sherman's work, *Untitled Film Stills*, as a prompt. In this series of sixty-nine photographs, Sherman embodies different clichéd representations of women of the film noir genre. After discussing terms, the photographs, the power of images and representation, we asked students to pick names of other students from a hat. We then asked each student to act out or represent the person whose name they had chosen. We were able to engage in such a risky activity only because these students had been together more than a semester and had developed a tight bond.[4]

During this activity, Antoine picked Marcus's name. Marcus was an out queer, femme young man who came to us from the Triangle

---

[3] "Bomb" is the vernacular used by our students meaning fabulous.

[4] Alternate forms of this activity can be adapted to reduce risk. For example, students might choose to represent two different aspects of themselves in photographs or to create a collage of two or more of their many 'selves.'

Program. Antoine came to me panicked and said, "What do I do, I got Marcus's name?" He knew that it would be offensive and way too easy to rely on time-worn homophobic stereotypes to represent Marcus. But, he also wanted to participate in the activity. I asked him to think about Marcus's personality—what he was like as a person. Antoine lit up when he said, "He's always so proper." So I pushed him a bit and asked, "How can you represent that aspect of him?" With a deep breath, Antoine took off his baseball hat, pulled up his pants so that for the first time his underwear was not exposed. He stood up tall and proudly put his arms at his side. He couldn't hold back his enormous grin. It was one of the most powerful moments of my teaching career. Antoine had worked with us the semester before in our course. Not only had he retained the content, but he chose to take an anti-oppressive stance in a moment where it would have been so easy not to. Antoine and his peers continued to surprise us with their generosity of spirit and willingness to push themselves, each other, and us in our own process of teaching and learning. This is where the hope lies for us when we are sometimes broken-hearted activists in the neo-liberal times which constrict and brutalize these students.

WHAT DOES THIS ALL MEAN

In a conceptual framework developed by Vanessa and her colleagues, safe, positive, and queering moments in schools refer to the kinds of approaches educators employ with their students to challenge homophobia and heterosexism. Perhaps the approaches most often invoked by educators in the fight against homophobic oppression are rules and policies (creating *safe moments*). When kids call each other fag or dyke or say things like, "That's so gay," educators can easily turn toward school codes of conduct and anti-bullying policies. Through these types of tools, students are told that homophobic words and action are inappropriate. Teachers might, on occasion, send the offending students to the office. The problem with such a course of action is that the moment the teacher leaves the classroom and the students are left on their own, the name-calling will undoubtedly return because the students' actions are buoyed by their own homophobic ideas and by those of the schooling system.

Unfortunately, far less frequently are incidents like the ones just described turned into teachable moments where students are told why these words and actions are inappropriate, hurtful, or unacceptable (creating *positive moments*). And still less frequently are students given the skills to critically analyze how these actions are supported by different institutions including the family, education, media, religion, and so on (another way to create positive moments). In the moment we worked together, we attempted to embed anti-oppressive concepts and pedagogical approaches at different points across the curriculum in order to help our students understand and address homophobic ideas, actions, and institutions. What we were not able to anticipate—but what took our breath away—was the impact of a particular combination of elements: the presence of out queer teachers; the use of the arts and digital media; our constant vigilance and care for our students as they moved in and out of crisis; and our approach to homophobia, which examined its intersections with race, class, gender, ability, and Aboriginality. The impact of such a precious combination of ingredients created explosions that disrupted the homophobic and heterosexist places and spaces at school and beyond (creating *queering moments*). These queering moments resound loudly and mightily for both of us as they continue to inform our pedagogy, curriculum, and practices in our current work in schools, teacher education programs, and community organizations.

"There is no fast lane that leads
    to a destination where LGBTQ-based
prejudice and discrimination
    at school are remedied; queer roads
and signs require new spaces,
    time to erect, and require workers
to build its foundation."

TAKING CHANGE TO THE STREET: KICKING HOMOPHOBIA AND HETEROSEXISM TO THE CURB

Jenny Kassen AND Alicia Lapointe

ILLUSTRATIONS BY Jenny Kassen

E ven before the first day in the teacher education program, we knew that homophobia and heterosexism—thinking that everyone is or should be heterosexual—might create speed bumps on our road to becoming educators. We were unable to foresee just how pervasive they would be in our school experience. Sexual- and gender-based inequities were largely unnoticed by the straight majority, yet were for us, inescapable.

Within this gridlock, faced with these barriers, we sought to change the heterocentric backdrop of schooling by organizing and leading LGBTQ-focused initiatives at a faculty of education. We challenged our peers' homophobic language use and their heternormative frames of reference—attitudes and behaviours that make heterosexuality seem normal and natural—to clear the way for more inclusive ways of thinking.

This is an account of how, as sexual minorities, we chose to navigate within a predominately straight school culture, and the actions we took to queer the professional landscape of Canadian postsecondary education.

Both situations left us at a fork in the road: either let oppressive situations pass or directly challenge LGBTQ-negative attitudes and behaviors. Our choices were to: *Swerve and Avoid, Reroute and Distract*, or prepare for a *Head on Collision*—terms we invented. *Swerve and Avoid* means to let the situation run its course. If someone assumes that you are heterosexual and

SWERVE AND AVOID: Let the situation run its course. Do not correct heterocentric assumption or homophobic slurs.

REROUTE AND DISTRACT: Redirect the question or situation to someone else. Do not "out" yourself.

HEAD ON COLLISION: Deliberately stop LGBTQ-based prejudice and discrimination. Brace for impact.

335

asks you if you have a boyfriend, simply say "no." They will move on and think you are single, not gay. Unfortunately, this fails to disrupt the straight framing embedded in the question. *Reroute and Distract* is passing or failing to answer the question. This can be done through redirecting the conversation to something that does not require you to "out" yourself. Finally, when preparing for a *Head on Collision*, you deliberately stop LGBTQ-based prejudice and discrimination.

For Alicia, the road to becoming a teacher did not start in her first class or on practicum; it began when she decided to hit the gas and steer the conversation into a new direction: Queer Street; a road seldom travelled down by teacher candidates at the faculty. She chose to interrupt and challenge her peer's heteronormative assumptions by stating that she had a girlfriend, after which her colleagues began the *process* of using more inclusive language. The response had a variety of ways it could have played out, and that is the risk of a *Head on Collision*: there is no telling what the damage will be. Answering the "partner" question with full disclosure and honesty was a risky venture because Alicia couldn't know whether her peers would respect and accept her sexuality, would wonder why they had been burdened with this personal information, or whether the table would empty and the space would be revealed as being unsafe for her.

The comment made by Jenny's peer caught her off guard: the individual was genuinely kind, and this homophobic expression was the last thing she expected to hear casually thrown into conversation by him, and at a faculty of education of all places. The whiplash hit with her peer's explanation: as if his relationship with an LGBTQ-identified person justified the use of a homophobic phrase. Though he was apologetic, her peer's response and subsequent justification of word choice demonstrated the need for a change of gear from unintentionally oppressive to intentionally aware and inclusive. This was not an isolated incident—anti-gay slurs like these were common in the faculty.

It can be difficult for others to understand that their homophobic language and/or heteronormative framing is the real issue; language can confine people in restrictive gender and sexuality boxes, where many people do not fit. When LGBTQ people attempt to disrupt queer exclusion and insensitivity, it can feel as though people are bothered with this information and as if we are the ones to blame for another's inappropriate behaviours or assumptions.

These homophobic and heterocentric situations inspired us to reflect on what it means to be LGBTQ in school, and what we could do to raise awareness of queer educational issues so that homophobia and heterosexism would come to a screeching halt at a permanent stop sign. We wondered how teacher candidates' heterosexist ways of speaking and behaving affected elementary and secondary students if they were negatively impacting us? If educators are unaware that their language is problematic, can we assume that they will use inclusive and non-oppressive language in the classroom? Will they recognize homophobia and challenge it if they encounter it? Do they know and/or care about the consequences of heterosexism, or were these issues hiding in their blind spots?

When we became teacher candidates and started attending school, we began to question the taken-for-granted notion of safe, inclusive, and equitable education. We became sensitive to the fact that the majority of our peers did not speak our language. "Hetero-talk"— conversation regarding marriage, fairytale weddings, and children—was omnipresent. As queer women, it was difficult to participate in discussions about marriage and family because they have been and continue to be heterosexualized institutions. It was isolating; if in daily conversation our voices were marginal to the straight impetative, how would LGBTQ insights be received in our classes at the faculty? Would issues beyond blatant homophobic bullying, even register on anyone's radars as a "worthwhile" topic to tackle in class?

Without a professional community to draw on, our experience was insular; the underwhelming queer community affected our ability to teach because there wasn't a co-pilot with whom to hash out how to negotiate our sexualities at school. We were not provided guidance in this area, and our experiences became as invisible as they were isolating.

In January 2012, we found each other through our individual desires to expose other students to queer knowledge while Jenny was completing a Bachelor of Education (BEd), and Alicia was finishing her Masters of Education (MEd). One conversation was all it took to legitimize and validate what had up until that point been a lonely experience. We realized that there was strength in numbers and that, in order to cultivate change, we had to take action. Student-directed activities and initiatives had the potential to queer the school community and raise awareness of LGBTQ issues in education, especially if staff supported them. Collaborating with faculty members and students, Alicia spearheaded the organization of an event that drew attention to LGBTQ concerns in schooling and highlighted practical insights for creating safer, more inclusive

and equitable learning environments for LGBTQ youth and their allies. Later that winter, Jenny organized a session for student teachers on LGBTQ-inclusive sex education, which also blurred rigid heteronormative boundaries. Alicia and another MEd student facilitated a workshop at a Professional Development Day (PDD), to help engage student teachers with queer knowledge. This session persuaded attendees to interrogate their ethical and pedagogical practices to better service and support LGBTQ pupils.

Working on these projects was an empowering experience because it made local-level change possible and observable. These events slowly cleared the way and made queer paths accessible to students at the faculty. Though the progress was good, we were aware that, with a new cohort, the trail we were carving out ran the risk of growing over and disappearing. LGBTQ and allied teacher candidates would be starting at square one, with just as little frame of reference as we had.

In order to pave this road, LGBTQ inclusion had to be more concretely placed within the map of the faculty. We co-founded the first Gay-Straight Alliance (GSA) for both teacher candidates and graduate students in November 2012 at the faculty, to continue creating an LGBTQ-inclusive environment at school.

The GSA was created so that LGBTQ students and their allies would have a safe and supportive space to educate themselves, transmit their learning to the wider school community, and practically apply knowledge in their teaching profession. The specific objectives of the club have shifted throughout the two years it has existed. The focus of the first year was on student-directed discussions and activities that assisted members in learning about sexual and gender minority issues. Each week had a theme (e.g., "coming out" as queer or as an ally, speaking out and addressing anti-gay behaviors at school, reaching out and supporting queer and ally youth, and teaching "out"—queering lessons, providing positive LGBTQ class content, and exercising teachable moments). Whereas the first year primarily involved internal education of club members by club members, the second year currently aims to transform the larger school community by providing educational events for students.

The queering of the faculty did not happen over night; it was a purposeful and planned process that evolved over time. There is no fast lane that leads to a destination where LGBTQ-based prejudice and discrimination at school are remedied; queer roads and signs require new spaces, time to erect, and require workers to build its foundation. Schools can be more equitable places for LGBTQ youth if we consider the consequences of our preconceptions and actions. Student teachers must first learn about queer issues in order to be an ally to LGBTQ youth. Thereafter, they can begin to advocate for better learning conditions for sexual and gender minorities. LGBTQ content must be integrated into the regular curricula at faculties of education. This way, teacher candidates will develop their understanding about queer issues and feel more comfortable including LGBTQ content in their classrooms and disrupting heterosexist assumptions. The provision of equitable education depends on current and future teachers' ability to pave a more just path for LGBTQ youth. PDD sessions must incorporate queer perspectives and help student teachers challenge homophobia and heterosexism. GSAs can be formed at faculties of education to foster safe and supportive intellectual and physical spaces for LGBTQ teacher candidates and their allies, and provide education for students in order to motivate them to advocate for justice. The change must start in faculties of education by providing more teacher candidates with the maps and legends necessary for travelling through this landscape, and if those maps are not satisfactory, we can change them or draw new ones.

When we teamed up to queer the roads of our faculty, we found that the ride did not need to be dark, illuminated only by half-functioning low beams. All it took was a conversation. Once in the carpool lane of collaboration, it is a short distance to an exit marked, "Change." Assemble a convoy and build new roads. Take change to the street.

ACKNOWLEDGEMENTS

From an early age, I was conscious of the impact of poverty and the hardships of rural living, both as a sexual orientation minority, and one who suffered from epilepsy and rheumatoid arthritis. My resolve to advocate for human rights for lesbian, gay, bisexual, transsexual, transgender, trans*, intersex, interested, queer, questioning, two-spirited, asexual, or allies (LGBTTIQQ2SA) children and adults, strengthened when I became a teacher at an intermediate school in St. John's, NL, while in my early twenties. Now, as a university educator, I have embraced what I term, "a pedagogy of love." A number of years ago, I was especially pleased to make the acquaintance of Rebecca Rose, President of Breakwater Books Ltd., a person who shares this loving passion for social justice and equity. Without Rebecca's persistence, camaraderie, and collaborative vision, this anthology would likely not have seen the light of day.

The manuscript of this anthology could not have passed muster without the able critique of James Langer. I thank Rhonda Molloy for the eye-catching beauty and simplicity of the covers, and interior book design. I thank Egale Canada for their partnership in this venture, and specifically Helen Kennedy and Susan Rose, who assisted with a nationwide call for essays and much more. I would like to thank my angel, Sebbi, for his endless devotion, loyalty, and calming presence as I steadfastly worked on this anthology over the past year(s). I am enormously grateful for all the contributors who took the time to write their stories and for their willingness to share them with the world. I am humbled by their stories of pride, courage, and social justice, by their sacrifices, navigation of treacherous ups and downs, and by their sheer narrative talent.

After all, this anthology is about their voices, and sharing them with you, the readers. Thank you all.

Douglas Gosse
Brantford, Ontario, 2014

INDEX

DOUGLAS GOSSE, PH.D., is the author of *Jackytar* and a professor of social justice and cultural studies at Nipissing University. He has won numerous awards for his research on diversity and inclusion, and using the arts in academic writings. He is a frequent speaker and writer on human rights, particularly for marginalized men and boys, and the LGBTTIQQ2SA community. He lives in Brantford and Toronto, Ontario.

CONTRIBUTORS

LOUISE AZZARELLO is a media educator working from an interdisciplinary and equity framework. Louise was a member of the writing team who produced the new Gender course developed by the Ontario Ministry of Education. She has worked closely with the TDSB Aboriginal Education Office on a number of initiatives and has presented numerous workshops for educators on critical pedagogy, equity, media, and interdisciplinary curriculum.

VALÉRIE BAH was born in Ottawa and raised in a Haitian-Beninese household. She currently lives, works, and writes in the Democratic Republic of the Congo.

JENNIFER A. BARNETT is an Associate Professor in the Faculty of Education at Nipissing University in North Bay, Ontario. Her area of research includes studying how society and culture educate an individual as to her or his identity. In her spare time, she is an active member of St. Andrew's United Church and sings in the Integrity in Politics choir.

DR. JASON BEHRMANN is a post-doctoral fellow at McGill University's Institute for Gender, Sexuality and Feminist Studies. Funded by the Canadian Institutes for Health Research, his research focuses on advancing LGBT rights in medicine and health policy. Beyond research, his interests centre on the arts, fitness, and cooking.

NOELLE BICKLE is a writer and a certified Amherst Writers & Artist (AWA) Creative Writing Facilitator. She works with reluctant, emerging, and established writers in community centres, local workshops, and writing circles. Her passion is working with youth-at-risk, in order to provide them with an outlet to share their voice and personal stories through expressive writing.

SARAH BLACKSTOCK lives with her partner, Juana Berinstein, and their daughters, Isa and Nica. Together they are a mighty, joyous team. Sarah's expertise in advocacy and strategic communications has been put to use in various social justice campaigns. Currently, Sarah is Director of Communications at Unifor.

VINCENT BOLT is an active member of the LGBTQ2 community in Sudbury, Ontario. He is the group facilitator for TG Innerselves, a transgender organization in Sudbury. He is also the LGBTQ2 Program Facilitator at the Sudbury Action Centre for Youth. He has a BA in English Literature, and is currently completing a BSW at Laurentian. He likes to spend his leisure time with his adopted rabbit.

Born and raised in Halifax, Nova Scotia, TUCKER BOTTOMLEY spent most of his childhood attending Neptune Theater School. He later pursued his interests in music and began playing bass guitar in bands and performing around the city. Despite the difficulties of trying to make a career out of the arts, he spends most of his time playing all genres of music with his friends.

HUBERT BRARD is an educator in the public system who has taught all grades from JK to twelve. He now finds himself on a leadership journey in his school district. A graduate student with a focus on LGBTQ leadership, he advocates for LGBTQ equity for school leaders.

Born in Toronto, JOANNE BRIGDEN was the fourth of five Catholic-raised children. She has mined her various neuroses for comedy material and has written for comedians such as Joan Rivers, Rodney Dangerfield, and Jay Leno.

JANE BYERS lives with her wife and two children in Nelson, British Columbia. Her first poetry collection, *Steeling Effects* has been published by Caitlin Press (2014). She is the recipient of the 2014 Richard Carver Emerging Writer Award and has had essays and poems published in a variety of literary journals across Canada, the US and the UK.

ADAM CARROLL is a working actor and comedian in Toronto, Ontario. He's the creator of the YouTube channel "Let's Have a Moment with Adam Carroll" where he talks random topics and performs sketches and characters. Adam is currently enrolled at Humber College in the Comedy: Writing & Performance program. Once he graduates, he plans to focus on "Let's Have a Moment" and produce live stage versions of his channel.

BOGDAN CHETA's work moves through different media as he investigates the world around him. His projects are a blend of magic and myth, fact and fiction, blurring the distinctions between art and life by positioning art in relation to everyday experiences. Consisting of anecdotes, explanations, aphoristic musings, memories, declarations, confessions, analysis, diaristic observations, working thoughts, and maze like questions, his writing often emerges like an intimate form of personal companionship.

CHRISTINE L. CHO, PhD, is an Assistant Professor at Nipissing University's Schulich School of Education in Brantford, Ontario. Her research in teacher education contributes to current educational conversations on racial, ethnic, and linguistic representation in schools, and explores the constructions and understandings of teacher identity within school structures.

TOM CHURCHILL is a writer, ghost writer, and editor. His poetry has been published in *The Antigonish Review*. He lives in Toronto and is thankful for family, friends, and the freedoms he enjoys as a gay man in Canada.

DORIAN CLIFFE is a queer failure misfit who's travelled from a forgettable small town in rural Southern Ontario to the gay promised land of Church Street Village. Tripping over every milestone along his path, Dorian now writes short stories that point towards how the system is a game with rules we will never win. He works with fellow creative partners in crime at the Institute for Misfit Studies.

KATY CRAGGS was born in and grew up in Goose Bay, Labrador. She is currently a Licensed practical nurse (LPN) and in the process of getting her nursing degree, after which she hopes to become a registered psychiatric nurse and use her empathy obtained from personal experiences with mental illness to help those suffering with same. Katy currently lives in St. John's with her four cats and is working on her first novel.

JESSICA DEL ROSSO is a gay-rights and youth in care activist. She has a passion for equality, public education, and awareness. Her personal life experiences have led her to become engaged in public speaking as well as government and local advocacy. She believes that everything in life happens for a reason. That belief is what motivates her to continue trying to make a positive change in the world.

NICOLE DOUCETTE is a fourth year Mineral Engineering student at the University of Toronto. She enjoys creative writing in her free time, and is a science columnist for her school paper, *The Cannon*. An avid adventurer, Nicole hopes to spend her life travelling, writing, and learning.

NATHAN DOWNEY is a writer and editor living in St. John's. A native of Alberta, he finds the Newfoundland winters worse, but the people more tolerant. He loves the ocean and misses the mountains.

LUKAYO FAYE CATHERINE ESTRELLA is a shapeshifter birthed in Maharlika islands (Bicol, Philippines) who lived under the shadow of the Mayon volcano. They were sent over half way around the world to a sky-scraped settler city on Turtle Island at the age of three. By the age of eighteen, they migrated to unceded Algonquin territory (Ottawa, Ontario), and for the last decade the desire to decolonize with a raised rainbow fist and a peaceful trickster grin exploded out of them as community outreach, poetic performances, and consensual solidarity/support work.

PAUL EDWARD FITZGERALD has always had a passion for writing. He has always felt the best stories are those that are meaningful, come from the heart, and possess a quality we all can relate to on some level. In his spare time, Paul is no stranger to the stage, having always had a flare for the arts and a love for the applause and laughter of a crowd. Aside from writing and the theatre, Paul also loves working with children, and feels that all work involving children is its own reward.

ANDRÉ P. GRACE is Director of Research at the Institute for Sexual Minority Studies and Services, Faculty of Education, University of Alberta. He is national consultant on sexual and gender minority issues for the Canadian Teachers' Federation. He served as expert advisor for the 2011 and 2012 Chief Public Health Officer's Reports on the State of Public Health in Canada.

SASSIMINT GRACE is a fifty-four-year-old wife, mother, and grandmother who fiercely loves and advocates for the vulnerable and disenfranchised. She believes that humanity is on the verge of discovering we are all connected, and what we do to the earth and to each other, we do to ourselves. Grace has spent many years exploring the paradox of a Creator who draws us closer by stretching our faith through adversity in a game of Peek a Boo.

JANE EATON HAMILTON is the author of several books of fiction and poetry. She won first prize in fiction in the CBC Literary Awards and the Prism International short fiction award. Her book *July Nights* was shortlisted for the BC Book Prizes and *Hunger* was shortlisted for the Ferro Grumley Award. Jane is also a photographer and visual artist and was a litigant in Canada's same-sex marriage case. She lives in Vancouver.

JACLYN HAYNES is happily in a same-sex relationship with her partner, Lizzie. Food is one of their passions, from creating new recipes to trying new restaurants. She is working in a permanent position as a Registered Early Childhood Educator in an Early Learning Centre. Jacklyn has also graduated with a M.Ed., and B.A. (Junior/Intermediate) from the University of Ottawa. She has a B.A. (Hon.) in Child Studies from Carleton University. In her spare time, she enjoys volunteering with Girl Guides of Canada as a Girl Guide Leader in a Brownie Unit.

ANDREA HAYWARD completed her M.Sc. in Molecular and Medical Genetics at the University of Toronto and spent a number of years counting fruit flies before switching to squish bugs of the silicon variety. She now works as a systems analyst for a major Canadian health authority, when she isn't killing dragons in *World of Warcraft*.

GEMMA HICKEY, a St. John's native, was born with a fire in her belly. A widely known activist and up-and-coming poet, Gemma has served on a variety of boards and committees nation-wide and has received a number of scholarships and awards, including a Queen's Diamond Jubilee Medal in 2013 for her contribution to gay rights in Canada. She is currently Executive Director of the arts-based youth charity For the Love of Learning and founder of The Pathways Foundation, an organization offering support to survivors of clergy abuse.

FRANCISCO IBÁÑEZ-CARRASCO mission is to inspire and connect. He is a lifelong educator specialized in online and social media, an AIDS activist living with HIV for thirty years, a writer, and a social scientist. His research focuses on rehabilitation in the context of HIV, mental health, autopathography, and HIV research methodologies. His latest creative non-fiction effort *Giving It Raw* is a tell-all memoir. He lives in Toronto with his 17 lbs., blue-eyed cat, Orion.

JULIAN KITCHEN, PhD, is an associate professor in the Faculty of Education of Brock University. He is the Director of the Tecumseh Centre for Aboriginal Research and Education and lead author of *Professionalism, Law and the Ontario Educator*. His research and writing focuses on teacher education, Aboriginal education, and queer issues in education.

JENNY KASSEN is an Intermediate/Senior teacher and freelance illustrator. She has teachables in Visual Arts, English, French, and Special Education, and is currently a supply teacher in Ontario.

ALICIA LAPOINTE is an Ontario Certified Teacher and a PhD Candidate, specializing in Equity and Inclusive Education.

JAMIE B. LAURIE is a young writer and poet who recently published *The Big Summer*, his first novel. His work has been included in numerous collections, including a recent first-place finish in a national writing competition. He lives in Montreal where he enjoys spending time with the people he loves, travelling, and exploring the arts.

KIM CHEE LEE is an eighty-two year old gay Eurasian man from St. Boniface, Manitoba who came out to and was accepted by his family as a teenager. As a young child, he was sent to live in a small village in South China, only returning to Manitoba for high school. He moved to Toronto at aged twenty-four and has been active in the gay community, volunteering with the 519 Community Centre, the AIDS Committee of Toronto, the Inside Out Film Festival, and many other special events over the years. His personal interests include Chinese brush painting, tap dancing, Zine program, short film production, and short-story writing.

DAVID LE makes it a rule to follow his heart, which has, in turn, led him to buffet lines all around Canada. He is an INFP and sits on a Virgo-Leo cusp. Recently, he's been very into puns and have asked people, "What does Petrie call his father?" To which he answers, "A pteroDADtyl!"

CARL LEGGO is a poet and professor at the University of British Columbia. His books include: *Growing Up Perpendicular on the Side of a Hill; View from My Mother's House; Come-By-Chance; Teaching to Wonder: Responding to Poetry in the Secondary Classroom;* and *Sailing in a Concrete Boat: A Teacher's Journey.*

NICOLE MACFARLANE is a graduate of University of New Brunswick's English and Sociology programs. She currently resides in Halifax, Nova Scotia, with her partner and their two cats, but she grew up in Fredericton, New Brunswick. Her passions include equality, activism, and social justice.

JENNA MACKAY is a researcher, writer, activist, educator, and artist living in Toronto, Ontario. She loves baked goods, bike rides, and her rescue cat, Mushu.

KRISTA MCCRACKEN is a bi-sexual writer and public historian living in Northern Ontario. She is passionate about community engagement, collective memory, and local history. Krista's work frequently draws on her experience living in small town Canada.

KATE MILLER is a Child & Youth Worker originally from the Niagara Region. She is also a bisexual, hard-of-hearing artist who creates things under the name Kate Mildew. Kate has been a part of the inspiring team at *Shameless Magazine*, a politics and culture magazine for girls and trans youth.

KERRI MESNER is a doctoral candidate at the University of British Columbia, a minister with Metropolitan Community Churches, a theatre artist, and a queer activist. Kerri's current arts-based research includes the creation and performance of a new play exploring the intersections of queer, Christian, and artistic identities, as well as the impact of anti-LGBTTIQQ2SA violence.

ANTHONY MOHAMED has a successful career in the field of health equity and lives with his partner and their neighbour's cat in Toronto.

PAUL NATHANSON is a professor at McGill University's Faculty of Religious Studies. His research with Katherine Young has focused broadly on the relation between religion and secularity. From this perspective, political ideologies often become "secular religions" (of the fundamentalist variety). Considering one pervasive ideology in this way, the research has focused on misandry (the sexist counterpart of misogyny). This context has not led Nathanson to feel "at home" in the world, but it has led him to discover the meaning of his life not only as a gay man but as a man.

MARGARET ROBINSON holds a PhD from the University of St. Michael's College and is a Postdoctoral Fellow with the Re:searching for LGBTQ Health team at the Centre for Addiction and Mental Health in Toronto. She is a long-time bisexual activist and former co-chair of the Toronto Dyke March. She is passionate about Indigenous self-government, cultural reclamation, animal welfare, and LGBTQ liberation.

VANESSA RUSSELL completed her PhD in 2009 at the Ontario Institute for Studies in Education at the University of Toronto (OISE/UT) and has worked as a teacher educator at both York University and OISE/UT. She has held a number of leadership positions at the Toronto District School Board and has taught at the Triangle Program, Canada's only dedicated classroom for queer students "at risk." Vanessa has published and presented extensively in the areas of anti-oppression education, embodiment, and ethics.

In addition to teaching history at the secondary level, KAEL SHARMAN also enjoys researching the history of technical and vocational education in Ontario. The role of schools in maintaining social categories such as gender is also a recent academic interest.

IONA SKY is a queer social worker and activist who is deeply committed to social justice and creating change through education and advocacy. Iona lives in Ontario and is the proud mother of a young son who is her inspiration to continue to fight for acceptance and inclusion for all.

MELISSA SKY is a proud femme, indie artist. She's also a mother, a dreamer, a fighter, and a tea fanatic. She has a PhD in English literature and teaches at the Ontario College of Arts & Design (OCAD). Check out Femme Fatale Creations for more about her films and writing.

KAYLIE SORRENTI is a student at Western University who was born and raised in London, Ontario. Through their experiences living in London, they realized firsthand the injustices that occurred towards transgender youth in psychiatric facilities. Kaylie is currently writing for *Shameless*, a not-for-profit magazine for girls and trans* youth.

AMY SOULE is a proud gay Jewish resident of Hamilton, Ontario, where she's lived her entire life. For two and a half years, she had the privilege of working as a substitute Educational Assistant. Though she's held various volunteer positions, her favourite is to serve as musical leader at her synagogue, something that enables her to reach out to God above, while simultaneously helping people here on earth.

Toronto teacher and filmmaker, LAURIE TOWNSHEND writes, directs, and produces documentaries and narrative films for a growing audience. Her take on human connectedness is explored in an online collection of two-minute vignettes featuring strangers titled, Human Frequency Streetdocs. Her cinematic offerings extend to include acts of courage made visible through crisis. Townshend's short film, *The Railpath Hero* (2013), is a gripping portrait of the threads of hope that hold a young hockey player's life together in the wake of childhood sexual abuse.

LEANNE TAYLOR is an assistant professor in the Faculty of Education at Brock University. She teaches graduate and undergraduate courses addressing diversity and equity issues in schooling, marginalized youth, and the interrelationship between pedagogy, culture, and identity. Her research has appeared in a variety of publications.

CHANTAL VALLIS is a youth worker who lives in Guelph, Ontario. She graduated from Queen's University in 2009, where she earned a BA in Global Development Studies and English Literature. In her spare time, she volunteers with the Ten Oaks Project, a charitable organization that connects children and youth from LGBTQ communities.

JOHN L. VITALE is an Associate Professor of Education at Nipissing University (Brantford) where he teaches Music Education and Curriculum Methods in the Bachelor of Education Concurrent Program. He is also a member of Nipissing University's Graduate Studies Department in Education where he teaches general "Research Methods" and supervises a number of student dissertations. As a professional musician, John continues to perform in national and international venues each year.

Born and raised in Nova Scotia, LISA WALTERS has spent all of her life there and all but three years in the city of her birth. Married to a wonderful woman, they co-parent a four-legged fur baby. Working as a teacher and aspiring writer finishing a novel set in Nova Scotia, she loves to spend time outside walking and biking, particularly with their puppy, and playing soccer.

SHANNON WEBB-CAMPBELL is a writer, poet, and Canadian Women in Literary Arts critic-in-residence 2014. Currently, she is earning her MFA in Creative Writing from the University of British Columbia, and holds an English Literature and Journalism degree from Dalhousie University. Her writing has appeared in the top Canadian magazines, anthologies and quarterlies such as *Riddle Fence*, *Quill and Quire*, and *Room*, among many others. She lives in the north end of Halifax.

As a father of twin seven-year-old boys, ALEX WHEY gets to see the world through very tiny eyes sometimes. He hopes to reach out his hand through words on paper and touch someone deeply, ultimately creating a more beautiful world for his sons. Education is key.

VALERIE WINDSOR is a lesbian, feminist, mom, and grandmom. She has written general interest stories for *Wayves* magazine and loves telling stories, especially about her childhood in a fishing village in Newfoundland. Windsor spends most of her spare time walking her cocker spaniel in the park and wishing Wanda Sykes was her girlfriend.

CPSIA information can be obtained
at www.ICGtesting.com
Printed in the USA
FSHW011951191120
76137FS

9 781550 814873